About the contributors

Alexander Parker and Tim Richman have authored several books between them, and written for publications in South Africa, the UK, Australia and New Zealand. They are especially interested in the lessons to be gained from popular history.

Zapiro is South Africa's premier political cartoonist. Among numerous accolades, he has won the Principal Prince Claus Award (Netherlands) and the International Publishers Association's Freedom to Publish Prize.

All three contributors currently live in Cape Town, South Africa.

50 PEOPLE WHO MESSED UP THE WORLD

Alexander Parker
& Tim Richman

with cartoons by

ROBINSON

ROBINSON

First published in South Africa in 2017 by Mercury, an imprint of Burnet Media

First published in Great Britain in 2017 by Robinson

ISBN: 978-1-47214-071-5

Typeset in Minion Pro 11 pt on 14.5
Printed and bound in Great Britain by CPI Group (UK) Ltd, Croydon CR0 4YY

Papers used by Robinson are from well-managed forests and other responsible sources

Robinson
An imprint of
Little, Brown Book Group
Carmelite House
50 Victoria Embankment
London EC4Y 0DZ

An Hachette UK Company
www.hachette.co.uk

AP: To Bronwyn, Olweyn, Elizabeth & Dair

TR: To Jules & Nicholas

– our antidotes

Contents

Introduction
by Alexander Parker & Tim Richman

AS A BOY GROWING UP IN BRITAIN in the 1980s, Alexander never really understood the value of history. That particular revelation came during a memorable year spent on the Zulu War battlefields of KwaZulu-Natal in South Africa in 1994. There, a historian and storyteller of some legend by the name of David Rattray illustrated the power of history by making him feel its discernible presence in present-day lives. It was a lesson that stuck, and it's one that informed the premise and production of this book – the notion that history matters, not just because it's bloody interesting when it's told right, but as a way to make sense of the present and guide us into the future.

We're living in a time of enormous change in the West, a time in which entrenched elites are being asked to justify themselves, and have been found wanting by many people in many different places. At the same time, we appear to be suffering from what might be called peace fatigue, which manifests itself in astonishing levels of entitlement and an alarming disregard for the true meaning of reckless political language. This may be the price to pay for avoiding any serious homefront wars since 1945. In other parts of the world, the near eradication of violence that is taken for granted in the West simply doesn't exist. Sharing time and viewpoints between First and Third World is, therefore, one way to gain some perspective on things, and it is with a foot in both that we have undertaken this project.

If this – let's be honest – unserious book achieves one small thing, it is our hope that it serves to remind readers of the place you get to when you enthusiastically pile onto the populist express. We want to underline the point that when political extremists, racial or religious demagogues and radical activists suggest that *this time it will be different*, they are lying –

they have always said that. When they diminish or question the record of history resulting from the implementation of similar politics, they expose themselves as definitely dangerous and quite probably evil. When they ardently present simple solutions to long-standing, sometimes intractable problems, they demonstrate either that they don't understand or, worse, that they don't care. There are a lot of people in these pages who started out sounding a lot like this.

Then again, there are also quite a few who, by comparison, would appear harmless. Next to the likes of Stalin, Pol Pot and Talat Pasha, Justin Bieber may seem an innocent bystander. But is he? *Is* he? Of course we could not sensibly or fairly draw moral equivalences between Stalin and the Bieb, or the Kims of Korea and Kim Kardashian, or Hitler and Donald Trump – no matter how many times that particular comparison has been made already. But establishing who has messed up the world isn't just an exercise in counting corpses. We could have gone that route, as others have, but it gets monotonous. Damage is done to life and society in various ways, and if you say that music – in our first example – isn't a profoundly important facet of humanity and a measure of culture then we're just going to have to agree to disagree. Hence young Justin's place here among many other arguably unlikely entries.

Of course any selection of a mere fifty people who messed up the world will be cause for debate and possibly even anger. Where, some will demand, are Tojo, Mussolini, Eichmann, Mountbatten, Castro, Nixon, Putin, Ayatollah Khomeini, Imelda Marcos, Muammar Gaddafi, Pablo Escobar, the moron who spawned anti-vaxxing, Steve Jobs, Sepp Blatter, Nicolas Cage, Shonda Rhimes and Kanye bloody West? Well, Kanye's just in view in the Kim Kardashian cartoon, but otherwise good questions, the lot, with no simple answers. So first let us explain the parameters we set ourselves.

Our arbitrarily assigned, but necessary, cutoff date for inclusion was the turn of the 20th century, but given the diminishment of effect over time, not to mention how self-involved we all are these days, there was always going to be a natural inclination towards more recent personalities. In the end, this was a far more complicated job of exclusion rather than inclusion, and many individual entries (Mengele, for example) are obliged to hold the place of an entire class of messer-uppers (Himmler, Göring, Goebbels, Eichmann…).

Given what we have found in our research, we will no doubt stand accused at some point of being Eurocentric and, equally, of being borderline-middle-aged white men with a crushingly bourgeois outlook. That would be entirely accurate. While we're on the subject of our supposed weaknesses, we should probably confess up front to being committed to the increasingly uncool ideas of liberal social democracy and the importance of personal responsibility, parliamentary procedure, limited government, independence of the judiciary and freedom of the press, markets and enterprise. We believe that dangerous things ought to be regulated, the second-most dangerous of which is government – the first being its absence.

So, vent on Twitter if you must. We are what we are.

But while we acknowledge our perspective, we should also state our belief that there are historical facts and – gasp! – even moral judgements that should be considered empirically true. Throughout this book, therefore, we've tried to find the centre ground, to be *The Economist* in a world that was, not long ago, *The Guardian* versus *The Telegraph* but is now *Left Wing Nation* and *Everyday Feminism* versus *Breitbart* and *InfoWars*. We are not fans of the extremes of political and ideological discourse and we expect, therefore, to offend those on either side. It is a feature of the modern world that this isn't very hard to do.

Discerning what 'centre ground' means has been a fascinating journey through cognitive bias and prejudices of various kinds – our own, and those that we believe exist out there in real life. We've discovered just how powerfully the digital world is designed to keep you reading within an ideological echo-chamber and that stepping out of it requires an active effort, but that it is ultimately good for the soul. We've tried to remember a time before this new cultural era of intolerant certainty, and to write with open minds. Our book is best read that way, too; just as long as you agree with us about Josef Mengele, the rest is up to you.

So, here they are. Our collection of some of the baddest bastards to ever set foot on our wonderful planet. And Justin Bieber. To hell with the lot of them.

September 2017

Idi Amin

c. 1925 – 16 August 2003

Leader of Uganda 1971-1979; vainglorious mass-murdering ethno-xenophobe and economics dunce; personification of modern African mayhem; lunatic

WELL, THIS IS AWKWARD. How do we start a collection of global stuffer-uppers with an African without getting ourselves into trouble? Any fair-minded reading of that continent's history will conclude that it has been, by some measure, more a recipient of stuffer-uppers than a net contributor. And yet here he is, Idi Amin, leading a gurning zombie-phalanx of some of the most egregious samples of humanity the world has issued forth.

Whereas it might feel more just, not to mention chronologically sensible, to open proceedings with, say, a suppuratingly awful example of the plight of Africa under colonial rule, such as King Leopold II of Belgium, Cecil

John Rhodes or Hendrik Verwoerd (all to come), we are constrained here by the alphabetical nature of this list – and, yes, the Western-Anglosphere perspective thus inherent. Before we get drawn into a self-flagellating whirlpool of guilt-ridden relativism, let's be clear that nobody here gets a free pass because of where they're from, or their race or religion. Unlike the new morality Big Brother roaming our social-media byways looking for intersectional crimes against wokeness, we believe people of all races and creeds are capable of taking responsibility for their actions, and by that measure Idi Amin fairly pole-vaults into these pages like the deranged, bloodthirsty tyrant he was.

To adopt David Attenborough's wheezy authority, then, *our story begins in Africa*, as all stories of humanity must. And if the story of humanity started in Africa, then it follows that buggering things up started in Africa too. Long before the horrors of the millennium-long Arab slave trade and early-stage colonialism, and longer still before the centuries-long Atlantic slave trade and the imperial savagery of the Scramble for Africa, it is our contention that Africans were probably doing a fine job of cocking up the place for their own purposes. But of course the slavers did their thing and the pioneering colonisers made inroads along West Africa and the likes of Jan van Riebeeck set up camp in the Cape of Good Hope in 1652. And there followed an ongoing disaster for the continent as various European powers divided it up for their own ends, a story that only began to unravel midway into the 20th century when those imperialists, weakened by two disastrous world wars, considered the expense of empire and the morality of the idea of empire, and found it wanting on both counts.

In *The Better Angels Of Our Nature* Steven Pinker describes the 'decivilizing anarchy of decolonisation' as a process that many recently decolonised countries tend to suffer, notably in Africa. This is a concept that may leave the odd African intellectual and Twitter offence-seeker bristling, especially in the face of evidence that relatively peaceful transitions are possible, as we have seen in Botswana, Namibia and South Africa. It is, however, hard to argue with Pinker's analysis that the alternative has been common, and it has surely been exacerbated by the risible leadership the continent has seen, in the main, since Ghana set the (sub-Saharan) independence dominoes falling in 1957.

The story of 20th-century Africa has repeatedly seen, in historian Martin Meredith's words, 'a flamboyant, autocratic figure, accustomed to living in style and demanding total obedience' emerge as head of state, 'tolerating neither opposition nor dissent, rigging elections, emasculating the courts, cowing the press, stifling the universities, demanding abject servility and making themselves exceedingly rich'. And, we would add, doing a fair bit of murdering in some cases. Whether democratically elected or taking power in the time-honoured military coup, this Big Man syndrome is visible all across Africa, from Angola to Zimbabwe – but in the 1970s Uganda endured the foulest monster of the lot.

With Idi Amin, the Ugandan people were dealt a leader who became a caricature of the African Big Man, a hyper-inflated impression of all the worst post-colonial clichés. His distended ego and general lunacy was on a par with that of Jean-Bédel Bokassa of the Central African Republic and Colonel Muammar Gaddafi of Libya, and his rule was about as catastrophic as Mobutu Sese Seko's of Zaire. But he turned out to be more racist, brutal and violent than any of his fellow tyrants.

Before Amin's arrival, Uganda had been a British Protectorate from 1894 to 1962, famous in Blighty for being home to the source of the White Nile. Early in this colonial phase, some 30,000 Asian, mainly Indian, labourers had been brought in to British East Africa on indenture contracts to build the Ugandan Railway. The name was a bit of a misnomer, representing access to the protectorate only, as the entire length of the track lay in what is now Kenya, connecting Mombasa on the Indian Ocean to Kisumu on the eastern shore of Lake Victoria. But the nation of Uganda, like so many African countries drawn on a map by distant colonisers, is itself something of an illusion. Ostensibly based around the ancient kingdom of Buganda, it was a political minefield of distinct and competing ethnic groups, with a broad differentiation between the Bantu groups in the south of the country, and the Nilotic and Sudanic groups in the north. Numerous subdivisions within all three confuse matters further, as does the fact that the rivalries within the north and south are often as intense as those between the two.

Such a typical colonial nation-construct was always going to prove tricky to manage after independence, and this same problem echoed across the continent as country after country gained independence. Uganda's turn came in 1962 with the election of Milton Obote as prime minister, followed in 1963 by the installation of the Bugandan king, Cambridge-educated Sir Edward Mutesa II, as a ceremonial president. This agreeably diplomatic arrangement didn't last long.

The Bugandan relationship with the colonial creation of Uganda as a whole had always been difficult, and various British administrators had never really addressed the tensions. Facing challenges from within his own party, Obote, a Lango from the north, ousted Mutesa in 1966 and proclaimed himself president, chasing the king into exile in the UK.

Where Amin would become the supersized African tyrant in time, Obote was your regular serving. A seemingly decent egg to start, he led a thriving Uganda in his early years in charge. But he turned out to be a fellow who enjoyed the taste of power, felt a one-party state was the most effective form of governance, and steadily, and violently where necessary, crushed any form of resistance to his rule. In 1967 he simply abolished the kingdom of Buganda, removing that particular thorn from his side. All standard operational procedure from the post-independence playbook, then.

To do his dirty work, Obote had found the ideal man, a British-trained colonel from the West Nile region by the name of Idi Amin. Amin was enormous – six-foot-four, with the build of a heavyweight boxing champion, which he was as a younger man – and seemed just the right kind of semi-literate thug for the job. When Obote needed the king's palace ransacked and some Baganda disposed of, Amin was the man. But Obote underestimated his henchman's ambition and thirst for power. By the time he came to be threatened by it, the corrupt Amin had grown himself an ethnic power base within the Ugandan army.

When Amin discovered that Obote was intending to have him arrested on charges of stealing army funds, he readied his coup. He waited until Obote was out of the country to strike, then took over Entebbe airport and the Kampala radio stations and declared a temporary military government. It was 1971 and Amin was in his mid-40s.

In contrast to so many of the other famous African Big Men, Amin's reign of horrors was short: a mere eight years. And it began quite positively, in fact. The British and many Ugandans were happy to see the back of Obote, respectively considering him to be dangerously left-leaning and a monumental shit, and Amin put on a good initial show. But the promising start is yet another cliché of African dictatorship, and it was only a few short months before the paranoia and megalomania displaced the diplomacy and goodwill, and people started dying and disappearing.

Amin didn't muck about. He announced that the former president's powers now all vested in him, and that he was commander-in-chief of the military. He promoted himself to Field Marshal and, having appointed a well-qualified cabinet, then ruled by decree. Military law, it was announced, superseded judicial law, and parliament was dissolved. Most worryingly, he established a large and overlapping network of plain-clothes secret police units with ominously nondescript monikers such as the State Research Bureau and the Public Safety Unit, which could do – and did do – very bad things. Inevitably, they were staffed by men from Amin's own district. The courts and the press were suppressed as required, and the killings began.

A Muslim of Nubian descent, Amin was wary of other ethnicities. He feared opposition forces within the Ugandan army, in particular possible Obote supporters. Within a year he had had several thousand soldiers in his 9,000-strong army executed, removing entire ethnic groups in the process. He also set about eliminating other enemy groups, perceived and real.

Rather than digging graves, it seemed easier to dispose of both corpses and evidence by feeding truckloads of bodies to crocodiles in the Nile, but the scale of the murders was so vast that the crocodiles weren't up to the job, and the bodies tended to collect, a little inconveniently, on riverbanks and in dam shallows. Putting a final number on a genocidal regime's death toll is, as we will see throughout the pages ahead, seldom a straightforward task. Hitler's Nazis were just about the only mass killers who kept accurate count because, being Germans, they couldn't help themselves. In Amin's case, the crocodiles-in-the-river method of body disposal was one of several complicating factors. In time, the International Commission of Jurists would put Amin's death toll at around 300,000. Amnesty International believes it might have been as high as 500,000. Either way, it's a number that's too large to be meaningfully contemplated. Even working out all the *types* of people who were killed on his orders isn't easy.

Those who died included his military and political enemies; prominent politicians, tribal leaders and churchmen; important administrators,

'He read very badly and clearly had a hard time just signing prepared documents. As his first Principal Private Secretary, I never ever received a handwritten note from him. Amin had no idea how governments were run.'
— *Ugandan cabinet secretary Henry Kyemba*

businessmen and intellectuals; anonymous farmers, shopkeepers and students; Ugandans from other ethnicities; foreigners who dared get in the way; and people who offended or upset him. Wherever pain could be inflicted it was, and Amin's lackeys revelled in their torturous duties. A favoured routine was forcing one prisoner to bludgeon another to death, after which that prisoner was bludgeoned by the next. They took their inspiration from their leader himself: Amin's reputation for personal violence was universal, and Ugandan rumour had it – and still has it to this day – that, as a younger man under the guidance of his sorcerer mother, he killed his first-born son and ate his heart as a means to achieving personal power. It's a story that speaks volumes for the man's reputation, whether apocryphal or not.

In 1972 Amin had Uganda's chief justice, Benedicto Kiwanuka, also the country's first prime minister, dragged from court to be killed. One version of the story has Kiwanuka shot by Amin himself; another has him castrated, disembowelled and tortured to death. In other prominent cases, Anglican Archbishop Janani Luwum met his fate in a staged car accident – his body was riddled with bullet holes – and the vice chancellor of Uganda's only university, Frank Kalimuzo, was simply disappeared. When Amin's estranged wife, Kay, was found dismembered in the boot of a car, he had her sewn back together and put on display for him and his family. Two other wives survived attempts on their lives. (Amin had five wives, numerous mistresses and dozens of children. He liked to be called 'Big Daddy'.)

'Systematic and deliberate killings by government forces began in the first month of President Amin's military government and the practice was rapidly institutionalized as a means of eliminating opponents and potential opponents. The victims included members of ethnic groups other than those from which Amin drew support, as well as religious leaders, judges, lawyers, students and intellectuals, criminal suspects and foreign nationals. The impunity with which the security forces were allowed to kill political opponents and criminal suspects created the conditions in which many other people were killed by members of the security forces for criminal motives or simply at will.'

– summation of the opening years of the Amin regime by Amnesty International, 1972

Of Amin's numerous personality faults, his bloodlust was most striking. But a further defining trait was his unquenchable xenophobia. In 1972 Amin declared that he'd had a dream in which Uganda would expel all Asians. He mentioned this to some senior soldiers later that day, and by evening it was national policy.

Those affected were mainly of Indian origin, often third- or fourth-generation descendants of the men who had worked on the railways. They made up the merchant class in Uganda and held considerable control over large parts of the economy. Amin evidently mistook the free movement of people, ideas and capital as something pernicious and planned, a common misunderstanding among those with little economics literacy and a large chip on the shoulder.

Fifty or sixty thousand Asian residents with British nationality, even those with Ugandan passports, were thus given ninety days to leave the country on pain of who-knew-what. The scale of the personal tragedy this entailed for those families is, of course, unimaginable, but the socio-economic consequences for the entire country were even worse. Countless professionals – technicians, doctors and the like – were lost. Businesses were seized and handed out to Amin's cronies, and inevitably, as with farms given to Robert Mugabe's henchmen years later in Zimbabwe, they were simply stripped of their assets and left to ruin. This was all part and parcel of what Amin called his 'economic war of liberation'. Properties and businesses belonging to Europeans were also confiscated. Many locals, in fact, supported these moves – though his passions were extreme, Amin wasn't uniquely xenophobic – but the empowerment of indigenous African Ugandans that was supposed to follow never did. Instead, wealth fled the country like birds before a storm, and the economy collapsed.

In response, Amin had more money printed, believing this would fix the problem. Politically ruthless he may have been, but he really was a thicko.

As Jimmy Carter would later put it, Amin had 'disgusted the entire civilized world', and his regime, observed with grim fascination from abroad, became internationally isolated. The US cut off all aid in 1972. The UK, initially cautiously supportive of Amin, also retreated, despite Amin's natural affiliation with the country. He had served in the King's African Rifles (and wore its tie for the rest of his life), and had served against the Mau Mau in Kenya. (His claim to have served in Burma was, however, a lie.)

Critical Israeli investment was also withdrawn after Amin's unreasonable demands for financial and military assistance were rebuffed, and he ejected all Israelis from the country in response. He turned to Muammar Gaddafi for support, becoming his first African ally and fiercely anti-Semitic in the process. He expressed admiration for Hitler and support for the Palestinian terrorists who abducted and murdered Israeli athletes at the Munich Olympics in 1972.

This was a political position that culminated disastrously for Amin with his involvement in what became the Entebbe incident, when a hijacked Air France Airbus travelling from Tel Aviv to Paris was allowed to land at Entebbe, Kampala's main airport. The subsequent Israeli commando raid on the airport on the evening of 3 July 1976 has gone down in history as one of the most audacious and extraordinary military operations of all time. Having flown 4,000 kilometres to get there, the Israelis ended up evacuating 103 hostages – three were killed – and shooting dead all the hijackers. They also destroyed eleven Soviet MiGs while they were at it. The Ugandan army did eventually manage to return fire, killing one Israeli commando, the 30-year-old soldier-poet Yoni Netanyahu, brother of future Israeli Prime Minister Benjamin Netanyahu.

One lone hostage remained, a British grandmother by the name of Dora Bloch, who also held Israeli citizenship and who had been taken to hospital in Kampala after choking on some food at the airport. Outraged and humiliated by the turn of events, Amin ordered her execution. At the age of 74, Bloch was dragged screaming from her hospital bed and brutally murdered, her body dumped outside of Kampala. This was too much for the British, who broke off diplomatic relations in 1977. In response, Amin awarded himself a VC, a 'Victorious Cross', and the title 'CBE', a variation of 'Commander of the British Empire'; in this case he was 'Conqueror of the British Empire'.

This type of overblown tendency to the absurd enhanced Amin's reputation as the bemedalled, big-headed buffoon, and he was without doubt on various levels laughable. He was a strutting self-obsessed martinet who bestowed upon himself endless meaningless and invented titles and investitures: his official appellation was eventually 'His Excellency, President for Life, Field Marshal Al Hadji Doctor Idi Amin Dada, VC, DSO, MC, Lord of All the Beasts of the Earth and Fishes of the Seas and Conqueror of the British Empire in Africa in General and Uganda in Particular'.

The Bloch affair convinced many that Amin was mad, and both Israeli and British intelligence reports supposed that he suffered from syphilis-induced insanity. He variously claimed the crown of Scotland, and gave himself a Doctorate in law. Rumours that he was a cannibal never disappeared, and he didn't help by denying it later in life thus: 'It's too salty for my taste.' Other reports have him describing human meat as 'saltier than leopard flesh'.

He developed the amusing habit of sending telegrams to world leaders.

To Henry Kissinger: 'You are not intelligent because you never come to see me when you need advice.'

To Queen Elizabeth: 'I hear that England has economic problems. I'm sending a cargo ship full of bananas to thank you for the good days of the colonial administration.'

To Leonid Brezhnev and Mao Zedong: 'If you need a mediator I am at your disposal.'

It's important to be careful here. It *is* kind of funny, all this puffed-up nonsense, this idea of an uneducated assistant cook from the Kings African Rifles, as he had been, adopting – but kind of messing up – all the pomposity and affectation of the worst European royalty. But in the grander scheme there's very little that's funny about Idi Amin, and the temptation to roll the eyes and breezily dismiss him as ridiculous is to dismiss the scale of his crimes as somehow unimportant.

The truth is that Amin is but one of a particularly unpleasant gang of Big Man thugs who have done massive harm to Africa in the post-colonial period. They count among them Bokassa and Mobutu and Gaddafi and Mugabe and Zuma, utterly woeful gangster lowlifes driven to the fringes of policy insanity, and ultimately motivated by the most craven needs for wealth and power.

'Capricious, impulsive, violent and aggressive he certainly is, but to dismiss him as just plain crazy is to underestimate his shrewdness, his ruthless cunning and his capacity to consolidate power with calculated terror.'
– *British journalist Christopher Munnion,*
writing after he had been held at the notorious Makindye Military Prison.
Four of Munnion's cellmates were killed with sledgehammers

Zuma

Jean-Bédel Bokassa proclaimed himself as emperor of the impoverished Central African Republic and re-enacted the coronation of Napoleon in 1977 at a cost of one quarter of the country's annual national budget. Mobutu Sese Seko built himself three palaces and an airport to handle Concorde landings in his home village of Gbadolite, while looting Zaire to its core and leaving it a dysfunctional, anarchic husk. Muammar Gaddafi's plundering of Libya was staggering: after his overthrow and nasty death in 2011, his net worth was estimated at more than $200 billion, more than the (supposedly) three richest men in the world combined at the time, while his most notable bequest to our planet was a failed state and an endless supply of desperate emigrants. Robert Mugabe, still going strong in his mid-90s, has reduced Zimbabwe from the breadbasket of Africa to yet another basket case, while expropriating land from white owners and redistributing it to his friends and family. And Jacob Zuma has managed to bring the most sophisticated economy on the continent, South Africa, to its knees by divvying up national assets among his patrons and cronies.

They are buffoons, the lot of them. Blunderers, plunderers, philanderers, dissemblers, hypocrites and, ultimately, the scourge of the continent. A cartoonist's bread and butter, yes, but it's difficult to know when to laugh – especially with Amin, a man who represents the abject failure of post-independence Africa and the chaos at the heart of humankind.

Idi Amin's rule came to an end after he invaded Tanzania in 1979 as a means to placate his factious army. Julius Nyerere's Tanzania responded in kind with a large force and a battalion of Ugandan exiles only too keen to be rid of the awful dictator back home. (Nyerere, a controversial figure to this day, was a less typical African Big Man, though he ruled Tanzania for 24 years, leaving it corrupted and economically devastated.)

Despite assistance from Gaddafi, Kampala fell, and the invading troops were met with scenes of medieval atrocity when they smashed the gates of the dungeon below the State Research Bureau headquarters. Amin fled to Tripoli and then on to Jeddah, where the Saudi Arabians let him stay on condition that he shut

GADDAFI
LIBYA
42 YRS

up and keep a low profile, and so stop damaging the reputation of Islam with his outspoken lunacy.

Amin's departure from Uganda cleared the way for the disastrous return of Obote to power and the resulting Ugandan Bush War, which possibly saw even more people die than had under Amin, though their plight attracted less international attention. In 1986 Obote's nemesis Yoweri Museveni came to power, a relative moderate and a glimmer of light in a land that had suffered much darkness.

After his visit in 1907, Churchill called Uganda the pearl of Africa. Today, it enthrals those who visit it. People return almost evangelical about its beauty and the generous and friendly people who live there. Bordered by Lake Victoria and fed by the White Nile River, it is, as it always was, a lush and bountiful equatorial Eden, with plenty of minerals beneath its fertile soil. Uganda should be a place of plenty, yet it languishes in the depths of any measure of human development by country. Corruption and poverty are endemic, and it competes with Niger for the lowest median age in the world: around 15 years, half the global average. In 2014 Museveni, now into his fourth decade in power, signed into law the Anti-Homosexuality Act, which attempted to criminalise same-sex relationships with life imprisonment. A previous draft of the Act had sought the death penalty. The new version was declared invalid by the Constitutional Court, but its very proposal was one of several indicators, if any were needed, that Uganda is still struggling to catch up with the rest of the world.

Nevertheless, Museveni has been – amazingly, depressingly – considered a reasonably solid leader. Not horrendously corrupt, not a mass murderer, not entirely off his rocker. Such low standards come in the wake of Idi Amin, the Butcher of Uganda, a name that will forever be associated with madness and tyranny.

Amin died in Saudi Arabia in 2003, exiled but unrepentant. They say he weighed 220 kilograms. He is outrageously flattered by his posthumous image as a buffoon and a clown; he was, in fact, a savage and wanton example of the worst of humanity – and thus a worthy first entrant here.

See King Leopold II and Cecil John Rhodes.

Lance Armstrong

b. 18 September 1971

*Disgraced professional cyclist; cheat; bully; asshole;
'greatest fraud in the history of sports'; progenitor of
the world's most annoying people and their pastime*

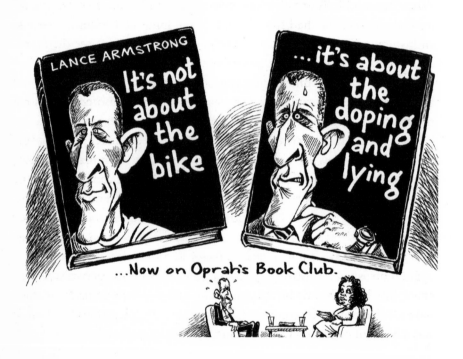

HE SAID IT WASN'T ABOUT THE BIKE, and that's true. It wasn't. It was about
the erythropoietin, the cortisone, the Andriol, the Actovegin, the human
growth hormones and the blood transfusions. Lance Armstrong's crimes
against professional cycling could earn his special space in this book on
their own. In doping his way to a record-breaking seven consecutive Tour
de France 'victories' – in the process becoming the most well-known and

revered cyclist of all time – he has comprehensively shattered the sport's reputation. He fought the rumours for years, but finally admitted the truth to Oprah in January 2013: yes indeed, he was a big old cheat. Ergo, the world concluded, professional cycling was a sham.

These days you just assume they're all on something. And if they're not *all* on it at this very minute – because Armstrong's Icarian plunge has frightened the horses, you see, or because your lawyer has pointed out that you shouldn't tar all cyclists with the same drug-taking brush – you imagine they'll be at it again soon enough, don't worry.

And yet Armstrong is the worst of the lot, not just because he was the best cheat with the highest profile, but because of his frighteningly casual inability to care about the people to whom he gave hope and inspiration. When he won his Tour victories between 1999 and 2005 after fighting off testicular cancer that had spread to his brain, lungs and abdomen, he was an inspiration to millions. Which ordinary person couldn't see the power of that story? Which cancer sufferer wouldn't see hope in such an outcome? When other cyclists from all over the world were getting caught doping and having their records expunged, the clean-cut, Nike-sponsored Armstrong remained unblemished and unconquerable. What a goddamned hero!

It was the stuff of fairy tales. Even if you didn't care much for the sport – because it's always been rife with dopers and cheats or, more prosaically, because it really is incredibly, incredibly boring – you couldn't deny the attraction of the Armstrong legend. He was an inspiration, not just for cancer sufferers, but for the average guy watching the telly. Here was proof of the power of the human spirit to overcome the greatest odds; to not just defy a killer disease, but to ascend to the peak of his sport...

But it turns out Armstrong was doping all along, his hypocrisy escalating exponentially each time he opened his mouth to defend himself. In 2001, Nike's 'What am I on?' commercial confronted the allegations head on. It was a brilliant concept – until it wasn't.

'This is my body, and I can do whatever I want to it. I can push it. Study it. Tweak it. Listen to it. Everybody wants to know what I'm on. What am I on? I'm on my bike busting my ass six hours a day. What are *you* on?'
– *Lance Armstrong, Nike commercial, 2001*

In 2005 Armstrong pulled the cancer card on *Larry King Live*, saying, 'If you consider my situation, a guy who comes back from, arguably, a death sentence, why would I then enter into a sport and then dope myself up and risk my life again? That's crazy, I would never do that.'

Later, he even used his children as the defence, explaining that he wouldn't be a worthy role model to them if he cheated. (Indeed, Lance. Indeed.) In 2012 Australia's ABC TV network quoted him berating 'the cynics and the sceptics' with the line, 'I'm sorry you can't dream big and I'm sorry you don't believe in miracles.'

Beyond the rampant hypocrisy and profound chutzpah came the seedy logistics of it all. The juicing up in trailers mid-race, with fans at the door looking for autographs, the evidence disappearing in used soda cans. Arranging for fresh supplies to be smuggled across international borders. Ordering in make-up to cover needle marks. And, critically, the bullying and cajoling of teammates to do the same so that his support crew was as unfairly advantaged, or as culpable, as he was. It may be true that it would have been impossible to win the Tour in his era without doping (because just about everyone was doing it), but falsely denouncing a young US Postal team masseuse as an 'alcoholic' and a 'whore' on TV when she dared to speak out against the drug culture in cycling, or telling ex-teammate

Tyler Hamilton, 'I'm going to make your life a living fucking hell' when he also spoke out, was tip-of-the-iceberg standard procedure for Armstrong. Countless others – pretty much anyone who threatened the Armstrong brand – were isolated and vilified, their reputations ruined.[1]

Hamilton has described how being asked to dope by Armstrong was like being accepted into a 'fraternity'. Long-time anti-doping activist and bona fide American cycling legend Greg LeMond puts it another way: 'This was an organised mafia and he literally tried to destroy people.' His wife Kathy has publicly described Armstrong as 'the greatest fraud in the history of sports'. We concur. Barry Bonds and Ben Johnson (and virtually every top 100-metre sprint champion barring Usain Bolt) had nothing on the guy.[2]

So not only is Armstrong a cheat, turns out he's a nasty piece of work to boot. And a wealthy one: he was estimated to be worth around $125 million shortly after his Oprah exposé. In 2013, the US Justice Department, acting on behalf of the US Postal Service which had sponsored more than $40 million towards Armstrong's team, launched a civil case against the man they would later characterise as 'a doper, dealer and liar'. Under the False Claims Act, Armstrong could be liable for nearly $100 million in damages, while many argue that he deserves jail time. Unfortunately, given the way the scales of justice tend to creak towards the famous and filthy rich, you wouldn't bet on either outcome.

The vast fraud and illegalities aside, though, it's important to save Armstrong's worst crimes for last: his cultural legacy. Yes, millions of people around the world – the majority of those who have followed his case – are shocked and appalled at his behaviour. But still he retains legions of fans who claim him as a great sportsman and a champion because everyone was doing it, because he still had to put in the training and hard work, because blah blah blah. Moreover, even those recreational cyclists who understand the simple human notion that wrong is wrong and that, therefore, what Armstrong did was unconscionable and inexcusable, have merrily appropriated the man's self-obsession, and his wilful disregard for other people and the rules at large. These are the Lycra-clad weekend warriors. The people who use the road as their personal gym while flouting its laws and expecting special dispensations from those who are actually going somewhere for a meaningful purpose. The countless brow-furrowed senior accountants and marketing directors, who spend their days cycling four abreast on single-lane uphills in their sanctimonious little pelotons, while the rest of the world's road-users entertain baseball-bat-out-of-car-window fantasies behind them.

Who are these unsmiling assholes bent over their dynamos of smugness, vacuum-wrapped like the flaccid contents of some giant novelty condom?

Who are these hairless androids pulling into the local coffee shop on a Sunday morning after four hours in the saddle, sitting down for a muffin and cappuccino in their psychedelic budgie-smugglers – with helmet still on?

They're the spawn of Lance Armstrong, that's who.

'Quite simply, I believed I had a responsibility to be a good person, and that meant fair, honest, hardworking and honourable. If I did that, if I gave back to my community or to some cause, if I wasn't a liar, a cheat, or a thief, then I believed that should be enough. At the end of the day, if there was indeed some Body or presence standing there to judge me, I hoped I would be judged on whether I had lived a true life.'
– from It's Not About The Bike by Lance Armstrong, published in 2000

Justin Bieber

b. 1 March 1994

Millennial pop star; YouTube sensation; voice – and death – of modern pop music; 'the King Joffrey of Pop'

BACK IN 1963 A NEW BAND CALLED THE BEATLES released an LP called *Please Please Me*. This LP – or album, for the youngsters reading this – contained a series of hits, including *She Loves You* and *From Me To You*. It was harmless bubblegum stuff played by nice-looking young men in suits – a primitive boy band. One of the band's two key songwriters, John Lennon, would admit matter-of-factly years later that he and Paul McCartney didn't really think too hard about what the songs actually said: 'pop songs with no more thought to them than that – to create a sound. And the words were almost irrelevant.'[1]

Oh boy, though, did The Beatles grow up, with their final few albums together embracing diverse and brave musical influences and expressing increasingly complex and profound meaning. This was pop music that became the greatest and most influential music of the century; music that's still relevant and celebrated fifty years later.

It's good to acknowledge that musicians, like writers and sportsmen, and in fact anyone in a particular field of human endeavour, flourish into their field given time and support. The artistic evolution that took place in just a decade, between the sweaty bars of Hamburg and the Cavern in Liverpool in the early 1960s and the Beatles' break-up in 1970, is extraordinary to behold.

But after ten years of Justin Bieber we're still waiting.

Since the Bieb was discovered on YouTube in 2008, it's been a decade of self-indulgent 'co-written' schmaltzy wallpaper, evolving from a nasal pre-teen of limited talent to a mock-intense, industrially produced twenty-something, self-conscious, affected breathiness. In that time he has endowed on the world one lonely, solitary, single song that transcends his fandom – one song that people who don't follow or really know Bieber could hum along to (if only under duress). The Beatles have at least twenty, Michael Jackson fifteen. Wham have five; even Britney Spears has three or four. Bieber has *Baby*. That's on a par with Dexys Midnight Runners and Billy Ray Cyrus. And yet this guy – *the* 'teenage heartthrob' of our time – has a mind-bogglingly large following of hysterical proportions and a profound cultural influence (not to mention a quarter of a billion dollars in the bank).

The internet created Bieber, and it's on the internet where you'll find his worst abusers too. Much of the vitriol that appears is revolting, as you'd imagine, it being the internet. He presents a version of maleness that some hairy-arsed folks just cannot seem to handle, all of which came spilling out in 2015 when he wore a *Metallica* T-shirt in public.

Let's distance ourselves from that kind of bro-dom. Our disdain for Bieber is simpler. Everybody has to be young and promising once, but talent, practice and the passing of ten years can turn *I Wanna Hold Your Hand* into *The White Album*. Bieber, by contrast, still speaks to the tweens who buy his albums after all these years. He has yet to formulate an adult insight that doesn't centre the world back on Justin Bieber. His famously gormless inscription at the Anne Frank House museum in Amsterdam – that in his view Ms Frank was 'a great girl' – was not improved by his expression of hope that 'she would have been a Belieber'.[2] No words, Justin. No words. (This is both our reaction here and advice to you.)

Pea-brained self-absorbed thinking of this type is perhaps not surprising in an era when our pop stars are sourced at ever-younger ages from Disney and Nickelodeon shows and YouTube channels, whisked out of school and given a platform and a microphone to utter their inane nonsense, be it as guestbook messages or actual music. And yet Bieber has observed the likes of Britney, Christina Aguilera, Justin Timberlake, Miley Cyrus, Selena Gomez, Ariana Grande and the rest, and seems, in our estimation, intent on reducing things to previously unheard of levels.

Even at just 23, there is something of the Peter Pan about Bieber; the boastfulness and the inability to grow up. All that changes are the haircuts and the try-hard tattoos. The core of Bieber – middling talent, unimportant material and huge production – never seems to change. He is, in so many ways, 'the King Joffrey of pop', as comedian Jeff Ross phrased it, and so he represents its potential death.[3]

If Justin Bieber is the Beatles of the 2010s then we can at least be grateful that we're not teenagers today. Discerning/grumpy older men that we have become, we'll take our 1980s Rick Astley and Depeche Mode, thank you very much. Still, we can't help thinking that if the Aztecs and the Incas and the Romans and the Mongols were listening to pop music before their civilisations fell apart, they would've been listening to Bieber.

Osama bin Laden

10 March 1957 – 2 May 2011

'Holy warrior'; civilian mass murderer; history-changer; mastermind of the new age of hyper-terrorism; one-time bogeyman of the world; the guy who made air travel such a pain

'OSAMA,' WHISPERS THE MAN in the dark. 'Osama...'

He is crouching at the top of the stairs in a three-storey house in Abbottabad, Pakistan, his silenced Heckler & Koch HK416 assault rifle pointing out into the darkness. Beside him, a second man also crouches. 'Osama,' he whispers one more time, before a tall figure appears in the gloom. He fires a suppressed shot, then another, and, just like that, Osama bin Laden is dead. Not with a bang, but with a quiet *bap*.

This, then, is the way the life of the world's most wanted man ends according to the Kathryn Bigelow-directed Hollywood action-thriller *Zero Dark Thirty*. It's riveting viewing, both because it is the climax of a superbly shot 25-minute raid sequence, and because there is an enormous and very human sense of validation in what has just happened. This is a take on Hannah Arendt's 'banality of evil': the uncontested, almost silent demise of the man who brought terror to the Western world; whose life work was to bring about the deaths of thousands of innocent people, and who came to represent the most refined evil of our time.

It's not true, of course, this depiction of Osama bin Laden's last moments. Though there were probably five key witnesses in reality – three American special forces operators, bin Laden's youngest wife, Amal, and another female family member – it seems unlikely that a definitive account will ever be possible. Two of the Americans involved, usually anonymous members of the US Navy's SEAL Team Six, have identified themselves since retiring from the military and told their stories. But they, and other experts, can't seem to agree on the details, which probably isn't that surprising given the circumstances: it was the middle of the night, they were wearing night-vision goggles with limited field of vision, there were numerous unidentified people on the scene, and they were there *to kill the world's most wanted man*. There is also the politics of two ex-SEALs speaking about a classified operation in public to consider. Both men, Robert O'Neill and Matt Bissonnette, have faced severe criticism for their decisions and there appear to be competing agendas among everyone with an opinion.*

Nevertheless, the death of Osama bin Laden went something like this. An unidentified point man, probably still an active SEAL, reached the top of the stairs first, with O'Neill second and Bissonnette third behind him. When bin Laden peered through his bedroom door, the point man got off a shot, which either missed or winged him, and both the point man and O'Neill quickly pursued him into the room. Specifically alert to the likelihood that people in the house might be wearing suicide vests, the point man aggressively pulled the two women in the room aside to protect

---

* In a 2016 settlement between Bissonnette and the US Defense Department, Bissonnette had to pay over $6.6 million in royalties he gained from the 2012 release of his book *No Easy Day* for publishing military information that was not vetted. O'Neill's approved book, *The Operator*, was published in 2017.

the others, as O'Neill shot bin Laden twice in the forehead, and then a third time as 'insurance'. Bissonnette arrived a split second later to fire a few rounds into the falling or fallen body.

There was more chaos, and probably two more people, than the movie depicted, and in his assessment of the recreation of the event O'Neill also noted that none of them had whispered for bin Laden, as they had for his son, Khalid, further down the stairway. There are several other technical faults in the extended raid scene. The soldiers' tattoos are laughably small. The assault team's security dog, Cairo, is a German Shepherd when it should have been a Belgian Malinois. A member of the team calls out before a breaching explosive is detonated, which wouldn't happen.

Do these minor particulars matter? Are we not splitting hairs? Notwithstanding the plot and character conflation in the movie necessary to keep it to a reasonable viewing length, *Zero Dark Thirty* is a remarkably authentic account of the hunt for and assassination of Osama bin Laden. The film-makers could hardly have done a better job – so we're not criticising them. We're just fussing over the details a little because never in the history of the world has one man attracted the resources that bin Laden did to track him down, never has an entire nation distilled their fear of the enemy into one man rather than the war machine around him, and never has the violent death of an individual been anticipated so long in advance. For millions of Americans, the death of Osama bin Laden on 2 May 2011 – arguably an unlawful extrajudicial killing – was an essential point of justice and a necessary part of the recovery process after the world-changing acts of September 11 ten years before.

On that day, two Boeing 767s were flown by al-Qaeda hijackers, 17 minutes apart, into the second- and third-tallest buildings in America and the symbolic representation of the country's financial centre, the Twin Towers of the World Trade Center. Within two hours both towers, each more than 415 metres tall, had collapsed, destroying all five other buildings in the complex, catastrophically damaging ten other large buildings in the area, and engulfing Manhattan in an apocalyptic dust cloud. For perspective, the *third* tallest building entirely destroyed on the day was the 190-metre '7 World Trade Center'; the loss of that skyscraper alone, for any reason, would have made world news for years. A third plane hit the Pentagon, and a fourth crashed into a field in Pennsylvania after the passengers learnt of the other attacks and tried to take back control of the aircraft; its intended target was either the White House or the Capitol Building in Washington, DC. All together, the attacks killed 2,996 people and caused incalculable financial damage to New York, the United States and world markets.

Osama bin Laden had spent half a million dollars on planning and executing what came to be known as the 9/11 attacks. The US government would spend half a trillion dollars, and launch two protracted wars, in hunting him down.

In many ways, Osama bin Laden was a worthy super-villain. The Saudi son of a Yemeni billionaire construction magnate, he gave up a potential life of luxury at the age of 22 to fight as one of 'the Afghan Arabs' after the Soviet invasion of Afghanistan in 1979. In the decade-long war that followed he became revered as a mujahideen senior, funnelling money to the cause, constructing guerrilla trails and installations, training volunteers and fighting in battle. He was injured in the foot and he inhaled napalm which left him with throat problems. He claimed to have survived a 120mm mortar shell that landed in front of him but didn't explode. (What the world might have been but for a properly primed Russian bomb.)

According to author Peter Bergen, a member of the CNN team that arranged bin Laden's first interview on television, 'the Sheik' was vain and

notoriously stingy, a narcissist who dyed his beard to hide the grey and used a herbal aphrodisiac to help him satisfy his wives (of whom there were three by the end). Critically for a man who would come to represent pure evil in our time, he was filled with hate for those who didn't embrace the strictest forms of Islam and believed non-Muslim civilians, specifically Jews, were legitimate targets (and if a few Muslims were lost as collateral damage then at least they'd be going to paradise). He had found his calling fighting the Soviets and was enamoured with the notion of defeating an anti-Muslim 'superpower' through attritional guerrilla warfare.

In 1988 bin Laden co-founded al-Qaeda, 'The Base' or 'The Foundation', a transnational militant Salafi jihadist organisation which sought to return Muslims to a conservative 'true' form of Sunni Islam. He believed in a literal Wahhabist interpretation of Islam that saw non-adherents as heathens and thus the enemy, and he would go on to issue two fatwas in its name. Initially, religiously corrupted or secular Middle Eastern states such as Saudi Arabia and Iraq were the focus of his organisation's ire. But after the 1991 Gulf War bin Laden shifted focus and declared holy war on the 'unjust, criminal and tyrannical' United States government, identifying its large presence on the holy soil of Saudi Arabia as the reason. His talent was the ability to tap into a specific seam of fervent West-hating righteousness within the Islamic world, and he mobilised this extremist consciousness across national boundaries in a way and to an extent that had not been done before.

Having abandoned Saudi Arabia, he moved to Sudan for a time before being ejected and returning to the only country that would have him, Afghanistan, under the rule of the troglodytic Taliban. By the time of the CNN interview, March 1997, bin Laden had links to the earlier 1993 bombing at the World Trade Center and militant training camps in Sudan and Afghanistan, and had called for jihad against US troops in Saudi Arabia. He railed against being defined as a terrorist by the United States, which he deemed a terrorist government in return, but in time every credible government and relevant global institution categorised al-Qaeda and its many offshoots as such.

Major al-Qaeda attacks, besides those on 9/11, include the bombings of US embassies in Nairobi and Dar es Salaam in 1998, the bombing of the *USS Cole* in Aden in 2000 and a series of truck bombs in Istanbul in 2003. Al-Qaeda-affiliated attacks include the Bali bomb in 2002, Madrid train bombing in 2004 and the London Underground attacks in 2005. There have been countless others throughout the world, and specifically in Iraq where 'al-Qaeda in Iraq', under the leadership of the psychopath Abu Musab al-Zarqawi, played a critical role in the insurgency against US troops and helped foment Sunni-Shia violence.

With or without his most famous act of chaos, Osama bin Laden had rivers of blood on his hands. But there have been far more deadly menaces in our times, so his legacy is less about the individual bodies he racked up than the universal fear he sowed and the shift in the geopolitical landscape that came of his actions. In introducing us to the new age of hyper-terrorism, he somehow reached down into our collective id to elevate the world's anxiety levels beyond any rational justification – so much so that in the year after 9/11 the number of US road fatalities increased appreciably as Americans chose to drive instead of fly. (A German risk specialist put the indirect toll of 9/11 at 1,595.)

The more profound and insidious effect of this universal neurosis is the way the Western world's attitudes to immigration and defence have evolved in recent years. Most fundamentally, bin Laden changed the history of the modern world, lending George W Bush the excuse and support to launch 'the War on Terror', including costly and protracted wars in Afghanistan and Iraq, forays that have sunk trillions of American dollars and distracted the country from, well, being sensible and going about its business.

'My brother Osama, how much blood has been spilt? How many innocent people, children, elderly, and women have been killed… in the name of al-Qaeda? Will you be happy to meet God Almighty carrying the burden of these hundreds of thousands or millions on your back?'
– *Salman al-Odah, Saudi cleric and one-time mentor of bin Laden, in an open letter, 2007*

There are several ironies to bin Laden's story. Famously, the CIA spent billions of dollars funding the mujahideen's war against the Soviets in Afghanistan so, whether directly or indirectly, America helped sponsor and effectively trained the architect of 9/11 for many years. A lesser-known irony was that he wasn't, in fact, the architect of 9/11. The brains behind the details and management of the operation were those of his equally hateful extremist associate Khalid Sheikh Mohammed, who was captured in Pakistan in 2003 and is currently locked up in Guantanamo Bay. (Bin Laden was certainly the sponsor and inspiration of 9/11.)

A third irony, perhaps an appropriate one, is that he died at the hands of soldiers who had become the best in the world at what they do – quietly stalking through houses killing people – because they had adopted this approach (over the flashbang method) and refined these skills repeatedly throughout the long wars that bin Laden had ignited. In his last few seconds alive, once his ten-year run from American vengeance had come to an end and he had been hunted down to that house in Abbottabad, bin Laden came face to face with men as inured to killing people as he was – men who had become the best in the world at doing exactly that due to his actions.

In those last moments there was fear in the air, according to O'Neill and Bissonnette – 'chaos, people screaming'. Bin Laden knew the Americans had come for him but he was paralysed in response. Rather than arm himself with either the submachine or pistol he kept in his bedroom, he used his wife as a shield when the SEALs came through the door. These are the details that engross and possibly offer some deal of therapy to those affected by 9/11.

'There's never any closure to this,' explained Maureen Santora, after meeting Robert O'Neill and hearing his story of the raid soon after he had

Hannity: Did you feel when you were standing over him that you had shot the embodiment of evil?

O'Neill: What I felt was a sense of pride to be part of such an amazing team, and that that team was picked to be the means to an end... We were the FDNY, we were the NYPD. We're the punch right now and we're here to deliver justice.

– Sean Hannity interviewing Robert O'Neill, 2014

revealed his identity in 2014. 'What this has done is put another piece in our healing, and it's a very large piece.' Santora's 23-year-old son Christopher was a firefighter, off duty at the time, who responded to the attacks on the Twin Towers.[1]

After bin Laden was killed, one version of the story has it that subsequent SEALs came into the room and riddled his body with bullets, possibly a hundred or more. That even the most professional soldiers in the world may not have been able to restrain themselves in the presence of the great nemesis of our time is probably not surprising. But there is a caution in there about violence begetting violence that remains worryingly unheard…

Al-Qaeda was a shell of what it had been by the time of the Abbottabad raid, its leadership largely vapourised from above by invisible American drones and its capacity to deliver lethal terror raids greatly diminished. But maybe it is impossible to truly kill a bogeyman. Today, the spirit of al-Qaeda and its emir Osama bin Laden has been consumed and rebirthed in a raging new breed of internet-savvy jihadi, the murderers of ISIS. When they go, as inevitably they will, there will unfortunately be other monsters to inherit the mantle.

'You killed the devil, and I salute you for that, sir.'
— *Weeping US citizen talking to Robert O'Neill at Ground Zero*

See Tony Blair, George W Bush & Mohammed Emwazi.

Ritt Bjerregaard

b. 19 May 1941

European Commissioner for the Environment 1994-1999; bureaucrat behind the push for diesel cars; embodiment of the law of unintended consequences

RITT BJERREGAARD IS A RETIRED SOCIALIST Danish politician and grower of organic apples. She seems like a decent, well-meaning kind of person who, when young, was fired with the outrage of somebody who grew up (relatively) poor and managed to make it to university, where the unfairness of wealth inequality struck her hard. All fair enough, and Bjerregaard's inclusion here isn't because we think she holds untenable political views or believe she is an especially unpleasant individual. It's because she's caused so much harm by accident. It's because she's a standard-grade political meddler of no particular egregiousness whose well-intentioned decisions have contributed to uncountable deaths over the last two decades.

If you drive a diesel car, Ritt Bjerregaard is most likely the reason. She's the reason you took what you thought was a wise, environmentally sound and economically sensible decision to buy your car. And she's the reason you've been pumping excessive amounts of carcinogenic filth and dangerous toxic gases into the atmosphere your children breathe.

Now, diesel engines are remarkable things. They are very efficient in crude fuel-efficiency terms and their power delivery is perfect for certain applications. Because they produce a lot of torque, as opposed to outright power, they're great for commercial vehicles; if you're in the market for a tractor, say, or a combine harvester, diesel certainly makes sense. They're getting better in cars, too, and are unbeatably efficient on long motorway runs and for towing trailers and caravans.

As good as diesel engines may be these days, however, diesel cars are still actually pretty terrible. They're clatteringly noisy, they fall asleep after 3,000rpm, and they're enormously complicated to put together and will inevitably break, at great cost, after a few years. And, really, how often do you tow a caravan that you need to do this to yourself?

More pertinently, for this entry, and life in general, diesel is horrible, horrible stuff, a fact we have understood for a long, long time. Your first clue is the overwhelming stink. How often have you sat in traffic with the air on recycle because of the stench of the black cab in front of you? Methamphetamine sales are down in central London because if you want to get absurdly high and vomit all over the pavement you just need to go and stand on Tottenham Court Road for twenty minutes. That's not actually true, of course, but the point stands.* This is your body telling you to stop breathing in clouds of nitrogen oxide and diesel particulate, which together cause breathing problems, asthma, bronchitis, heart disease and lung sicknesses, including cancer.

So in summary: diesel cars are rubbish to drive and they depreciate badly and they fall apart and they're expensive to maintain and they make a stupid noise and they stink and – oh yes – they kill your children.

Only the European Union could have promoted something this shit.

Bjerregaard's story serves to illustrate the sheer scale of unintended consequences when governments decide to *do something*. It is a tragedy of modern life that no politician would enjoy being remembered for a legacy of leaving people alone to make their own decisions. More's the pity.

In the early 1990s there was growing concern that something called Global Warming was a real thing, that human activity was responsible for it, that specifically human production of carbon dioxide (CO_2) was the principal driver of this phenomenon, and that if we didn't do something about it soon the world, and humanity with it, would be doomed. This sense of crisis resulted in the United Nations Conference on Environment and Development, a.k.a. Earth Summit, in Rio de Janeiro in 1992, at which

---

* According to the European Environment Agency, the most polluted street in Europe, as of 2016, was in fact London's Marylebone Road, with levels of nitrogen oxide more than double the EU's legal limit.

certain principles were laid down about sustainable development and the protection of forests. Ever since, the environmental movement has been chasing legally binding targets on what it believes causes Global Warming: so-called greenhouse gases, the number-one culprit, according to the orthodoxy, being carbon dioxide.

Now it's pretty clear to everyone with a brain that climate change, as it's now known, is a real thing. The cause and extent of it is something argued about by people who are experts in meteorology, climate science, atmospheric science, geoscience and science in general. So, to be really, really clear: that categorically excludes the worst gibbering eco-commie groupies of the likes of Greenpeace and the World Wildlife Fund (WWF) who consider all human progress an affront to rare Guatemalan butterflies, as much as it excludes the alt-right assault-rifle-toting anarcho-libertarian whack-jobs who see an attack on human freedom every time someone points out that it's a bit warm this afternoon.

When it comes to climate issues the best course of action is to adopt powerful scepticism – not for the science (which, being science, is naturally sceptical), but for the pub professors and the Twitter conspiracy nuts. Anybody who starts shouting or hurling pejoratives – be it 'climate denier' or 'warmist' – is almost certainly an idiot and unlikely to have the requisite PhD. It's absolutely critical to ignore them in the same way you'd ignore somebody with a diploma from a catering college who has an opinion on open-heart surgery.

The more nuanced element of the climate change debate, in an age in which nuance doesn't hold a candle to volume, comes in considering how we balance humankind's shorter- and longer-term needs. What and how much can we do to slow climate change without compromising the health and wellbeing of humans everywhere? Yes, we want to save the planet and not get tipped into the sea but also we want to increase, or at least maintain, global human living standards (ascribing, as we do, to the idea that life has got better, not worse, with the advancement of human civilisation).

Great minds have been thinking about this for some time now. So have politicians who want to be seen to be doing something… By happy coincidence for the latter, the year that the Earth Summit took place in Rio, 1992, also saw the European Economic Community (EEC) transmogrify into the European Union (EU) through the adoption of the Maastricht Treaty. No longer did this entity regard itself as merely an economic union;

it was now an overtly political union – and for some in its corridors of power, the Rio Declaration would have come as a serendipitous manifesto for change.

Perhaps sensing the shifting breeze, it was into this milieu that Ritt Bjerregaard began to move, tossing off her anti-EEC feelings to join the Danish European Movement and become its chair that same year. Bjerregaard has claimed the reason for her embracing the European project was the success of the reunification of Germany in 1989. But by the looks of her rapid rise from leftist politician in a small country to the position of European Commissioner for the Environment in 1994, the EU was plain and simply good for Ritt Bjerregaard too.

By 1995 Global Warming was all the rage and carbon dioxide cast as the devil's fuel that powered it. Bjerregaard was decidedly interested in listening to the arguments of trigger-happy environmentalists and she believed in their interpretation of the science. Though automotive emissions were responsible, according to the commission's own statistics, for no more than 12 percent of all carbon dioxide emissions in the EU at the time, on Bjerregaard's watch the commission would begin to flex its muscles and force manufacturers to substantially reduce emissions and increase fuel economy in their cars.

In a communication from the time, Bjerregaard made her position clear to the European car industry with this Orwellian gem: 'For the industry, entering into an ambitious CO_2 commitment is an opportunity to prove their environmental credentials. We will closely watch the progress which they are making.'[1]

In the same communication, she laid out the commission's strategy, explaining that tax would be used as a weapon to make 'a less fuel consuming car' more affordable. And, while a general motivation for more fuel efficiency seemed logical enough – even if you don't give a continental about Mother Nature, it makes economic sense – the unmistakable means they were imposing was diesel cars, which are more expensive to buy because they are more complicated to build.

That, in the short telling of it, is how we ended up in a situation where diesel is taxed less than petrol at the pumps, and diesel cars fall into lower tax brackets than their equivalent petrol models: because Bjerregaard's environmentalist advisers had bludgeoned her with their impression of the truth, that no matter how disgustingly filthy diesel engines are, at least they

> 'Diesel cars should attract less vehicle tax than their petrol equivalents because of their better CO_2 performance.'
>
> *– Gordon Brown, then Chancellor of the Exchequer, speaking in 1998. He introduced tax incentives in the UK to buy diesel cars in 2001*

emitted less carbon than a petrol engine, and that this was more important than public health generally.

The result, unsurprisingly, has been a proliferation of diesel cars on European and ultimately the world's roads. Once incentives were introduced in the UK in 2001, diesel car numbers accelerated from 3.45 million to 8.1 million in the following decade and a half. According to figures from the European Automobile Manufacturers' Association, 23 percent of new cars in the European Union were diesel in 1995, rising to a peak of 56 percent in 2011. In Bjerregaard's Denmark, the figures leapt from a paltry 3 percent to 47 percent.

One wonders what she might think of this today, when suddenly everyone is upset about diesel, and not just because car manufacturers like Volkswagen have been caught out cheating on their real-world emissions tests. The new studies have been coming in – most damningly in 2012 – and it turns out diesel is even more revolting than we thought. It's difficult to quantify the sickness-causing effects of a certain type of pollution, and particularly the difference between 'acceptable' levels of pollution and those that exceed the defined regulations, but the boffins have been giving it a go and the figures are frightening. Researchers at King's College London and the International Council on Clean Transportation estimate that more than 9,000 people a year die prematurely in London alone, and as many as 60,000 across the UK, due to pollution caused primarily by diesel traffic. In Europe the figure appears to be in the hundreds of thousands.

That right there is the cost of listening to eco-fascists who use the environment as a veil for their political objectives – people who denigrate others as 'deniers', deliberately comparing them to those who would question the veracity of the Holocaust if they dare to examine their ministrations in a little detail rather than nodding in dumb acquiescence.

Now cities are coming under enormous pressure from – if you can actually countenance the nerve of it – the European Commission (and

'The scientific evidence was compelling and the Working Group's conclusion was unanimous: diesel engine exhaust causes lung cancer in humans. Given the additional health impacts from diesel particulates, exposure to this mixture of chemicals should be reduced worldwide.'
– *Dr Christopher Portier, Chairman of the International Agency for Research on Cancer Working Group, commenting on the World Health Organization's 2012 decision to upgrade diesel to a Group 1 carcinogen to humans, in the same category as tobacco, mustard gas and plutonium*

Greenpeace, naturally) to reduce harmful pollution, and are taking aim at diesel cars as the principal target. Londoners are having to pay double the congestion charge to drive their diesel cars through the city. Paris, Madrid and Athens have plans to outlaw them entirely, and the powers that be are putting in place regulations to have diesel phased out across the continent.

Ah, hindsight, you might argue. It was worth a try. But no, it wasn't really. Because we've always known that diesel was disastrous for our health. And yet the only thing the EU was really worrying about when power was vested unto them to regulate an entire continent in the early 1990s was carbon emissions. Human health be damned. If that doesn't underline the vast and awful scale of the misanthropy at the heart of the Soviet-style environmentalism so frequently peddled in our time, what will?

In a final, depressing illustration of the extent of this futility, it is now being argued that diesel cars in fact produce *more* carbon dioxide than petrol cars when the entire 'well to wheel' process is considered because diesel is more energy-intensive to refine and drivers tend to buy heavier diesel cars. In the words of one expert, 'what you actually find is diesels are not lower CO_2 than gasoline, they're just more fuel-efficient at the tailpipe'.[2]

Make no mistake, if Ritt Bjerregaard had stayed in Denmark in the 1990s, waiting for another crack at the Education ministry where she first made her name, or simply farming those apples, somebody like her would have come along and done the diesel thing. She's not a mass murderer, and she wasn't the architect of this disaster so much as the name on the building.

But after her five-year stint at the EU shaking up the car industry and making a name for herself, she did once again become a minister in the

Danish cabinet after a twenty-year hiatus. Later she became Lord Mayor of Copenhagen. These lofty assignments are perhaps not incidental to the moral here.

The story of Ritt Bjerregaard is thus a lesson in the dangers of unintended consequences; a cautionary tale for those holding extreme positions and wanting to *do something* in any environment – such as the environment – in which the real facts can only be accumulated and made sense of slowly and incrementally. In crude terms, the rule could be: if your proposed change will kill a lot of people soon, don't do it. A more sophisticated version would involve the gathering and analysis of information over time, an enjoinment that, in matters of great importance, leaping should be performed only after looking, and that the Truth and your desire to be at the centre of it will always transcend your limited time in office.

'It turns out we were wrong.'
– Sir David King, the UK's special representative for climate change and chief scientific adviser under Tony Blair and Gordon Brown, speaking about diesel cars, April 2017

Tony Blair

b. 6 May 1953

Prime minister of the UK 1997-2007; the politician who got our hopes up; the politician who gave us spin; the most compromised politician of modern times; Bush's legitimiser; really just a PR guy

WHEN TONY BLAIR WAS PHOTOGRAPHED wearing a gold-cross necklace while holidaying off the coast of Sicily in August 2016, UK columnist Jan Moir described him as looking 'like a half-baked Mafioso, a Tony Mezzo-Soprano'. Well played, Jan Moir. Well played. Layered. Why, that may have been the wittiest bon mot of the summer.

The greater point she was making is that jewellery on a man – aside from a gentleman's cuff links, watch and wedding ring, that is – doesn't just enhance the possibility of you looking like a half-baked mafioso. No. 'Almost without exception, it [is] a cry for help; the external manifestation of a bleak chunk of self-doubt.'[1]

It's hard to disagree.

There are, we'd suggest, three broad categories of male jewellery wearers: rappers, the mistaken and the insecure. Rappers are, of course, all of the above, whereas Blair, a man whose political career will be defined for being the very opposite of what he chose to project (honesty), is surely the latter.

Who would have thought? When this vibrant confident-looking son of a tax inspector reinvented the UK's Labour party as New Labour in the early 1990s, he appeared as a breath of fresh air in the stale politics of the day. Here was, it seemed to people everywhere, a charming, direct and intelligent contender unencumbered by the cynical backroom machinations that seemed to prevail at the time. Moreover, he had what seemed like a workable plan to steer Labour from apparently delusional far-left socialism towards a centrist social democracy based on some kind of market reality, having convinced his party, in the words of Ross Clark, 'that profit is not a dirty word but the source of the tax revenues which pay for social programmes'.[2] He was, in short, a genuine alternative to the establishment and just what the UK – and the world – was looking for. 'We were all convinced that Blair would find a way of reconciling the divisions in Britain and making us a more honourable and less cynical country,' remembered veteran political commentator Peter Oborne two decades later.[3]

Labour's return to power in May 1997 after eighteen years in opposition was by landslide, its greatest electoral victory ever. 'A new dawn has broken,' Blair declared on the day he was elected to be the UK's youngest prime minister in 185 years. He went on to describe his incoming administration as 'a government that seeks to restore trust in politics in this country'.[4]

And for a little while, at least, they did that.

When Blair appeared before a battalion of cameras in the aftermath of the death of Diana, Princess of Wales in August that year – the inexperienced prime minister's most public moment to date, transmitted to a stunned world – the endearing impression was... honesty. Here was a leader who understood people, and yes, was someone you could trust.

Only the bitterest Establishment man might have denied that this was a talented politician ushering in a new era. And that he certainly did – an era that might have been remembered in time to come for the introduction of the minimum wage in Britain, the end of the troubles in Northern Ireland and the birth of a viable form of social democracy in Britain.

But didn't he just pawn this glorious opportunity?

When Blair was eventually eased from office ten years later, cheese-grinned and Brown-harassed, his reputation was tarnished beyond what could ever have been thought possible. Instead of charming, direct and intelligent, he was viewed with almost universal contempt: manipulative, evasive and, if not downright stupid, then having misjudged both the politics of the Middle East and the court of public opinion. Above all he was seen as dishonest: the man once known as Bambi was now BLIAR, as those who marched against him so succinctly put it.

For Blair, the big smiles and the nerdy, cheery demeanour had, it seemed, merely been cynical strategy – spin. He was the beaming face of New Labour but in the background he let loose one of the most odious men of modern Britain, Alastair Campbell, his bad cop, to spin and spin and spin. Under New Labour the truth was postmodern, something to be manufactured. In time it came to be assumed that everything Blair and the Blairites said or did had to be interpreted through a lens of public-relations chicanery. The most infamous deception (and the one most important in global terms) was his passionate exhortation for the invasion of Iraq based on the 'sexed-up' fact that Saddam Hussein possessed weapons of mass destruction that he could deploy against British troops (in Cyprus) on 45 minutes' notice. This would, in time, be proven to be unequivocally wrong.

By this stage of Blair's premiership, many observers – perhaps the majority – were already refusing to take anything significant he might say at face value, given the long list of deceptions, distractions, evasions and manoeuvres that had taken place on his watch to date. For them, every proposal or call to action was mere lip service, and the ultimate goal was not even about governance. As *The Economist* put it in a 2007 review of Blair's time in charge, 'Everything was done with the aim of winning the next election.'

Of course, when Blair made his move, his shot at greatness, he hitched himself to the coattails of one of the gigantic plonkers of modern history, George W Bush. In forming an unlikely special relationship with the cowboy president, he was happy to play the role of respectable and competent partner in the global war on terror, skilfully deflecting from Dubya's embarrassing performances at press conferences and conferring respectability on his international policies. In so doing, he gave himself the greatest chance to become a global player and a big man of history, the messianic figure he longed to be. Only in partnership with Bush could he find himself in US Congress, the greatest of political stages, receiving a standing ovation.

We may speculate that Blair believed he could manipulate the intellectually inferior Bush and bend him to his will – perhaps even for an intended good, if we're being generous. But for the partnership to work it meant backing him come what may, and if that meant invading Iraq, so be it.

Some say that Blair's famously stated belief that Saddam Hussein possessed weapons of mass destruction and was ready to use them within 45 minutes' notice was a lie; others say it was a bloody great big rotten lie. Whatever your take on the justification for invading Iraq, it's hard to argue that Blair didn't compromise his country's reputation and his own ethical standing in stumping for war.

The real crime, however, was the embarrassing lack of planning for what happened next. Perhaps if Blair had arranged for a few of his famous focus groups to be run in the Shia and Sunni communities of Baghdad, he might have come better prepared. Because no-one argues that the consequences of the Iraq War and its aftermath have been catastrophic: somewhere between 500,000 and a million deaths, and sectarian chaos that has destabilised the entire region and bred a new generation of West-fearing extremists. (See *George W Bush* for more on all this.)

Blair himself has admitted that it was a disaster, though the concession was delivered – to Sir David Frost, no less – during an infinitesimally small lapse of PR protocol.

David Frost: But so far it's been, you know, pretty much of a disaster.
Tony Blair: It has, but you see what I say to people is...
– Al Jazeera interview, discussing Iraq, 2006

> 'Blair's strong, passionate often, advocacy of the [Iraq] war carried a lot of weight. Without Blair's vocal support and participation, they might not have been able to carry it off.'
>
> – *Noam Chomsky, 2016* [3]

In a move of farcical inappropriateness, shortly after leaving office in 2007 Blair was appointed special representative of the Quartet of international powers – the United Nations, the US, the European Union and Russia – that seeks to negotiate a peace agreement between Israel and the Palestinians. In other words, he was chosen to be Middle East peace envoy in a region that he was instrumental in destabilising.

The release in July 2016 of the Chilcot report, the UK's official inquiry into the Iraq War, excoriated the UK government. It found that it had, along with the United States, undermined the authority of the United Nations Security Council, and that the war had been initiated needlessly and on the flimsiest of evidence. In short, what we all knew already.

In his official response, Blair adamantly refused to apologise for the invasion itself, claiming he would do it again based on the same evidence, but he did accept blame for the disastrous management afterwards. 'For all of this I express more sorrow, regret and apology than you may ever know or can believe,' he said, his voice cracking with emotion.[5]

The last three words are his most revealing admission of all. We can't believe him, and he doesn't expect us to – he knows he has sold for silver the faith in him that the average observer once had.

Today Tony Blair jets around the world trading on the contacts he made as prime minister, and later as Middle East peace envoy, to earn obscene amounts as a consultant for international investment companies and governments. The reported figures are astounding: speaking fees of more than £200,000; annual consultancy retainers from finance company Zurich of £500,000 and investment bank JP Morgan* of $5 million; a $1 million brokerage fee for the three hours he spent facilitating the Glencore-Xstrata merger in 2012.

---

* The JP Morgan name pops up in minor asides throughout this book like a bad penny – a part player, it seems, in numerous global catastrophes. Make of that what you will.

But it's the ethically bankrupt associations with dubious governments and low-level tyrants around the world that have raised the most contempt from observers and perhaps reveal the most about the man himself. In 2016, leaked documents showed that Tony Blair Associates was charging more than £5 million a year for advising the Kazakhstan government of Nursultan Nazarbayev, in power since 1989. In one instance Blair offered PR advice on how to manage the aftermath of a massacre of unarmed protesting mine workers. In 2010 it was reported that his firm would be paid £27 million by the Kuwaiti government for consultancy work, an ethical conflict of some note given Blair's role in removing Saddam Hussein, a long-term Kuwaiti enemy, from power. (If you glossed over that, read it again: that might be considered a thank-you honorarium of some proportion.)

'There's an honour about the prime minister of Britain and a dignity about being a former prime minister of Britain,' says Oborne of this track record. 'Mr Blair is using that dignity to go around the world advising torturers, dictators, murderers – in return for hard cash.'[3]

On entering office in 1997, the Blairs were not wealthy. Today they are what many consider to be offensively rich. Plausible estimates of the Blairs' wealth peg it at upwards of £50 million, while some have speculated that it is twice that. As New Labour tried to make clear on its emergence, profit should not be considered a dirty word – but this is surely taking the piss.

> 'No former British prime minister has come close to Blair for sheer, naked avarice. If there was a fortune to be made at the bottom of a sack of shit, Blair would dive in head first (having been given a helpful push by his wife).'
>
> *– journalist and long-time Labour Party member Rod Liddle, writing in The Spectator*

In 2016 *The Guardian* reported that the Blair property portfolio included ten houses and 27 flats, with an estimated value of £27 million. The Blairs' London residence, in Connaught Square, was alone valued at more than £8.5 million. In 2014 Blair made it known through a spokesman that his net worth was only around £10 million, but given his track record, one suspects there may well be some obfuscation in the declaration; that the figure has perhaps been sexed down rather than up. Perhaps, for instance, *his* net worth was £10 million but his wife Cherie's was a whole lot more. Or perhaps the money is technically held in the various companies and partnerships that form the complex corporate structure that he has created that conceals what he earns. Or perhaps by £10 million he actually meant £100 million and when the error is discovered he will express more sorrow, regret and apology than we may ever know or can believe.

In summary, Tony Blair's great sins were twofold: first, he holds responsibilty for the Iraq War and its consequences; and second, and perhaps most damningly, where he once offered the promise of a new dawn of political trust and goodwill, he ultimately gave us the opposite, an age in which we have never been more wary and cynical of those in power. He is certainly the key figurehead behind the UK's current malaise, both left-wing and right, and we would contend that he has contributed as much as anyone to this feeling across the globe. Who else embodies the smug and insincere political opportunist like the erstwhile prime minister of Britain?*

---

* According to the 2007 Edelman Trust Barometer, in the year Blair left office UK respondents rated their government the least trustworthy of all eighteen countries assessed. Other countries represented were the US, France, Germany, Italy, Spain, the Netherlands, Sweden, Ireland, Poland, Russia, China, Japan, South Korea, India, Mexico, Brazil and Canada. The UK government received a score of 16/100, the lowest score across all 90 metrics polled, which were: government in general, media in general, business in general, NGOs and religious institutions. (The UK also had the least trusted media.)

Sensible people aren't surprised by the Putins, Kims or even Trumps of the world – with them you know what you're getting (respectively shamelessness, madness and a combination thereof). And yes, most of us are of the opinion that all politicians are truth manipulators of some or other ilk, guided by expediency and self-preservation. But in working so hard to inveigle our trust from us, Blair has set new standards of betrayal. By offering us that vision of a brave new world, he took us for fools, and for that he will never be forgiven – by his own party (who seem to hate him the most), by his electorate and by the greater world who bought into what he was selling. Blair was the man who wrestled Labour from left-field delusion in the 1990s and yet because of him his party is now run by Jeremy Corbyn, a man divorced from reality who looks like he slept in a hedge with a huddle of red-socked vagrants – but who is there, with disturbing levels of support, because he at least retains some kind of personal integrity.

Twenty years after resurrecting Labour and ten years after leaving it in tatters we see Blair for the fundamentally flawed individual he is. A man whose self-doubt and insecurity is reflected in his cynical avarice – and his jewellery.

In his quiet moments of reflection, as he fingers his gold chain on the deck of his client-friend's yacht, you can imagine him wondering what might have been: the real greatness that lay in arm's reach, which he lacked the strength of character to grasp. Perhaps we must conclude that Tony Blair was never meant to be a politician. Rather, he is a businessman – just a good PR man, really.

See George W Bush.

'In the court of public opinion, he is despised.'

– Clare Short, Secretary of State for International Development under Blair. She resigned in 2003 in protest against the Iraq War [3]

Nick Bollettieri

b. 31 July 1931

*High-profile tennis coach; mentor of Monica Seles,
Maria Sharapova, the Williams sisters and others who
have made modern women's tennis unwatchable*

a-Yaaah!
Nnggggg!
a-Yaaah!
Nnggggg!
a-YAAAAAH!
Nngggggggggggg!
a-YAAAAAAAAAAHHH!

Thus we have, as readers who follow their television sport might have
deduced, an onomatopoeic approximation of the average rally between the
contemporary superstars of women's tennis, Maria Sharapova and Serena
Williams. Delightful, no?

Now rewind a generation to this:

hah-EEha!
[sound of ball on racquet]
hah-EEha!
[sound of ball on racquet]
hah-EEha!
[sound of ball on racquet]
hah-EEhaaaaa!

That of course is the one and only Monica Seles, who started this madness in the women's game back in the early 1990s, when she made her caterwauling entry onto the international circuit as an all-conquering teenager. However on earth was this allowed to be?

Women's tennis is hardly a sport beset with controversy, but what room for dispute there has been has tended to be gender-rights related. In the 1920s the radical change in attire from pre-war corsets, belts and floor-length dresses to looser-fitting skirts that revealed some ankle got the old-timers all hot and bothered.

In 1973 the contrived 'battle of the sexes' between Billie Jean King and Bobby Riggs proved that a woman at the peak of her career could beat a self-promoting chauvinist has-been and attract a large audience in the process.* From this came the battle for women players to be paid the same as men, a moderately heated and sometimes logic-confounding topic – but it doesn't pay to overthink things when you're operating in the unfathomable waters of professional sport remuneration. In 2017, a decade after tournament organisers conceded to equal pay, the Wimbledon singles champions earned £2.2 million each – about 75 times more than the average man's annual salary in the UK and 85 times more than the average woman's salary at the time. (The real discussion should be about paying lower-ranked players, men and women, more.)

Once these minor quibbles are set aside, there is, however, one consistent low-level controversy that has for the past couple of decades unsettled the women's game like an annoying background drone – or, if you'd rather, like an annoying foreground shriek. That would be grunting. And we can trace its roots to the aforementioned Monica Seles.

When the bunny-toothed, Graf-busting Seles arrived on the scene in the late 1980s, she quickly became known for her ferocious double-handed groundstrokes and the remarkable collection of farmyard sounds she introduced to the court. Having turned professional in 1989 while barely adolescent, she beat Steffi Graf to win her first Grand Slam, the French Open, a year later. The tennis-viewing world was taken aback. Here was a 16-year-old Yugoslavian upstart rolling over the unrivalled queen of the

---

* King was 30, Riggs was 56; he claimed to have made $1.5 million from the match – upwards of $8 million today. He had hoped to make it an annual event, presuming he'd win.

game, winner of eight of the previous nine Slams. And making a helluva lot of noise in the process.

In 1991 Seles won the Australian, French and US Open. In 1992 she repeated the feat, and she might have won Wimbledon, too, had veteran Martina Navratilova not complained about her screeching in their semifinal. As a result, Seles toned things down for the championship decider against Graf and the German won easily. Seles subsequently described her efforts to keep quiet during that match as one of the great regrets of her career.

She, and the grunters who would follow in her sonorous wake in the years to come, considered shrieking an integral rhythm-generating facet of her playing style. Like a shot-putter in full cry or a gym-bro on the bench press, it supposedly helps create maximum force at the point of impact.

Navratilova, however, has always called foul. She has described it as 'cheating, pure and simple' and is adamant that excessive grunting is gamesmanship. More war cry than shot technique, it is off-putting to competitors, disguises the sound of ball on racquet, and violates the spirit of the game.[1]

At the height of her powers, Seles smashed and screamed everyone into submission, winning eight Grand Slams before the age of twenty, usurping Graf's throne and looking set to dominate the game for the decade ahead. And let's not begrudge her the successes: audio excesses aside, she was a champion player.

Then, in April 1993, she was stabbed in the back with a boning knife, during a break between games at a tournament in Hamburg. They say a deranged fan did it because of his love for the magnificent Steffi.

Seles was, in the words of Blair Henley of *Tennis Now*, 'the godmother of female grunting', but she wasn't a match for the worst offenders today. Next to Sharapova she is like a mouse roaring at the tyrannosaur in *Jurassic Park*. The Williams sisters in full cry aren't far off, and the array of bizarre vociferations that their competitors have developed varies from the obnoxious to the quite extraordinary. Take your pick from the dog-summoning high-pitched *Ohhh*-ing of Victoria Azarenka, the end-of-the-evening retching of Francesca Schiavone, or the affected falling-bomb whistle of Michelle Larcher de Brito (loudest of the lot), and there you have, in short, the soundtrack of the modern women's game.

> ## 'Every time she hits the ball it sounds like a little girl fell off a cliff.'
>
> *– online post describing Portugal's Michelle Larcher de Brito*

Seles also didn't invent the habit. Exactly who did is difficult to ascertain, though the player who first made it famous was, in fact, a man, Jimmy Connors, who roared his way to winning the Australian Open, Wimbledon and the US Open in 1974. Later, Andre Agassi announced his arrival on the tennis scene with a throaty bellow, and he had a run-in with Ivan Lendl during the 1988 US Open that was a forerunner of the Seles-Navratilova dispute at Wimbledon. (In that case, however, Lendl won. Appropriately, Agassi had beaten Connors in the quarters.) Today, many high-profile grunters are men. Indeed, Rafael Nadal and Novak Djokovic in battle can sound like a musk ox rut at dawn – and yet it's the female players who have always faced the criticism.

Is it sexist to complain that grunting has ruined women's tennis? Are we latter-day Bobby Riggses to point out that anything more than some light parping from the ladies detracts from our viewing pleasure? In this age of self-identifying sexuality (when the options are no longer just X or Y), when the movement that (absurdly) claims men and women to be identically capable seems to gain ever more traction, this contention may appear a trifle archaic.

There are those who argue that men can get away with grunting because of an aural technicality: men's grunting is, they explain, less an assault on our audio senses than women's because of its pitch – the lower the pitch, the less maddening it is to the human ear. Do we believe this? Is our hearing inherently sexist? Is this somehow unfair? Either way, it makes no practical difference to the problem at hand: viewers are put off more by women's grunting than men's. And this being a book on people who have messed up the world – in this case, admittedly, at the cheekier end of the scale – we need to blame someone. Or at least find a representative to point fingers at. So we're going with Nick Bollettieri.

Long-time tennis fans will know Bollettieri as probably the most successful coach of the modern age, and certainly the most famous before the likes of Becker, Lendl and Edberg started giving tips to Djokovic, Murray and Federer. The Nick Bollettieri Tennis Academy was established in Florida in 1978, and was so successful that it was purchased in 1987 by the sports and entertainment company IMG, which evolved it into a sprawling sports academy and boarding school. Bollettieri remained integral to the tennis academy and when you take a closer look at some of its most successful alumni, in light of what you've read above, you may spot a common trend. Andre Agassi, Monica Seles, Maria Sharapova and Serena and Venus Williams (as well as Michelle Larcher de Brito, whose emanations, by the way, really are worth looking up for yourself) have all spent plenty of time under Bollettieri's tutelage. Agassi, he noted in a 2016 interview, trained for barely two hours a day, while he considered Seles a weak athlete but mentally very strong. She started at the academy at age twelve, Sharapova at age nine.

It would seem to many observers of the game, therefore, that Bollettieri has intentionally trained his players to grunt, and that his academy has become 'a production plant for the world's screamers and shriekers'.[2] He has been regularly asked for comment on the matter over the years and, for the record, has always denied the charge, though he has spoken about the importance of 'exhaling'. Whether or not you believe this trifle suspicious response, we see no way around blaming him for the phenomenon: either he has purposefully trained at least some of his students (the best ones!) in this technique, or some magical concatenation of universal energies has conspired to produce it in his players. Ergo, Nick Bollettieri – in our opinion, at least – made grunting in tennis a thing.

And as inconvenient as this truth may be for some, women's grunting really has ruined the women's game. In 2012, CEO of the Women's Tennis Association Stacey Allaster admitted as much to ESPN. 'The fans are telling us pretty clearly that they would like us to address the noise level,' she said. 'There's no doubt on this particular issue, there seems to be a growing concern from fans around the world. They don't like it. It's too loud.'

'Her higher pitched scream, complete with warble, conveys anxiety, and could plausibly be confused with a new-born foal sinking in quicksand.'
– *The Telegraph on Venus Williams*

According to the BBC, television viewership for the 2015 Wimbledon ladies' singles final (Serena Williams v Garbiñe Muguruza) was considerably less than half that of the men's (Djokovic v Roger Federer). Though an extreme example, this pattern is reflected in all the major tournaments to a greater or lesser degree, and while it's difficult to figure out just how much of this is due to aural offensiveness, it surely plays a considerable role.

Sharapova, for instance, has been widely criticised by fans, commentators and fellow players for years, generating a decibel count that has been compared to an airliner taking off or a chain saw. Banned for 15 months in 2016 for a mild case of doping, she strikes us as the type of hyper-competitive show pony who'd do just about anything to gain a competitive edge, niceties be damned. *This is how I play and if you don't like it – even if you're the paying fan – get stuffed*, appears to be the attitude. (Bollettieri describes her as 'an antisocial personality, but very disciplined'.[3]) It's the same inconsiderate me-thinking you get from the guy manspreading on a packed tube or teenagers playing music on their phones at volume 11.

The latter examples may be the realities of the modern world, but is it too much to ask that we keep tennis a game of gentlemen and gentlewomen? Navratilova, the original complainant more than two decades ago, hasn't stopped calling for something to be done about excessive on-court noise, and the solution, she believes, is simple: 'I guarantee you, once you start giving out point penalties, they're gonna stop it.'[4]

Finally, it seems, change is coming. Very slow change. The Women's Tennis Association is now aiming to eliminate 'excessive grunting' from the next generation of female players. The current crop are a lost cause, is their logic, so they've chosen to cultivate a new breed who simply exhale when they stroke the ball, rather than summon the demons of Mordor. In 2012,

WTA officials specifically approached players and coaches at Bollettieri's hugely influential academy to establish a way forward. If things have gone according to plan – and for the love of all that is good, please let this be the case – new players should be entering the game on a quieter footing, and in time the noise-makers will be steadily phased out, like solar panels replacing diesel generators. Until then the abomination that is women's tennis in its current form continues.

The stabbing of Monica Seles was, hardly surprisingly, an incident that caused irreparable damage to her tennis career. Followers of the game were appalled by the act, and the women's game, having lost a fearsome competitor in her prime, was considerably worse off for it. The Seles-Graf rivalry was reduced to being one of modern sport's greatest hypotheticals, and without her Yugoslavian challenger, Graf became a racquet-wielding superhero (or villain) without a nemesis, winning ten of the next thirteen Grand Slams that she entered.

Meanwhile Seles suffered from depression and bouts of binge-eating. It took her two-and-a-half years before she returned to the women's tour, and though she competed well, winning the Australian Open in 1996, she could never reclaim her former glory. She eventually retired without much fuss in 2003.

These days Seles looks remarkably like Celine Dion and is married to American billionaire businessman Tom Golisano. They make the news when he has to sue the interior decorator of his 240-foot mega yacht for overcharging. So you'd think she's doing okay.

But is she? Had she not been stabbed, she might have become the greatest women's player of all time. Does her unfulfilled potential ever keep her up at night? Or is it the nightmare visage of Nick Bollettieri, appearing in her dreams to teach her the banshee wailing that she is most remembered for?

George W Bush

b. 6 July 1946

*President of the USA 2001-2008; Dubya; the Decider;
the Bush family dunce and yet the one who got two
terms; initiator of the Iraq War and non-planner for
its aftermath; the guy who didn't understand what
'mission accomplished' means*

IN 1942, FOLLOWING THE JAPANESE ATTACK ON PEARL HARBOUR, a young
Connecticut man by the name of George Herbert Walker Bush put on hold
his plans to study at Yale University so that he could join the United States
Navy and fight in World War II. In June the following year, not yet 19 years
old, he became the youngest aviator in the Navy to date and would go on to
fly 58 combat missions against Imperial Japan. In August 1944 Lieutenant

Bush was at the controls of a Grumman TBM Avenger torpedo bomber in a mission to attack installations on the island of Chichijima when the plane was hit by anti-aircraft fire and went down in flames over the Philippine Sea. His two crewmen died in the crash, one in the plane itself and the other falling to his death when his parachute failed to open, and Bush spent several long hours floating in the Pacific before being rescued by a lifeguard submarine, the USS Finback. He stayed on the Finback for another month to aid in rescuing other pilots and was eventually awarded the Distinguished Flying Cross for his actions, to accompany several other service awards.

After the war, Bush made money in the oil business in Texas before following his father, Prescott Bush, who had by then spent ten years as US Senator, into politics in the mid-1960s. By 1988, after loyal political service including, among other positions, member of the House of Representatives, US Ambassador to the United Nations, director of the CIA and vice president to Ronald Reagan, George Bush was elected president of the United States. The war hero had become leader of his country and the free world, and the circle of patriotic service was complete. Unfortunately for HW, he dropped the ball when it came time for re-election in 1992, and he lost out to the charming and serial-philandering Bill Clinton. So this intelligent, business savvy, true-blue American hero who had devoted himself to – indeed, had come so close to losing his life for – his country saw only one term in office. (His critical error: reneging on an election promise, his famous 'Read my lips: no new taxes' pledge.)

With Prescott and George HW, the Bush political dynasty had a proud and esteemed beginning, and for knowing observers of the family it was the latter's second child, John Ellis, who seemed groomed to carry the Bush mantle proudly forward. Jeb was 'the smart one', a good man by most accounts, and he would do well to become the first two-term Republican governor of Florida from 1998. But he had narrowly lost his first shot at the title in 1995, which would ultimately keep him from the presidency. Because, before Jeb was primed, it was his older brother, George Walker, who somehow got himself into the Oval Office in 2001.

So. Dubya.

In contrast to his father, George W Bush managed to avoid being drafted to Vietnam by joining the Texas Air National Guard in 1968, where he missed drills and lost his flight status. His finest military achievement was, many believe, being honourably discharged. Afterwards, he developed a reputation for hitting the bottle, underwhelmed his professors at Harvard Business School, ran an oil exploration company into the ground, and was investigated (and cleared) by the Securities and Exchange Commission for insider trading. On the plus side, he married well, eventually made money investing in the Texas Rangers baseball team, and found his way into full-time politics in the early 1990s. His decision to run for governor of Texas in 1995 was a surprise to many – notably his family, who were then prepping Jeb for greatness – but Dubya was likeable and had a good dose of gee-whiz charisma (and campaign strategist Karl Rove). He ended up winning by a landslide. After that he somehow snuck his way into the White House in 2000 – winning the decisive and controversial Florida recount by 537 votes – and then he was re-elected in 2004.

Of all the Bushes, Dubya would be the two-termer president. It was a shock to many, including George Senior.

'I know how hard it is to put food on your family.'

– George W Bush, 2000

'There's an old saying in Tennessee – I know it's in Texas, probably in Tennessee – that says, fool me once – shame on – shame on you. You fool me, you can't get fooled again.' *– 2002*

'Our enemies are innovative and resourceful, and so are we. They never stop thinking about new ways to harm our country and our people, and neither do we.' *– 2004*

'I want to thank the president and the CEO of Constellation Energy, Mayo Shattuck. That's a pretty cool first name, isn't it, Mayo? Pass the Mayo.' *– 2005*

Dubya was famous from the start for fluffing his lines and sounding... really quite simple at times. Watching him in action was inevitably cringe-worthy, and it was often impossible to sit through a presidential Q&A session without wanting to hide behind the sofa or mute the sound. But perhaps contrary to much popular opinion, and despite the special wonderfulness of his belief that he was 'misunderestimated', George W Bush is not dumber than the average man in the street. He may not have excelled at Harvard, but he was the first US president to gain an MBA, and those who know him describe him as a voracious reader. The famous picture of him reading a children's book upside down was, tragically, a hoax. The claim that he had an IQ of 91, which was circulated in 2001, was too.

According to a credible 2006 paper on the matter, which analysed plausible estimated IQs of all 42 US presidents to that point, Dubya has an IQ of around 120, roughly average university graduate level. There is some relief in learning that there are sufficient filters in the American electoral system to prevent a borderline moron from entering the highest office, but within the presidential subset Dubya was near the bottom of the class, with only Warren Harding, James Monroe and Ulysses Grant trailing behind. Harding, the most recent of the three, died on the job in 1923. The top three were John Quincy Adams, Thomas Jefferson and John F Kennedy, all estimated to have IQs above 150, while Dubya's predecessor, Bill Clinton, was also on the cleverer side, a full 20 points ahead of him. This was 'a disparity that may have created a contrast effect that made any intellectual weaknesses all the more salient', according to the paper's author, Dean Simonton, professor of psychology at the University of California, Davis.

Tellingly, Dubya had the lowest score of the lot for 'openness to experience', a key metric that indicates curiosity and willingness to learn new things, and correlates closely with presidential performance. He received a resounding 0.0 out of a possible 100 points. (Clinton scored 82.0; Jefferson 99.1.) 'Bush's specific score is indicative,' observed Simonton, 'of someone who discusses issues without taking alternative points of view into serious consideration.' Besides describing pretty much everyone on Twitter, this, then, would also be a good estimate of someone who might invade a country with the intention of 'liberating it' without considering what those being liberated might think of the invasion.

And so we come to the reason for George W Bush's presence in these pages: the invasion of Iraq in 2003.

Alphabetical lists have their inconveniences, as we've already discovered. In this case, however, transitioning in relatively quick succession from bin Laden to Blair to Bush is for our purposes, ideal. The first was the excuse for the invasion of Iraq, the second was the enabler, and the third was the executor.

The 9/11 attack on the US mainland, masterminded by bin Laden, was always going to demand a major military response, and a suitable and appropriate target was immediately identified: Afghanistan. Three weeks and five days after the planes hit the Twin Towers in New York, Operation Enduring Freedom was under way with the aim of hunting down al-Qaeda forces and destroying the Taliban government that was harbouring them. As far as starting wars go, this was quick work.

The War in Afghanistan has hardly been a cakewalk. As of late 2017 it was still ongoing, the longest-running war in US history, in an isolated country that has tested and found wanting the might of the British and Soviet empires. But it was at least justified and sanctioned by international law, its people are generally better off for not having the odious Taliban in charge, and it has helped reduce al-Qaeda's operational capacity to almost nothing. The death of bin Laden, in Pakistan, was also a symbolic success.

The Iraq War, by contrast, has almost no redeeming features. Senior players in the Bush operation, most prominently Dick Cheney, Donald Rumsfeld and Paul Wolfowitz, had been advocating for invasion and the removal of Saddam Hussein not just before 9/11 but before Bush was even elected. It seemed to them to be a smart regional move, and there has been much speculation from various quarters exactly why: an opportunity for the US government to secure the Iraqi oil supply, or US businesses to milk that oil supply, or the American military-industrial machine to oil its cogs. Perhaps all of the above. Perhaps, even, some genuine intent to finally remove Saddam and bring political freedom to a long-oppressed country.

Whatever the true motivation, bin Laden's attack was the catalyst needed to implement their plans – and yet it didn't provide a legitimate casus belli. That would have to be manufactured, no easy task when you're trying to form an international 'coalition of the willing' and get the United Nations to sign off on your plans. The Bush administration tried, for instance, to claim a direct link between Saddam's regime and al-Qaeda when they in fact loathed each other; bin Laden believed that secular Muslim rulers such as Saddam were central to the modern crisis in Islam.

Ultimately, the best plan they could drum up was 'weapons of mass destruction' – the infamous WMDs wild goose chase. This was the point in the plan where the slick-talking Tony Blair played his critical role in moving things along, helping Dubya to sell the idea of WMDs to the world as though he were peddling informercial blenders or junket-marketing his autobiography. Together, the two used all their charm, persuasiveness, dirty tricks and political capital to convince the world that Saddam possessed weapons of mass destruction. At best this was dated intelligence-gathering (he may have destroyed the weapons before the invasion) mixed with wilful self-delusion (anything to get this war started!). At worst – and more likely, in the eyes of many observers today – it was simply a lie so they could start dropping bombs.

Ultimately, the schtick was enough to get about three-quarters of America approving of the plan to remove Saddam. So despite the international protests that saw millions marching against the plans for war in more than 600 cities around the world on 15 February 2003, and despite the objections from the UN and elsewhere, Bush sent in the tanks while Blair looked on approvingly. The invasion commenced on 19 March 2003, Baghdad was occupied within three weeks, and three weeks after that Dubya strutted his strut after landing on the *USS Abraham Lincoln* aircraft carrier in his dashing flight suit and then declaring to the world the goodies had won. 'Major combat operations in Iraq have ended,' he declared, beneath a MISSION ACCOMPLISHED banner. 'In the battle of Iraq, the United States and our allies have prevailed. And Iraq is free.'[1]

They were words to haunt the rest of the Bush II presidency, and words that will echo coldly whenever its legacy is considered.

Iraq, as history relates, fell into a rage of sectarian violence that outstripped anything Saddam had dreamt up in his cruel and unfortunate time in charge. The reason was astonishing: the Bush administration had no plans in place to manage the country. Apparently overwhelmed by groupthink, individuals within the administration had simply assumed everything would work out fine when a complex Middle Eastern nation was handed a slice of American liberty on a plate. Those who weren't so sure were too cowed to raise any concerns.

The sudden removal of the secular Ba'ath party left a power vacuum that soon saw different sects and ethnic groups pitted against each other and occupying allied forces. The majority Shiites, who had been suppressed under Saddam, were elevated to power, igniting a long and bloody Sunni insurgency. As noted before, up to a million Iraqis have died as a result of the war. Around two million refugees have fled to Syria, Jordan and beyond.

Saddam was a murderous brute who had ruled his country with little mercy for 24 years and made a good case for entry here under his own heading. In December 2003 he was found by US forces in a hole in the ground near the city of Tikrit, about 200 kilometres north of Baghdad. He would be handed over to the interim Iraqi government, convicted of crimes against humanity and hanged three years later, the video of his execution quickly leaking on to the internet. There is no doubt that he was a tyrant who deserved to be removed, but his downfall signalled the start of an era, still ongoing, of extreme chaos and suffering in Iraq, and his shambolic execution is symbolic of the violent disorder that consumed the country.

Noam Chomsky has described the invasion of Iraq and its aftermath as 'the worst crime of the 21st century'. Chomsky has made some quite profound errors of judgement in his time, but it's hard to disagree here.[2]

Despite their best efforts, Bush and Blair never found their nuclear or chemical weapons of mass destruction. It was a travesty that left many unsurprised, and it was enhanced by the terrible hypocrisy that it was the occupiers who, in fact, used chemical weapons from their arsenals: white phosphorous and depleted uranium. They are both controversial munitions. The former, used in certain explosives, burns through skin to the bone; the latter, used in armour-piercing projectiles, is toxic and causes widespread health complications to local populations when used in large quantities.

For the United States and the Western world the consequences have also been devastating, though lacking the equivalent death toll. The Iraq War lasted nine and a half years after the Mission Accomplished speech, with 4,800 coalition soldiers dying, the bulk of them American. In May 2003 the Pentagon put an estimated price tag on the Iraq War of $4 billion per month, which seemed a lot but somehow acceptable. By 2017 the total cost was probably more than $3 trillion – it's difficult to calculate these things – and likely to be trillions more once interest and benefit payouts for veterans are included. For context, this is considerably more than the gross domestic product of Germany, the fourth-largest GDP in the world by country.

And, then, the final irony: out of the Iraq War, the spectre of al-Qaeda terrorism, once used as motivation to topple Saddam Hussein, morphed into the hideous extremist ghoul of our times, the Islamic State of Iraq and

'The report concluded the United States gained little from the war while Iraq was traumatized by it. The war reinvigorated radical Islamist militants in the region, set back women's rights, and weakened an already precarious healthcare system, the report said. Meanwhile, the $212 billion reconstruction effort was largely a failure with most of that money spent on security or lost to waste and fraud.'
— *Reuters reporting on the Costs of War Project by the Watson Institute for International Studies at Brown University, March 2013*

Syria (ISIS), or the Islamic State of Iraq and the Levant (ISIL), or Daesh. Whatever your preferred nomenclature, this was brute evil in its most visceral form – and the Bush administration was directly responsible for its emergence. From al-Qaeda came al-Qaeda in Iraq, and from al-Qaeda in Iraq came ISIS, the Islamic caliphate that has brought horrors to much of Iraq and Syria and elsewhere in the Middle East, and transferred those atrocities to localised explosions of terror in Egypt, Paris, San Bernardino, Brussels, Orlando, Nice, Berlin, London, Manchester…

'ISIS is a direct outgrowth of al-Qaeda in Iraq that grew out of our invasion.'

– Barack Obama, 2015

George W Bush had a presidential approval rating of 90 percent after the 9/11 attacks, a phenomenal statistic. After that point, there was a steady, almost straight-line decline for the rest of his presidency, with a noticeable boost from the initial invasion of Iraq. Towards the end of his second term he bottomed out at 25 percent, equivalent to Richard Nixon when he left office. Dubya's ratings weren't helped by his inept management of the aftermath of Hurricane Katrina or the 2007/8 financial crisis, but Iraq will always be the deepest stain on his reputation.

In the final review, we can acknowledge that Dubya was a president who saw things in black and white. He was the Decider, as he famously put it, and you were either with him or you were against him. In an increasingly sophisticated, complex and interconnected world this is the type of attitude that poisons daily interactions for the average guy going about his business. For the most powerful leader in the world it is the type of attitude that heralds impending disaster, costing lives and wasting enormous amounts of capital, both financial and political. With Dubya in the vanguard, the Iraq War, sadly, was never going to end well.

What odds that his Republican successor, Donald Trump, has learnt these lessons?

See Osama bin Laden, Tony Blair & Mohammed Emwazi.

The call-centre drone

The human you eventually speak to, after navigating the labyrinthine hell-cycle of automated responses put in place to prevent you from doing so, when you call a helpline; Kafka's worst fucking nightmare

Your call is important to us.

Really?

Really?

Does anyone buy that line any more? Does the widest-eyed doe-blinking horoscope-touting Santa-believing teenaged fly-catcher still fall for it? Is there the smallest iota of honesty, or even meaning, vested in that godforsaken line?

Your call is so important to us that we've been ignoring you for seventeen minutes at your expense.

That would at least approximate something closer to the cynical truth, but for words to have any real meaning they need to convey a truth understood by those who speak them. In this case, there's a machine playing words but, if you'll indulge us a little pop-philosophy a moment, they're not really being *spoken*, are they? They're simply being initiated by a series of ones and zeroes programmed to execute a pre-recorded voice, a voice without any value whatsoever assigned to it because computers, even those vested with human qualities, don't intrinsically know what is important and what is not.

Your call is important to us? That's as absurd a notion as Sony being responsible for the genius of a Mozart concerto. Or a thousand monkeys on a thousand typewriters writing the greatest novel known to man. It's not even a lie. It's simply a great big digitally executed up-yours.

Sorry, silky-voiced and soothingly soporific electro-Scottish lady of some Call-Centre Land narcotic fever-dream, but what kind of blithering halfwits do you take us for? No, our call is not important to you. Our call is an irritant and, worse, a line item in an Excel spreadsheet of costs that need to be managed.

Wait! Hallelujah! Somebody is answering! Excuse me? Can you speak up? It sounds like you're in a Bangladeshi train station… Is that a goat? What, wait, you *are* in a Bangladeshi train station?

Okay. Hocus pocus time to focus. What do you mean is it plugged in? Of course it's plugged in! What do you take me for, a deranged toddler? Can you please just answer my question? No? You have a script, and if you stray from the script you'll lose your job? What? Are you selling me an upgrade now? Or are you telling me something about my actual problem? Wait wait, no, don't put me on hold…

What kind of modernist hell-with-elevator-muzak have we constructed here?

In the end, it seems, economics may win this argument for us. A misunderstanding of economics and the human capacity for tolerating surreal mental torture once made the operations director of GigantiCorp Corporation Incorporated outsource their call centres to Delhi or Dhaka or Paraguay or Pianosa, and in most cases this has made the experience so tormentingly ghastly for the customers of GC Corp that they're starting to buy other people's stuff. So the call centre in the Philippines got a rocket up its CEO to employ people who have at least met somebody whose aunt once knew somebody who spoke English, or they'll close down the call centre and open a workable one back home, write it off to experience, and cash their bonus cheque anyway.

You think we're making this up? Nope. In recent years, the movement has been for companies to start repatriating their customer service call centres due to overwhelming customer dissatisfaction. Not only do the locals speak a betterly type of the English but it ticks the patriotic job-creation box. These corporate honchos know how to follow a trend. And they have, of course, made up the budgeting difference with expanded exponentially unnavigable self-service technology (don't even bother, just press # repeatedly) and email communication that will be responded to

'Thank you for calling Megacorp. Your call is as unimportant to us as every human action and may be recorded for purposes that are unclear. All our operators have identical names right now. Please listen carefully to the following options although they all lead, eventually, to the same outcome. Press 1 to hear this message again, cyclically, for ever. Press 2 to keep perfectly still for seven years, listening. Press 3 to speak to your three-greats granddaughter, who is also your three-greats grandmother. Press 8 to experience the interpenetration of non-deterministic reality with rational unreality. Press 5 to be engulfed by a plot hole. Press 9¾ to find yourself amid a popular fantasy. For all other options, please sacrifice the goat that your family ate last week. After the tone, you will be executed by firing squad and reincarnated as a jaguar. Thank you for calling Megacorp.'

– Frank Upton, reader competition in The Spectator in which entrants 'were invited to take something mundane and filter it through the lens of magic realism'

within 48 hours (by someone in Bangladesh, no doubt, but at least he has a spell checker).

Now, we're not proposing here that home-stocked call centres offer a decent service by definition – some of them are in some ways worse, if only for their sheer lack of enthusiasm – but we *are* saying that it's easier to have an apocalyptically bad call centre at the far ends of the earth where it's always the middle of the night GMT, English proficiency isn't as common and there is no cultural connection whatsoever between caller and customer service agent.

Either way, at home or abroad, very rarely an extraordinary thing happens – a moment that fills your life with an ephemeral flash of dazzling light. You ring the number, a person who can communicate in English answers the phone and this glorious representation of all that is good about humanity has been actually trained to help you. They know the business and they know how to fix what's wrong. They sound like they actually care. Would I like a voucher as an indication of the company's regret that things went wrong? Really? I may literally cry. They laughed at your dumb joke? Just marry me.

This completely irrational adoration of your company, directors of GigantiCorp Corporation Incorporated, is yours for the taking. All you have to do is have a functional call centre staffed by nice people who speak a reasonable approximation of the language of your callers and who keep you holding for less than seventeen minutes. (The eighteenth minute is when the Michael Douglas in *Falling Down* meltdown kicks in.) Your customers will be so blown away that they will forget why they were upset in the first place. The power of good customer service – the outcome of which is the total reversal of a damaging narrative – is invaluable and, seeing as you have to have a call centre, why not just make it a good one?

Or, you know, don't. Make us email you. Yeah, we know. Our email is important to you.

Hugo Chávez
& Nicolás Maduro

Hugo Chávez: 28 July 1954 – 5 March 2013
Nicolás Maduro: b. 23 November 1962

Presidents of Venezuela since 1999; champions of
the poor; rockstar socialist demagogue of the South
Americas and his anointed successor; authoritarian
destroyers of a nation; timely lessons in history

IN OCTOBER 2016, IN HIS ACCEPTANCE SPEECH for the Philip Merrill Award
for Outstanding Contributions to Liberal Arts Education, the historian
Niall Ferguson outlined the 'decline and fall' of the teaching of history
at American universities, which he claimed was happening 'faster than
Gibbon's Roman Empire'. The number of history undergraduate degrees

was dropping at a steady and alarming rate – by more than 13 percent in 2014 alone at the country's most prestigious schools – and enrolment was falling dramatically too, he explained. And the trends didn't look to be stopping any time soon.[1]

Ferguson proposed a number of explanations for the fall but focused specifically on the changing emphasis of what's being taught. University professors of history are now specialising in what might have been considered marginal (or non-existent) topics in the past – the histories of culture, race and ethnicity, women and gender, and the environment – while more applied fields of political, intellectual and international history, which students find more interesting and practical, have fallen from favour in recent decades. At the time of his speech in 2016, for example, the Harvard history department, which includes more than fifty faculty staff, was offering courses on just seven of what Ferguson believes to be twenty 'significant historical subjects' of the last 500 years, from the Reformation in the 16th century to European integration in the 20th. A student wanting to learn about, say, the American or French revolutions, the American Civil War or either World Wars would have been out of luck that semester. The problems were similar at Stanford and Yale, where undergrads wouldn't have found too many broadly enticing classes to take but could have tried History 283: 'History of the Supernatural', History 260J: 'Sex, Life, and Generation' or History 41Q: 'Madwomen: The History of Women and Mental Illness in the US'.

'I do not wish to dismiss any of these subjects as being of no interest or value,' said Ferguson. 'They just seem to address less important questions than how the United States became an independent republic with a constitution based on the idea of limited government, or how it survived a civil war over the institution of slavery.'

Ferguson is of a more conservative persuasion than the majority 'liberal' professors he was none-too-subtly chastising in his speech, so it's worth pointing out that he is employed by Harvard, Stanford and Oxford. Which is to say, the world's major universities would presumably respect his take on things. Either way, we see that there are fewer students learning any history today at the most prestigious universities in America, and the history they *are* learning is, to be euphemistic about this, not as broadly relevant as it once was. (Ferguson calls them 'antiquarian or anachronistic options'. There are ruder terms.) Now, we would guess that if this analysis was applied at universities throughout the world, the outcomes would be similar in many, many places. Why do we think this? Because kids these days, we tell ya, they don't know their history. And if you consider the learning of history to be integral to the understanding of the present and the possibilities of the future – as we do – then this starts to become a problem. Because history teaches us what works in practice as opposed to what sounds nice in theory.

Take global politics today, for example. At various points throughout this book we consider the dismal state of politics in the US, the UK and the world in general. The consensus – hard to disagree with – seems to be that the status quo isn't working and people want change. They're *demanding* change. In America they voted in Trump. In the UK they voted out Europe. Throughout the continent fringe parties are suddenly looking appealing.

But this isn't the change the young voters – the youth, we'd call them, if we wanted to sound especially, er, un-woke – want. Young people today are particularly incensed at the injustices they see all around them and they want *real* change. They look at the Baby Boomer generation and think, *Screw you guys, you had it made with your easy money and affordable houses and guilt-free abuse of the environment, and now we've got university loans for life and corporate-crony politics and a ridiculous reality-TV president and Brexit…*

The answer, as they see it, is the knocking to the ground of the corrupted pillars of free-market democracy and its replacement with a dreamy and obvious solution: socialism. Where everyone is treated like a beautiful human being, with care and dignity, and a free house and medical treatment and a daily latte forever. Where the left admits that centrist politics of Clinton and Blair have failed and reaches for the true fair and equitable dream of humanity's destiny… So suddenly Bernie Sanders and Jeremy Corbyn are the heroes of the hour. The faces of change. The hope for a new generation.

Kids. Honestly.

If you *do* know a teeny bit of history, you've presumably worked out what we're getting at here: that it's the lack of basic knowledge of our past that has allowed the resurgence of loony-left thinking. Thus the great lessons in ideological indoctrination that marked the 20th century like a concentration camp tattoo now seem to begin and end with some vague understanding of Nazi fascism; as in, *You've offended me, you fascist!* And so a new generation reaches voting age and encounters what seems like a fresh new concept, socialism – which is, of course, an old and thoroughly debunked one.

We will get to the older examples in pages to come, but for now there is a timeous contemporary lesson to be learned in South America, a running example of just how socialism doesn't work, in the ongoing Hugo Chávez-enkindled conflagration of Venezuela.

It's important to note that when Hugo Chávez was democratically elected to the presidency of Venezuela in 1999, on a popular mandate of social revolution, Venezuela was in a right mess, riddled with corruption and inequality. (The people wanted change; they *demanded* change, etc etc.) The country's economic Achilles' heel was its dependence on oil, and the oil price had been on an extended slide since the mid-1980s. The month before he was elected, it hit a fifty-year low of $16.99 a barrel.

So no-one's accusing Chávez of stuffing up a well-run ship.

Equally important to note, though, is that on taking office – in what he might have considered a divine indicator of his righteous destiny to govern his chosen people – the oil price almost instantly began its ten-year rocket to more than $150 a barrel in 2008. In a country with more oil than Saudi Arabia, this makes a difference. When you're nationalising businesses and rolling out massive social reform programmes, it means you can actually foot the bill – at least for a while.

In this time, as Chávez made real the notion of '21st century socialism', he came to be widely revered by the poor, working and even middle classes. Healthcare and education was made free, poverty fell, food programmes were received with widespread gratitude and Chávez developed a messiah-like reputation that he revelled in. He saw himself as a philosopher-king, a heady mix of Símon Bolívar, Karl Marx and, when the mood took him, Jesus (hey, why not?). He was mobbed in the streets and his face appeared on billboards, walls, the facades of buildings, books, T-shirts, even tree trunks… The quiet grumbles of those who knew a little of the histories of Mao and Stalin and co were ignored.

'[G]enerally speaking, Chávez appealed to all those on the left who considered American society hopelessly unjust and inhumane and saw his regime as greatly superior.'

– *historian Paul Hollander*

> 'Chávez showed us that there is a different and a better way of doing things. It's called socialism, it's called social justice and it's something that Venezuela has made a big step towards.'
>
> *– Jeremy Corbyn, speaking the day after the death of Hugo Chávez, March 2013*

The Chávez government spent so much money delivering the dreams he had promised that the country always ran at a deficit. Prices of goods were fixed, as were exchange rates, while land and businesses were expropriated and nationalised – the type of policies to gravely concern a first-year economics student. The revolution saw basic amenities such as toilet paper, tampons, rice, sugar and medicine being given to citizens for free or almost free, but it didn't consider the plight of the businesses that would be forced to manufacture goods for unsustainably low prices. This was the child-minded policy of an ideology that can't see beyond the now. A decade and a half later and those and other products are frequently unavailable in stores, with no money to import them and businesses wiped out across the land.

After Chávez came to power, many of his prominent supporters in the United States – the likes of Noam Chomsky, Cornel West, Sean Penn, Oliver Stone – praised the way he prioritised poverty reduction, often in contrast to US policies, and his initial economic successes were seen as a valid threat to the capitalist orthodoxy of the West. Today poverty is far worse than it was when Chávez took over. In March 2017 *The Economist* reported that 82 percent of households were living in poverty, compared to 48 percent in 1998 (and 14.5 percent in the US today). But it's not just that poverty is worse; the country, once the richest in South America, is now crippled across almost every measure of human welfare index. Those with the means, approximately two million Venezuelans, have fled abroad.

Chávez died of cancer in 2013, at which point his chosen successor Nicolás Maduro, previously the vice president, assumed control. A former trade unionist, he avowed to continue the socialist revolution. At the time, one US dollar bought you 30 Venezuelan bolivars. By this stage the country was already careening towards economic disaster, but when the oil price tanked the following year, any last semblance of hope that 'Hugo Chávez's economic miracle' might endure evaporated. With oil production also reduced due to the predictable corruption, incompetence and mismanagement that comes with nationalisation, the country has since experienced one of the greatest peacetime economic disintegrations in history. By mid-2017 one US dollar officially bought you about 9,800 bolivars; on the black market, however, you could get 18,000 bolivars. You needed to carry your cash in a toiletry bag when you went shopping, and in a suitcase if you were in the fortunate position of making a bank deposit. Chávez had made a great deal of protecting the rights of workers but the fruits of his efforts by this stage saw the country's minimum wage equating to $1.50 per week. A quarter of the country earned less than that. The highest denomination banknote, 100 bolivars, cost more to print than it was worth and the real inflation rate was unknown, said to be around 300 percent by government but beyond four digits by economists.

Venezuela has now been number one on the World Misery Index, which measures 59 countries by inflation, unemployment levels, lending rates and GDP per capita, every year since 2013. In 2016 it returned a measure of 573.4; second-placed Argentina scored 83.8; the USA, in 39th position, scored 9.4. Demand and supply of all products had fallen off the charts. Canned corn and peas were luxury goods. Long-forgotten diseases such as diphtheria had returned, along with malnutrition; 'the Maduro diet' led to three-quarters of the population losing eight kilograms or more in 2016. Bizarrely, in this South American wonderland, cheap oil remains a Venezuelan 'birthright', and you could drive about 1,000 miles on a dollar's worth of petrol as of late 2016 – but mineral water cost a hundred times as much. Resourceful locals would buy cheap petrol to smuggle across the border for resale. In the final indicator of a desperate nation, Caracas had the highest homicide rate of any city in the world that year, and Venezuela the second-highest homicide rate of any country. Food riots, looting and million-people protest marches were now common.

Hugo Chávez had always positioned himself as anti-imperialist, anti-capitalist and anti-US, and he made all sorts of similarly minded friends in the process: Fidel Castro, Saddam Hussein, Mahmoud Ahmadinejad, Bashar al-Assad, Kim Jong-il, Robert Mugabe, Muammar Gaddafi. As Trotsky said about socialism, 'dictatorship is necessary', and Chávez, with the unblinking support of much of his country, firmly and skilfully steered his governance towards autocracy, suppressing dissent in the media and public as necessary. But at least he didn't resort to gunning down his citizens in the street when they started to complain. With the oil price on his side to help disguise the hollow promises he was selling, he didn't have to. When things fell apart, it would take Maduro to reveal the true colours of this particular revolution which, like every socialist revolution in history, was destined to end badly.

Maduro, adhering to the same anti-capitalist Marxist-Leninist ideals of his mentor Chávez, has stuck faithfully to the programme in the face of overwhelming evidence that it is ruining his country and killing his people, and it is for this reason that he gets his own special mention here. Whereas Chávez implemented the system that created the problem, Maduro has seen the problem come, without any measure of ambiguity, to fruition. And, unable to comprehend a lost wager, he has, like the most delusional gambler, doubled down instead of cutting his losses.

He has cracked down on all forms of dissent, used the most dubious of tactics to sideline opposition parties, and ignored all reasonable proposals to reverse the country's decline. He has ruled by decree since 2013, and although opposition parties won control of the legislature in 2015, he still commands the judiciary, which he has used to simply invalidate any laws they have proposed that don't really work for him. Having effectively committed a 'self-inflicted coup d'état' by taking over the country's congress in March 2017, Maduro followed up in July with an internationally condemned referendum that gave him the power to rewrite the country's constitution. Scores of citizens had died in anti-government protests by that point, and his regime was subsequently described by the UN Human Rights Office as using 'widespread and systematic use of excessive force' to quell dissent. Venezuela is now widely considered the dictatorship that Trotsky predicted.

Maduro has rightly been criticised from all quarters, and apologists of Chávez may try to argue that the utter catastrophe that is Venezuela today, a South American Zimbabwe, is more to do with his weak and destructive successor than the great man himself. That would be to miss the indicators that were apparent years before Chávez died. And, of course, the indicators that were apparent in every single truly socialist country of the 20th century.

And what about Chávez's original noble intentions? Was he simply deluded? Or was he your run-of-the-mill tyrant who just managed to steer clear of the violence? A review of the lifestyle and bank balance of one of his daughters, Maria Gabriela Chávez, is possibly revealing. She has been criticised within Venezuela and internationally for her luxurious and profligate expenses, and in 2015 she was reported by various media to be worth $4.2 billion. She appears not to have publicly denied this, which is quite something, given that it would make her, according to *Forbes*, the richest person in the country.

So yes, there it is. Is anyone with a vague eye to the past surprised?

For those flirting with the seductions of socialism, a historical review of the last century of human governance should be enough to set them straight. If that's too much to ask, or unavailable in their local university curriculum, then perhaps some history in the making will suffice. They just need to look to Venezuela for up-to-date lessons in how not to run a country.

Bill & Hillary Clinton

Bill Clinton: b. 19 August 1946
Hillary Clinton: b. 26 October 1947

US president (him); almost US president (her); cause of the global financial crisis (him, possibly); cause of the Trump crisis (her, definitely); standard bearers of the failed political establishment

AH, THE CLINTONS. Where do we start on this most divisive political couple? Their supporters – or even just objective readers of modern history – might kick off with a rundown of Bill and Hillary Clinton's greatest achievements. When Bill, the 42nd president of the United States of America, left office, they might offer, he left a country in better shape than when he began, one that was happy and prosperous and even had a modest budget surplus – quite the concept today. He'd helped bring peace to Northern Ireland and the Balkans and – another concept! – he'd avoided getting tangled up in any costly, wasteful wars. Hillary, they might continue, has in the meantime developed into a politician of great experience, one who has served her time and who, in a more equal era, could have been the prominent Clinton in the couple's early years, with Bill providing the support…

We *could* start there, but we won't. We're going with the financial crisis.

It's no great insight to say that the global financial crisis of 2007/8 was one of the great disasters of recent times. It would be an oversight not to give it some room here. Banks went into meltdown around the world, economies tanked and international financial systems came within a whisker of collapsing. The Great Recession lasted a year and a half in the US, far longer elsewhere, and forever, it seems, in Greece. The world suffered en masse.

You don't need an economics degree (or mortgage default history) to know this.

An economics degree does help, however, if you'd like to understand exactly *how* the financial crisis happened. Should you not have this qualification, we suggest you read and/or watch *The Big Short*.

For now, this will have to do: in the early 2000s lots of American banks gave lots of 'subprime' housing loans to lots of Americans who really couldn't afford them, on the assumption that housing prices would keep going up forever in which case they *would* be able to afford them (possibly). This was a classic financial bubble, like tulips in the 1600s and dot-com companies at the turn of the millennium, and everyone involved should have known better – but greed is good and all that. When housing prices stopped going up, the dominoes fell with a crash of epic proportions.

The economics degree-holders out there would, presumably, all agree that this explanation is inadequate. They would certainly agree that an episode with such dire global consequences would need to be covered in a book about people stuffing up the world. What they *won't* agree on is who exactly should take the bulk of the blame for the crisis. In other words, under whose name should we be discussing it?

Some blame the specific banksters at JPMorgan* who invented credit default swaps in the 1990s, which gave financial institutions the option to take insurance against loan defaulters (i.e. homeowners who don't pay their monthly mortgage instalments) and thus take on far riskier loans than they could previously. They did this because they were under the illusion that credit risk no longer existed. It did; it had just been transferred to the insurers, such as American International Group.

Some blame China for continuously undervaluing its currency, accumulating large dollar reserves and funnelling them back into the US financial system, so forcing US institutions to expand the borrowing pool with riskier clients (i.e. homeowners who probably wouldn't be able to pay their monthly mortgage instalments).

Some blame the banksters in general, always the cleverest and/or greediest people in the room, for coming up with ever more ingenious ways to package and sell toxic mortgage-backed securities (i.e. mortgages that eventually wouldn't be paid) as supposedly investment-grade debt.

---

* Probably JP Morgan's most incriminating mention in the book, this time in partnership with Exxon – though there are several more to come, including in this entry. *See Joseph Hazelwood.*

Some blame the size of the major banks, with their cavalier management and resulting inability to keep track of what exactly was on their books (i.e. lots of risky mortgages that eventually wouldn't be paid).

Some blame the regulators for failing to keep an eye on things. (The subprime mortgages shouldn't have been granted; the credit default swaps shouldn't have been allowed; the low-grade mortgage-backed securities shouldn't have been repackaged; the banks shouldn't have got so big; etc.)

Some blame Alan Greenspan, chairman of the Federal Reserve for twenty years until 2006, for lowering rates to such a degree after the 9/11 terrorist attacks that just about anyone out there who'd won $50 at the casino could afford a subprime mortgage. He also thought the banks would regulate themselves. (What a dummy!)

And, now that we're getting to individual names, some blame a certain William Jefferson Clinton. Bill Clinton? Of all the crimes we could put the charming and personable former president on trial for here the financial crisis may seem like a long shot.

What about the most infamous one of all, his relationship with White House intern Monica Lewinsky? Having initially denied, with much heartfelt vehemence, his affair with the woman 27 years his junior, Clinton went on to become the first US president impeached since 1868. In the process, he brought the office of the presidency and the country in general into disrepute, and inveigled the public into discovering all sorts of details we didn't really need to know about his spunk on Monica's dress and what he liked to do with his cigar. (He was ultimately acquitted of the charges but he was fined $90,000 for contempt of court for giving misleading testimony, and he lost his licence to practise law in Arkansas for five years.)

What about his disastrous foreign-policy decision to steer clear of international military interventions following the Battle of Mogadishu of 1993? There's a very strong case to be made that the Rwandan genocides of 1994 and 1995 would have been prevented or at least heavily curtailed without this call.

What about 9/11 itself? It may have happened on Dubya's watch, but the inter-agency dysfunctionality that allowed it to happen, so this often repeated argument goes, all developed under Clinton.

Those are three major, well-known points of attack. There are loads more, as any red-blooded Republican will bear testimony to, because every bad thing that has happened to America since 1992 was Bill Clinton's fault,

naturally. And if it wasn't, then it was Hillary Clinton's fault. But bear with us as we return to the financial crisis.

The economists who blame Bill Clinton for the crisis do so because his administration not only deregulated the finance sector in the 1990s generally – more so than any other president in history, according to those who push this line – but it specifically pursued affordable-housing targets as it did by reformulating the Community Reinvestment Act in 1995. Effectively, it ignored safe and sound financial practices by compelling government-linked institutions to grant subprime mortgages that a competent risk-aware lender would not have granted. Which is to say, the affordable-housing targets were unaffordable – but they certainly were vote-winners.

To cut a long story short: the Clinton government made the Federal National Mortgage Association (Fannie Mae) and the Federal Home Loan Mortgage Corporation (Freddie Mac) grant an ever-increasing percentage of their loans to poor people who ultimately had as much chance as a church mouse of paying them back in full.

So there it is. Noble intentions aside (road to hell, and all that), this was the cause of the financial crisis. Er, maybe.

Bill denies it, of course. And this is a *very* Republican line. So much so that we don't buy it. Apologies if we're flip-flopping a bit here, but if ever there was an entry where we have a little licence this must be it. But no, the financial crisis was the most complex of catastrophes and, to our mind, Bill

Clinton was at most a small causal link in a particularly long chain. So, as much as his political critics would like to force the case, Bill Clinton did not *cause* the financial crisis.

He does, however, embody it in many ways, along with his wife Hillary.

Now, Hillary. Well, for good and ill, deserved or not, Bill and Hillary will forever be conflated as the Clintons. Their political careers have naturally played off each other, and they share similar ideological beliefs, supporters, political tactics and bank balances. As a unit, they have come to represent one thing: the Democratic establishment.

Hillary may have paid her political dues, but she has achieved little of real significance while doing so, and yet it appears to many observers that by virtue of her surname and the immense diligence with which she worked the political system, she (and her supporters) felt entitled to the position of president of the most powerful country in the world. Also – and please note: this is a related criticism – she let Donald Trump win.

Hillary Rodham Clinton's political CV is, if we're now taking her opponents' perspective, as follows. She studied law at Yale in the early 1970s, where she met fellow law student Bill Clinton; she was politically active in her student years, flipping for the Republicans before flopping to the Democrats; she was persuaded by Bill to move to his native Arkansas and marry him, which she did in 1975. Erm… she was Bill's wife for a long time, while he was Attorney General and then Governor of the great state of Arkansas. Then, ahem, from 1993 to 2000, she was First Lady of the United States of America. Then she had the propitious fortune to be chosen by her party as a parachute candidate to run for the Senate in the state of New York, a virtually unloseable Democratic seat, in a strategy known in the US as carpetbagging*. After that, in 2008, she lost the Democratic primaries to an inexperienced Senator from Illinois, one Barack Obama, but was given the conciliatory position of Secretary of State. And then, eight years later, she ran for the presidency against Donald Trump and lost that. In both instances she was the can't-lose favourite.

---

* Carpetbagger *noun*: generally, someone who moves to a new place for opportunistic, usually immoral reasons; politically, someone who moves to a different state or district specifically for economic or political gain.

Of course, we're leaving out some of the detail here. Many Republicans, conservative observers and millennial lefties – her biggest haters – would paint a far less flattering picture of Her Royal Clinton... But to those still pining for her presidential what-might-have-beens, who may beg to differ with this assessment – who would like to unpack her many years in various political offices in more detail, and discuss gender parity in the 1970s, and point out that carpetbagging is actually relatively common and no big deal – our gist here is that impressions matter. And, in the end review, the impression Hillary Clinton has left on the US political landscape is very poor indeed. Today she is seen by many – including many who voted for her – as a political opportunist who has ridden on the coattails of her husband, ticked the boxes that needed ticking, and felt that would suffice to get her into the White House despite displaying a capacity for personal wealth accumulation that far outweighs her aptitude for the job.

In a nutshell, she managed to make a billionaire reality TV star partial to orange skin and gold curtains look like a man of the people, while offering in her campaign, in the memorable words of Michael Totten, 'microwaved establishment gruel that nearly everyone on both ends of the spectrum has been gagging on for years'. Moreover, as Andrew Sullivan put it, 'any candidate who can win the popular vote by nearly 3 million votes and still manage to lose the Electoral College by 304 to 227 is so profoundly incompetent, so miserably useless as a politician, she should be drummed out of the party under a welter of derision.' Totten and Sullivan were writing in *The Atlantic* and *New York Magazine*, which both, tellingly, lean towards the liberal left.

Hillary was defeated by her arrogance and entitlement, and by the rarefied bubble in which she and much of her support exists. To this disengaged, increasingly intolerant liberal elite, female voters were expected to vote for Hillary simply because she was a woman, not for anything she stood for. She told each niche demographic what they wanted to hear, without conveying a coherent economic message, and large swathes of the United States could be written off with a sneer as 'a basket of deplorables'.

With this kind of thinking to guide her, she campaigned in echo-chamber strongholds but didn't spend the required time in borderline states that she expected to win – the likes of Wisconsin, Michigan and Pennsylvania.

Most critically of all, next to Hillary Clinton, Donald Trump didn't look so bad – or, more accurately, he wasn't necessarily the worst possible option. So Trump's proposed policies were half-arsed and frequently delusional; Clinton's had conveniently evolved over the years to whatever was most expedient at the time. So Trump had a shady business empire and was grossly wealthy; the Clintons are also in 'the top 1 percent of the top 1 percent', having made at least $230 million since Bill's tenure ended, according to *Forbes* – the yields of decades of political crony-capitalism that voters today find increasingly offensive. So Trump was a congenital liar who made stuff up as he went along; the Clintons' political career was a smorgasbord of fibs, falsehoods and fabrications, so much so that

'I did not have sexual relations with that woman, Miss Lewinsky.'
– Bill Clinton, lying on national television, 1998

'It depends on what the meaning of "is" is. If the – if he – if "is" means is and never has been, that is not – that is one thing. If it means there is none, that was a completely true statement.'
– Bill Clinton, taking evasive action during testimony to a grand jury, 1998

'I remember landing under sniper fire. There was supposed to be some kind of a greeting ceremony at the airport, but instead we just ran with our heads down to get into the vehicles to get to our base.'
– Hillary Clinton, embellishing in 2008 her arrival in Tuzla, Bosnia in 1996.
In reality she was greeted on the tarmac by local children,
one of whom presented her with a copy of a poem

'Director Comey said my answers were truthful, and what I've said is consistent with what I have told the American people.'
– Hillary Clinton, taking liberties with the truth, about sending classified emails on her
private server, July 2016. The Washington Post rated this line 'Four Pinocchios'

Christopher Hitchens titled his book on them *No One Left To Lie To*. In the age of transparency, Trump's brash, almost idiotic fake news just seemed... honest compared to the Clintons' version. At least (so the equally idiotic thinking goes) he showed some *conviction*.

When it came time to place their crosses in November 2016, the American voter had a dilemma with only one sliver of redemption: at least, at the end of it all, whoever won would mean the other one didn't. Ultimately we would conclude, the American public voted for *not-Clinton* and against the political establishment. In the insanity of a Trumpian presidency, they figured, perhaps there was the vaguest promise of some kind of corrective action, if not in the politics that would govern the land over the next four years, then at least the politics that governs the politicians. The status quo is not good enough, was the verdict. Be better!

'We've never seen any reports on people, of which there are millions, [who] had to vote in Minnesota or Ohio, and had to hold their nose and almost on the verge of tears voted for Hillary Clinton because they thought, this is an awful person who doesn't give a shit about me and she's done terrible things, and yet I have do to this, I have to do this because the worst thing that could happen is that [Trump's] gonna win but this feels so awful.'

– *Felix Biederman, 26, Chapo Trap House podcaster*

Now, back to the financial crisis, where we kicked this entry off.

You probably have to be a true conservative partisan to consider Bill Clinton's administration a primary cause of the financial crisis. It's a long, long stretch. Nevertheless, in the public eye the Clintons themselves seem to be reflected in so much of it and its messy fallout. Together, we believe they represent the failure of both the political and financial establishment, the failure of the Democratic Party in particular, and the failure of modern politics in general across much of the free world.

After the financial crisis, economists and industry commentators, angry young Occupy Wall Street protestors and decent everyday citizens alike railed against the disconnected banks and unscrupulous banksters who

'[T]here's been a building reaction against Democrat politicians of the '90s who tried to make a compromise with corporate capitalism and then defined liberalism around cultural issues of diversity, immigration, women's rights and so on, while riding along with the shafting of the working class.'

– John Mason, professor of political science
at William Paterson University in New Jersey

played such fundamental roles in what had happened but who seemed to escape any real censure, emerging barely a year or two later with increased profits and business-as-usual bonuses. And it is these oleaginous elements of the political-financial industrial complex with which the Clintons have become so inextricably linked – they are, in the common mind, one and the same. Just days after leaving office in 2001, Bill was paid $125,000 to make a speech at Morgan Stanley Dean Witter, the first of many such presentations which brought in $106 million over the next fifteen years, according to *Forbes*. Hillary has made lip-service attempts in the past to take Wall Street to task about its excesses, but no-one's buying it when they know she, following Bill's example, rakes in $200,000 or more in speaking fees from the most darkly symbolic of the banking names: Goldman Sachs, Morgan Stanley, Deutsche Bank, UBS. It's hard to believe your solution when you are being paid millions of dollars by the problem.

Carl Benjamin, better known as YouTube podcaster Sargon of Akkad, sums it up like this: 'Hillary was the apotheosis of all the corruption in the system, literally.'[1]

Given that Bill was one of the most down-to-earth US presidents in memory, the transformation of the Clinton name over two decades – what it means, the emotions it generates – is quite astonishing. The Clinton way of doing politics, as with the Blair way in the UK, once promised much but has now been found wanting. Their defenders would argue that American (and international) politicians have long made expedient choices and shilled for the corporates; that there is nothing unique about this. Perhaps. But that's not good enough any more. They are the straw that broke the American public's back. Or they are the couple that simply took it too far. The voting public has tired of this corporate cronyism and elusive ethical backbone, and the Clinton decline is representative of the great existential soup sandwich in which the Democratic Party in particular and the American left in general finds itself.

In just sixteen years, the Democrats have lost two elections despite winning the popular vote, on both occasions letting an unsophisticated boor into the White House through the back door. As a result, the millennial left are up in arms, betrayed, they feel, by the Boomer generation of neo-liberals (really pseudo-liberals, in their estimate) who have backed the politically correct issues of social justice while selling out to Big Money and leaving them in the dwang: mired in student debt, jobless and fearful for the future. The solutions they propose as a result are generally off-the-reservation crazy – see the preceding entry, on Chávez and Maduro.

The right, meanwhile, somehow figured Donald Trump was an acceptable alternative.

In their contemptuous rejection of Clintonism, these extreme positions are frightening and have IMPENDING DOOM! written all over them – but they are, at least, understandable in their way.

America, once the world's great superpower, is teetering. To prevent its fall it needs a strong, moral Democratic Party. A strong Republican Party would also be nice. Either way, the time of the Clintons has passed.

Someone, please, tell Chelsea.

'[A] fact that has to be assimilated by both Labour and the Democrats is this: when Bill and Hillary arrived in Washington in 1992 they had little money. Now, despite remaining notionally in public service throughout, they are worth $200 million. Tony and Cherie Blair were also impecunious when they arrived in power in 1997. Today they are worth over $75 million.

'Think now of the working class voters whom the Clintons or the Blairs exhorted to vote for them in the 1990s: they are probably worse off now than they were then. In effect the Clintons and Blairs merely surfed on their grievances and inequities, making themselves rich and leaving their voters in the dust. Such contrasts have been duly noted, which is one reason that the old politics is no longer working now.'

– Historian RW Johnson, on Donald Trump's election victory, 2016 [2]

Jack Dorsey

b. 19 November 1976

Creator of Twitter; hero of the low-attention-span righteous; harbinger of the end of rational discourse

Jack Dorsey came up with the idea for Twitter at New York University, later developing it at his online vehicle dispatch business in Oakland, California, where he thought of drivers using short updates to communicate, like a mobile Instant Messager. In 2006, once smartphone market penetration made it viable, he created Twitter with several San Fran internet entrepreneurs. He was 29. Today he's a tech billionaire.

The original point of Twitter was to send a text to one number, which broadcast to all your friends/followers: essentially microblogging fun with mates, limited to 140 characters. Later it developed into a horse's-mouth news source, which remains its sole redeeming feature. But without room for complexity or depth, it's mostly a forum where holier-than-thous angrily correct the world, zombie socialism and alt-right racism continue their disturbing revivals, and rational debate goes to die.

Whoops, out of space. That's 140 words exactly. See? No complexity in 140 words, let alone 140 characters. For more on the evils of Twitter you'll have to read the rest of the book…

In the meantime, a last word to Jack Dorsey: Mr Dorsey, you may have had innocent intentions, with your supposedly innocent hipster beard, but we regret to inform you that you have created a monster.

See The Israel-Palestine letter writer & Mark Zuckerberg.

'We came across the word "twitter", and it was just perfect. The definition was "a short burst of inconsequential information", and "chirps from birds". And that's exactly what the product was.'
– *Jack Dorsey, 2009* [1]

'Twitter [is] a suppurating bubo of intense Satanic vileness in which bullies exult, idiots are hailed as sages and all decency, wisdom, insight, wit or modesty is drowned in a mucus flood of idiot received ideas, poisonous cant, vicious insults and sixth-form common-room glibness.'
– *James Delingpole, 2011* [2]

Mohammed Emwazi
a.k.a. Jihadi John

17 August 1988 – 12 November 2015

British-Arab jihadi; knife-wielding murderer; web-surfing loser; good PR for ISIS; bad PR for Islam

IN LONDON IN 2003 a former Guantanamo inmate called Moazzam Begg launched CagePrisoners, a non-governmental organisation now known as CAGE that describes itself on its website as an 'independent advocacy organisation working to empower communities impacted by the War on Terror'. Its broad aim is to 'highlight and campaign against state policies pertaining to the War on Terror'. Begg has, in various ways, argued that advocating for sharia law in Britain, the idea of a 'caliphate' (like the self-styled death cult in Iraq and Syria that calls itself ISIS) and jihad in general does 'not make people extreme'.[1] Indeed, he says that 'jihad is a noble concept'.[2] So, to be clear on this, behind the justice-for-those-wrongly-accused-of-terrorism shtick, CAGE is, by espousing such views and campaigning for terrorists who have actually pleaded guilty, in fact an advocacy group for Islamist terror and those who would perpetrate it.

Any impression Begg and his associates may have created that they were a serious human rights group fell apart when CAGE's relationship with a young man called Mohammed Emwazi came to light. They knew him long before he went to Syria. They knew him long before he horrified the world with the videotaped beheadings of ISIS prisoners. CAGE had been helping the man who became known as 'Jihadi John' for years.

It wasn't just CAGE that had been watching Emwazi. Britain's intelligence agency MI5 had been observing him too. In 2009 he was refused entry into Dar es Salaam after arriving drunk and belligerent at Tanzanian passport control in the company of known Islamist extremists. In that instance, he was sent home via Amsterdam and interrogated by Dutch and British intelligence officers, with MI5 also speaking to his fiancée. She – probably wisely – called the relationship off. After Emwazi's death, ISIS would confirm that he'd been trying to make contact with al-Shabaab, the Muslim terrorist group responsible for the attack on the Westgate shopping centre in Nairobi in 2013, which killed 67 people.

He hadn't been in Tanzania to go on safari.

Despite all this, in 2013 Emwazi managed to slip out of Britain and into Syria, where he rattled around with the al-Qaeda-affiliated group Jabhat al-Nusra for a while, before eventually settling down with the psychopaths of ISIS. Third time was a charm: he had found his spiritual home.

In August 2014 his year-long spell in the international spotlight began when he appeared in a five-minute video uploaded to YouTube that saw him, masked and clad in black, denouncing the Obama administration and the West in general before executing American journalist James Foley with a large knife. The beheading itself was not shown but the professionally shot and edited video stirred revulsion around the world. It is hard to begin to imagine what the experience must have been like for Foley and Emwazi's subsequent victims, journalists Steven Sotloff and Kenji Goto, aid workers David Haines, Alan Henning and Peter Kassig, traveller Haruna Yukawa and several un-named Syrian soldiers.

At first, Emwazi was anonymous, though his east London accent was a clue to his eventual identification. This was a man known to his captives in Syria as 'John', one of a group of four ISIS members with English accents nicknamed the Beatles. The tabloids soon branded him Jihadi John.

Slick use of the internet, as evident in the broadcasting of Emwazi's crimes, is a feature of the media-savvy ISIS, who took notice of the incredible visual power of the coverage of Osama bin Laden's hijackers crashing into the Twin Towers in 2001 and realised the recruitment potential and propaganda effects therein. The group has several media wings, with the al-Hayat Media Center specifically dedicated to creating propaganda for Western consumption. YouTube and other social media sites are important platforms for the group. In August 2014 Abdel-Majed Abdel Bary, from West London, posted a Twitter picture of himself holding a severed head. 'Chillin' with my other homie, or what's left of him' read the caption.[3]

It's probably only reasonable at this point to note that Emwazi's body count is pathetically small when compared to, say, Stalin or Hitler or the

'He was most probably one of the worst, who hit and tortured without the slightest restraint… He was the tallest, the calmest but also the most determined, without the slightest scruple.'

*– Didier François, French radio journalist,
who was held hostage for 10 months in Syria, talking about Emwazi*

active fighting that ISIS has been involved in in Iraq and Syria, but he finds himself on our list as a peculiarly Westernised jihadi, the kind who doesn't just travel abroad to take up arms, but often returns home to perpetrate the awfulness of terror attacks in Paris and Manchester and London and elsewhere.

How does a man like Mohammed Emwazi become Jihadi John? Born in Kuwait, he immigrated with his parents and took full advantage of Britain's liberal society, gaining a computer sciences degree from the University of Westminster. Like Omar Sheikh (LSE graduate, complicit in the murder of Daniel Pearl), Asif Hanif (King's College London, suicide bomber who killed three and injured more than fifty in Tel Aviv), Omar Sharif (Repton prep school, failed suicide bomber on the same mission) and Umar Abdulmutallab (University College London graduate, the 'underwear bomber' who tried to set off a bomb on a plane as it landed in the US), he was not oppressed by his adopted country. These are ordinary – indeed, privileged – Brits gone bad. As of mid-2017 about 850 young British men were believed to have travelled to Syria and Iraq to fight as jihadis.

There are complex reasons why disaffected young men become suicide bombers or align themselves with urban gangs or terror groups in a way that is likely to drastically shorten their lives. Sociologists and politicians are desperate to work out the causal links so they can do something about it. Former prime minister David Cameron liked to bang on about 'radicalisation', but the vast majority of Muslims who hear the hatred preached by local or cyber imams tend not to act on it. They certainly don't feel the need to decapitate an off-duty soldier in a London street, as happened to the unfortunate Fusilier Lee Rigby by two London converts of Nigerian descent, Michael Adebolajo and Michael Adebowale. So, in the absence of a better explanation, we must sadly conclude that Trump got this one right: Jihadi John and his ilk are, simply, enormous losers.

These are guys who can't relate to other people and have been rejected for being dull and a little weird, and who sit in their mum's attic and start reading nonsense on the internet. Guys who see a chance for some slice of power or glamour that they'll never achieve in the world they currently inhabit. And, of course, guys who have one or two important filters in their brain missing.

In a bizarre obituary in ISIS's in-cult magazine, it was claimed that Emwazi had a big heart because he gave his sex slave to an injured, unmarried soldier as a gift, a slave he had in turn received as a gift. This may have sounded familiar to the CAGE spokesmen who have described their boy Mo as 'kind', 'gentle', 'a beautiful young man'.[4]

The drunken brawl in Tanzania. The sex slave. The I'm-a-big-chap on-camera posturing. These are the clues that are suggestive not of a pious or religious man, but a lout and an outcast. It says a lot about a person that the only place on earth he can find some sense of purpose is the worst place in the world. That he and his fellow jihadi travellers are forced to adopt an extreme interpretation of Islam, one that is not compatible with the modern world – and one that the majority of Muslims reject with contempt – to feed their pathetic need for affirmation and their desperate quest for some passing consequence.

And CAGE? Well, they exposed themselves when their 'research director' Asim Qureshi went on air to explain how Emwazi was really the victim in all of this, a poor soul responding to 'a narrative of injustice'.[5] Yes, indeed. After all, being questioned by the security services really does leave a chap little option, in this view of the world, but to go and behead people in the

'This guy was a human animal. Killing him is probably making the world a little bit better place.'

– US Colonel Steve Warren,
speaking after the drone strike on Emwazi, November 2015

'It saddens me that here in America we're celebrating the killing of this deranged, pathetic young man... Had circumstances been different, Jim probably would have befriended him and tried to help him.'

– Diane Foley, mother of Emwazi's first video victim, James Foley[6]

name of ISIS, especially after one of the governments you're railing against paid for your family's housing and your university education. In the face of such intolerable oppression, what else is a man to do?

Perhaps this is the problem. Perhaps the sheer weight and scale of Western culture is so intimidating that certain minds simply succumb to the internet troll explaining to you all how very unacceptable it is. Can you imagine these people ever winning? To borrow from John Oliver's monologue in the aftermath of the Paris terror attacks in 2015: 'If you are in a war of culture and lifestyle with France, good fucking luck!' And the same applies in the UK and Germany and Spain and, yes, the United States. The people of Shakespeare, Beethoven, Picasso and Welles are equally unlikely to be persuaded of the joys of a medieval desert death-cult with rubbish food over their own, rather fulfilling, cultural existence.

Mohammed Emwazi 'evaporated' in a 2015 drone strike that, though not the justice he deserved, at least keeps him from causing further trouble. We would sincerely hope that, in a vaguely karmic universe, he didn't wake up after his death in paradise surrounded by dozens of slave-virgins. Instead, we prefer to think of him in a version of hell where his boss is a woman and he has to listen to Mozart all day.

As for CAGE, we wish them a declining membership and increasing irrelevance, to say the least.

And then there's ISIS itself, the post-bin Laden fundamentalists' club for wannabe Jihadi Johns. Theirs has been a reign of terror, in the most real sense of the word, and a plundering of one of humanity's earliest cradles of civilisation, that can ultimately only end in rejection. Let that day hasten forth so that they, like Jihadi John, may become an unlamented memory and nothing more.

Enver & Talat

Mehmet Talat Pasha: 10 April 1874 – 15 March 1921
Ismail Enver Pasha: 22 November 1881 – 4 August 1922

De facto leaders of the Ottoman Empire during World War I; two of the Three Pashas; chief prosecutors of the Armenian genocide; Hitler's inspiration

TO DENY THE HOLOCAUST TODAY is to mark yourself in a number of ways: anti-Semite, deluded, possibly evil, probably an enormous asshole. It's one of those reputation-ruining acts that puts you firmly in a box with the label DON'T TRUST ANYTHING THIS PERSON SAYS OR STANDS FOR. Rightly so.

By Holocaust, it is universally accepted that we are talking about the Nazi genocide of the Jews and other persecuted minorities during World War II. There is, however, another Holocaust that is worthy of the capital H – and can even be understood as a practice run for the Jewish Holocaust – which is not only much denied today but is barely discussed or even known. This is the Armenian genocide of World War I in which perhaps 1.5 million people were systematically exterminated during the dying gasps of the Ottoman Empire. It is the genocide for which the English word 'genocide' was coined, and yet it has become largely a forgotten genocide.

There's a compelling argument that sets the decline of the Ottoman Empire as the foundational cause of a great deal, even the majority, of the bloodletting of modern times. At its peak, in the late 1600s, it covered five million square kilometres of the earth, including Anatolia and Mesopotamia, vast tracts of territory in north and east Africa and Arabia, and much of Eastern Europe. In short, so the theory goes, the Ottoman contraction had by the early 20th century left a hodge-podge of small and vulnerable states in Eastern Europe, the Balkans, as fair game for the two predator empires that remained active in the area, Austria-Hungary and Russia. This unstable state of affairs came to a head on the back of a fluke assassination – *see Gavrilo Princip* – in the form of the Great War of 1914-1918, which was then rerun as World War II in 1939-1945, with knock-on effects in the form of the Russian Revolution and the atrocities of Stalin's communism along the way. How willing you are to follow this logic depends, probably, on your statute of limitations for geopolitical cause and effect.

One undeniably linked casualty of the Ottoman collapse, however, was the Armenian people. Life had long been complicated for the Armenians, a kind of buffer nation stuck in the middle, as they were, between the Ottomans, Russians and Iranians, and rather kicked around over the ages as a result. As the world's first officially Christian nation, dating back to the turn of the 4th century, religious victimisation was an added cross to bear. Within the predominantly Muslim Ottoman Empire, Christians were seen as second-class citizens, with the usual related rights restrictions and resentments as a result.

In the two decades before the genocide of World War I the Armenians suffered appalling pogroms at the hands of the Ottomans, with up to 300,000 deaths in the mid-1890s. That figure alone is staggering – on the scale of the Crimean War death toll or the depravations of Idi Amin – but it was the coming to power of the Young Turks in 1908 and, perhaps ironically, the radical political reform of the empire's absolute monarchy into something like a constitutional government that signalled their greatest existential threat. It was a threat that mirrored, and was ultimately caused by, the empire's very own parlous state.

The pre-war years were a time of political volatility for the Ottomans. Various governments had been formed under Sultan Memed V, and only a coup in 1913 by members of the Committee of Union and Progress party instilled some sense of stability into the foundering empire. The two most prominent instigators of this raid were the relatively young firebrands Ismail Enver Pasha and Mehmet Talat Pasha who, along with Ahmed Jemal Pasha, then assumed de facto leadership of the empire. They came to be known as the Three Pashas. The honorary term 'pasha' indicated a senior Ottoman ranking but would most accurately have translated to 'dictators' for this triumvirate. They were respectively ministers of war, the interior and the navy, but they held various posts and responsibilities in their time in charge. For our purposes, the former and the latter were the most influential: Enver as head of the Ottoman army and Talat as the most politically powerful of the lot, eventually elevated to Grand Vizier of the Ottoman Empire. Between them they ran the show with nationalist fervour, doing their best to 'Turkeyfy' the empire as a means to hang on to what was left of it, and entering the Great War on the side of Germany.

By April 1915 the war had delivered the Allied invasion at Gallipoli to the west and battle with the Russians in the Caucasus Mountains to the northeast. The Allies would eventually be repelled by Mustafa Kemal Atatürk, the future father of modern Turkey. The Russians, however, inflicted a defeat at Sarikamish in January of that year, which had been particularly humiliating for Enver, commander of the Turkish forces. As a result, the Armenians, who lived in the area, took the blame as treasonous collaborators, with Talat referring to them as 'enemies of the state'. Thus was born the required excuse to 'solve the Armenian problem' – the Ottoman forerunner, as we'll see, of Hitler's 'Jewish question'.

The systematic execution of the Pashas' plan began on 24 April 1915 with a 'decapitation strike' aimed at removing prominent Armenian leaders from Ottoman society. This first wave of deportations saw 250 Armenian clergymen, politicians and intellectuals moved from Constantinople to holding centres near Ankara. In July, once it became clear that the Allied forces at Gallipoli had been halted, the killings began in earnest. Armenians in the larger cities were rounded up by the thousand, to be shot in the countryside, whereafter the Armenian villages in the northeast were cleansed, as the modern parlance has it, their populations sent on 'relocation' marches into the Syrian desert to the south. Standard operational procedure was to separate the men early for execution, while the starving women and children were marched on to be killed later, abducted by local tribes

'You have already been informed that the Government... has decided to destroy completely all the indicated persons living in Turkey... Their existence must be terminated, however tragic the measures taken may be, and no regard must be paid to either age or sex, or to any scruples of conscience.'

– *cabled instruction from Talat to a prefect in Aleppo*

or simply succumb to the wild. To save ammunition, the Turks stabbed and beat to death their charges with bayonets, swords, axes, hammers and rocks. Thousands were burned alive in haylofts. Others were dragged to their deaths behind animals or roped together and drowned en masse, with one victim shot to drag down the others. At least two rivers, including the Euphrates, became so clogged with bodies that they changed course over several hundred feet. With the psychopathic jackboots of a genocidal regime let loose to do their worst, it almost goes without saying that rape and heinous torture were widespread. Elsewhere, Christian Greeks and Assyrians were also massacred in huge numbers.

The official Turkish response to the suggestion today, more than a century later, that the Ottomans committed a genocide of such outrageous proportions runs along the lines of *We will never accept an accusation like that* – which is in fact a direct quote (translated, but in context) from its president Recep Erdoğan. His position is that it was war, man, and bad things happen and Turks died too and 'measures were taken to restore order in Anatolia' and we can't really know everything that happened and let's change the topic. And, as with the best deceptions, there is some fudgy truth in there. The war it was set against was indeed the greatest the world had ever seen, the empire certainly was being decimated on all sides, and the Armenians did have a desire for their own nation-state. But not only is there overwhelming and conclusive evidence of the genocide itself, there is also evidence that the Three Pashas saw their entry into the war on the side of the Germans as the opportunity they had been seeking to institute it. This was the long-held plan to 'liquidate its internal enemies… without being disturbed by foreign intervention.'[1]

As historian Justin Marozzi describes it, 'The destruction of the Armenians, together with the ethnic cleansing and population exchanges of the Anatolian Greeks, was the "foundational crime" that facilitated the formation of an "ethno-national Turkish republic". One followed the other.'[2]

The US Ambassador to Turkey at the time, Henry Morgenthau, recorded much of the known detail of the atrocities in his memoir published in 1918, collating stories from American consuls, missionaries and travellers, and repeatedly broaching the topic with Talat and Enver (and others), to no avail. While avoiding the most direct charges of atrocity, Talat acknowledged his loathing of the Armenian people and his government's plans to destroy them. 'It is no use for you to argue,' he told Morgenthau in 1915. 'We have already disposed of three-quarters of the Armenians... The hatred between the Turks and the Armenians is now so intense that we have got to finish with them. If we don't, they will plan their revenge.'

In another exchange he had the temerity to request that Morgenthau arrange for American life insurance companies to pass on their lists of Armenian policyholders so that the Turks might collect the payouts now owing 'as escheats to the state'. Morgenthau refused.

And yet, as planned, with the war raging the Americans could do little to stop the horrors. As the Ottomans' ally, the Germans were in a position to do something, and several of their representatives complained and were critical in recording many of the horrors, but others preferred to take notes rather than intervene.

Given Turkey's 'fog of war' attitude to events and a lack of Nazi-style record-keeping, the number of Armenians killed under Talat, Enver and Jemal is difficult to ascertain. The figures vary from 600,000 to 1.8 million, with 1-1.5 million being the generally accepted range.

After the war all of the Three Pashas were found by Turkish courts martial to be, among other things, complicit in the strategic execution of the Armenian massacre. They and several other perpetrators were sentenced to death *in absentia* in 1919, and the widely recorded reactions of senior Turkish officials, including Atatürk himself, were those of shame and regret. The trials made global news. After the establishment of the Republic of Turkey in 1923, however, the history of the Armenian genocide was slowly disappeared from the Turkish collective recollection, and in time it faded from global memory.

During World War II the Polish lawyer Raphael Lemkin studied the massacres and coined the term 'genocide' – from the Greek *geno* for family, tribe or race, and *-cide* for killing – in an attempt to publicise it. The irony of the timing was as black as a Nazi swastika: Hitler himself had used the

'The "mission" in the circular was: to attack the convoys and massacre the population... I am ashamed as a Muslim, I am ashamed as an Ottoman statesman. What a stain on the reputation of the Ottoman Empire.'
 – *Turkish senator Reshid Akif Pasha, testifying about parallel orders intended to disguise the Armenian genocide, November 1918*

> 'We have this country absolutely under our control. I have no desire to shift the blame on to our underlings and I am entirely willing to accept the responsibility myself for everything that has taken place. The Cabinet itself has ordered the deportations. I am convinced that we are completely justified in doing this owing to the hostile attitude of the Armenians toward the Ottoman Government.'
>
> *Enver talking to US Ambassador Henry Morgenthau, 1915*

world's amnesia of what had happened as justification for his own insane acts just a few years earlier. 'Who, after all,' he said while contemplating the invasion of Poland, 'speaks today of the annihilation of the Armenians?'

Moreover, various architects of the Jewish Holocaust, including the future commandant of Auschwitz, were in Turkey in 1915 where, it seems, they learnt many of their foulest tricks. Methods of rounding up victims and suppressing news were noted. Talat, for instance, issued parallel government orders, just as the Nazis would, one set indicating 'official' logistical plans of no great malevolence, and a second with the real instructions to 'proceed with your mission'. There was even sinister inspiration to be had from what veteran Middle East correspondent Robert Fisk calls 'the twentieth century's first gas chamber': a large cave in the Syrian desert in which thousands of Armenians were killed by asphyxiation after their Turkish persecutors lit an enormous bonfire at its entrance.

No story of genocide can have a truly happy ending but there may at least be some grim satisfaction in the retribution dealt upon the chief perpetrator in this instance. The Three Pashas had all fled Turkey before their trials and travelled freely through Europe and Asia without threat of extradition. In response, the Armenian Revolutionary Federation political party established a covert assassination operation codenamed Operation Nemesis, identifying Talat as the principal target, along with Enver, Jemal and several others. Talat was tracked to an address in Berlin in March 1921 and was shot dead in broad daylight by 23-year-old genocide-survivor Soghomon Tehlirian. Tehlirian, who had lost dozens of relatives, including his mother and several siblings, was found not guilty by a German jury by reason of temporary insanity after a two-day trial. He emigrated to the US and died in San Francisco in 1960 an Armenian national hero.

Six others involved in the genocide, including Jemal, were assassinated before Operation Nemesis was brought to a close in 1922. Enver died violently that year fighting the Bolsheviks in what is now Tajikistan.

In 1991, following the break-up of the Soviet Union, Armenia became an independent republic. Wedged today between Turkey, Georgia, Azerbaijan and Iran, it has a population of around 3 million people, a quarter to a third of the world population of Armenians. Thus we see the enormity of the original modern genocide: not just the countless deaths and trauma at the time, or Hitler's inspiration two decades after the fact, but, more than a century later, the scattering of an entire people across the globe – the barely acknowledged diaspora that came of a barely acknowledged crime against humanity.

> 'Undoubtedly religious fanaticism was an impelling motive with the Turkish and Kurdish rabble who slew Armenians as a service to Allah, but the men who really conceived the crime had no such motive. Practically all of them were atheists, with no more respect for Mohammedanism than for Christianity, and with them the one motive was cold–blooded, calculating state policy.'
>
> – US Ambassador to the Ottoman Empire Henry Morgenthau

The guy who killed Concorde

b. in a time of adventure – d. in a time of soullessness

Emotionless, visionless, sensible-shoes bureaucrat who betrayed the wonder and potential of supersonic travel; mandarin too crushed by corporate life to imagine an extraordinary future

BLEACHING IN THE BRUTAL SUN OF THE MOJAVE DESERT stands a scrapped Continental Airlines McDonnell Douglas DC10 (N13067), an old warhorse of an aircraft that came to the end of its serviceable life in 2002. The predictable final destination of an ordinary passenger jet. In this case, however, this ordinary DC10 played a brief and fatal role in one of the most extraordinary aviation stories to ever play out.

In its otherwise unremarkable life, the DC10 in question lost a strip of metal trim, about 40 centimetres long and 3 centimetres wide, that was poorly affixed to an engine cowl as it took off from Charles de Gaulle airport one day in July 2000. The plane flew on, unaffected, to Newark. The strip of metal, however, stayed behind on the runway, and five minutes later would shred the tyre of an Air France Concorde jet airliner that was at that particular moment thundering towards its takeoff at approximately 330km/h and long past the theoretical point of no return known in aviation as V1.

The tyre exploded, sending a 4.5-kilogram hunk of rubber smashing into the fuselage of the plane at 500km/h, which in turn sent a shockwave through the full fuel tank, forcing it to rupture at its weakest point, sending fuel gushing all over the wing and the engine. The Concorde lurched into the air with flames pouring out the back, and the result, at Hôtelissimo Les Relais Bleus, about five kilometres from the airport, is well documented: 109 passengers and crew killed, along with four unbelievably unlucky people on the ground. It was a ghastly tragedy, as any deadly plane crash is, but it was more than that; it brought to an end Concorde's flawless run of almost thirty years of fatality-free flight, and ultimately it would signal the end of the plane's operational existence.

Jean-Cyril Spinetta, the CEO of Air France, had watched the catastrophe play out from his office at Charles de Gaulle, and the story goes that before the plane hit the ground he'd already told his secretary to call the French transport minister.

Unfortunately for him, it was a familiar feeling, as he had already seen two major air crashes in other roles, both involving Airbus A320s. Such are the risks of making a career in air travel administration. The duties of company directors in France are taken seriously, and lazy practice can end up in jail time if people are hurt as a result. French authorities make a habit of charging corporate executives and even ministers in their personal capacity with involuntary manslaughter in major transport incidents where they feel there might have been executive incompetence or shoddy practice. As such, we need to emphasise that Spinetta was not found to be liable in the earlier incidents, either as head of the French transport cabinet or CEO of Air Inter, and he would not be singled out in the crash of Concorde. Nevertheless, an observer could see how these dreadful events might turn Spinetta and his colleagues in aviation into men who were dedicated not to making Concorde safer and more profitable – or, more importantly, to seeking its replacement – but men so terrified of the mere possibility of something going wrong that they wanted Concorde out of the skies as soon as possible.

'Essentially, what Concorde is is a time machine, a wonderful time machine... Its [retirement is] really very, very, very sad, a huge backward step for technology.'

– BA chairman Lord Marshall, who has been blamed
as one of those instrumental in Concorde's early retirement[1]

Let's think a bit about Concorde. It was remarkable for many reasons, perhaps most obviously because it was the love child of the French and British governments working in relative, err, concord. (Put that in your Brexit and smoke it.) But as a technological marvel it was something else altogether. There's breaking the sound barrier. There's landing a man on the moon. And there's Concorde.

There was, in a way, an anthropomorphic love for Concorde. It was never 'the Concorde', or 'a Concorde'. It was always just Concorde. It was beautiful too, and loud to boot. As children living west of London, we'd run out into the garden to see the dart-shaped machine vanishing towards New York with a vast, earthquake-like rumble. It was fast. We know this, but it might be worth remembering just how blindingly, physics-bustingly quick it was: it would fly at 60,000 feet at 2,170km/h. Its pilots would speak of the surreal feeling of tearing through the sky and seeing, 20,000 feet below you, a 747, flying 1,300km/h slower, looking like it was going backwards. To demonstrate its potential, Concorde 002 made a legendary PR trip in 1974, leaving Boston for Paris at the same time as a Boeing 747 left Paris for Boston. Concorde 002 flew to Paris, spent 68 minutes on the ground loading up fuel and passengers, and returned to Boston, landing 11 minutes ahead of the lumbering 747.

It was an outlier. It would get you from London to New York in less than three and a half hours. Today, in 2017, the trip is still an eight-hour haul, just like it was for the DC10 when it first started plying the transatlantic route back in 1971. That's not progress.

Concorde was progress.

Concorde was the human spirit captured in flight.

A tiresome argument is 'who cares if some rich people now can't get to Harrods as quickly as they used to?' or some such snark. This is to miss the point of cutting-edge achievements like Concorde. When something is shiny and new and brilliant it tends to be expensive, which, in turn, tends to mean that rich people are the early adopters. What is supposed to happen – and indeed has happened in most spheres of technological advance – is that good disruptive technology is democratised, gets going with scale and scope, and prices diminish until what started out as a hugely expensive and unreliable 1920s Rolls-Royce ends up as a Kia Picanto in 2017.

But not so with Concorde, which is a rare case of a technological trajectory of blinding magnificence and potential just petering out like a dud firework.

In this case, it was a machine so far ahead of its time that the bean counters simply couldn't register its potential. Their logic could not compute that the demise of Concorde was harmful, not because paying thousands of pounds for a flight across the Atlantic while sitting next to Joan Collins was at stake, but because it stole the future of fast, affordable travel from those who might have enjoyed it. It delayed the future $1,000 return transatlantic supersonic flight, the there-and-back-in-a-day trip that ought to have been in the pipeline had Concorde followed a standard technology life-cycle. Imagine that. Imagine it and then weep, because a gang of frightened suits eviscerated by the fear of their own smallness simply didn't have the vision for such a future.

There was a great deal of corporate nonsense and politics involved to get Concorde out of the sky. Airbus became involved and, inevitably, so did British Airways, most notably its head engineer Alan MacDonald, who it was said didn't like the big hole in his maintenance budget that the Concorde operation left. It was, after all, an old, bespoke aircraft. To him, we imagine, looking after Concorde was a little like a Toyota dealer being asked to run a 1960s Packard Coupé. Possible – but a distraction.

The mechanics around the early grounding of Concorde remain murky, hence our inability to pin definitive blame on one person, even a representative. One particularly unimpressed Concorde lover and charterer, US aviation attorney Donald Pevsner, believes that Spinetta would have been desperate to retire the plane after the Gonesse crash, for fear of a second crash and possible prosecution under French law, but that this was well beyond his individual powers. Others had to be involved. There is, as a result, a rogue's gallery of assorted spineless suits, who could not between them match the vision of the politicians and the engineers who built Concorde, who we might finger. BA's CEO Rod Eddington and chairman Lord Marshall deserve a mention, as does Noel Forgeard, then boss at Airbus, who finally pulled the maintenance plug. Writing bitterly

> ## 'I've always thought of the Concorde as a magical object, a symbol, a miracle.'
>
> *– French designer Andrée Putman,*
> *who redesigned Air France Concorde interiors in 1994 [2]*

of 'French defeatism' in an article titled 'The betrayal of Concorde', Pevsner wasn't scared to implicate even former French president Jacques Chirac in the plane's demise. Chirac, coincidentally, had been onboard an Air France 747 on an adjacent taxiway before the crash. As it slewed down the runway, the doomed Concorde evidently missed his plane by mere metres before taking off.

There were, it is true, many headwinds for the old bird in the early 2000s. The terror attacks in 2001 in New York had battered the aviation industry, and more trying economic times had put pressure on the travel budgets of even the most profligate of Atlantic-hopping executives. There was, additionally, the fuel bill. Oil was up and Concorde used four times the fuel per passenger than did a standard Boeing 747, making up a full one-third of the cost of a ticket. And, of course, the maintenance bill was problematic. Concorde was by any other standard a 'classic', an old aircraft that required fastidious and costly maintenance, and encountered technical glitches and operational blips much more often than a shiny new Airbus might.

We can't say for sure, but it's hardly a vast stretch to imagine that Spinetta, Eddington and the maintenance people at Airbus were firmly of the opinion that Concorde must fly no more. 'The technical and financial challenges of keeping a Concorde airworthy are absolutely prohibitive,' Eddington said after being asked if just one plane could be kept airworthy for the purposes of charters and air shows. 'Airbus has told us that they are unable to support such a project, whether it be for British Airways or anyone else.'[4]

Air France stopped Concorde flights in May 2003, British Airways in October that year. It was the first time that a commercial aeroplane was retired without a successor.

The greatest sadness in all of this was that a plan to evolve Concorde had been in the works from the early 1990s. This, by any reasonable understanding of the true value of the investment that created Concorde, was as it ought to have been. But yet more faceless men had balked at the cost of developing Concorde's replacement, a 225-seater aircraft capable of a 2.5-mach cruise, with a range to fly from London to Tokyo.

Instead they downgraded their ambitions and in the process discarded, seemingly without thought, the foundations that would have built a supersonic future we might be living right now. So, now we can fly a 555-seater Airbus A380 to JFK, just like in the 1960s, in eight long hours. Gerard Blanc, another *grande fromage* at Airbus, damned himself to forever being remembered as the wrongest human in the entire sorry tale: 'Time will not have the same value as before,' Blanc said, when talking about the A380. 'There will be less disruption of your life, except for boarding and disembarking. You will rest, you will work, you will shower – you will be living your life as you would on the ground.' Have you ever read such *merde de vache* in your life? He should try an Air France economy seat, for starters. (You'll find them at the back of the plane, *monsieur*.)[1]

It's a fine aircraft, the Airbus A380, let's not deny this. It's quiet and efficient and carries a huge number of people, so it plays nicely with the sensible-shoes narratives about fuel consumption and emissions and the elitism of Concorde.

It's a disaster, either way. The real value of Concorde, for those who think in balance sheets, would only have been realised long after the life of Concorde, in the way that dental glues are so amazing because NASA decided to send Neil Armstrong for a walk in the 1960s, or that traffic fatalities in Europe are so low because Volvo decided to bear the cost of developing the three-point seatbelt. Orthodox liberal economists would probably have bristled at the idea of the state developing a supersonic jetliner at the cost of £1.1 billion in the 1970s. But having done so, throwing the whole project out as too expensive before its value can be realised at the next level just seems nonsensical.

Look, we get the whole idea of not throwing good money after bad. But spending money on Concorde wasn't bad; it was glorious! And this, ultimately, is more to the crux. The faceless suits who pulled the plug on Concorde at least ten years before it was due to run its course, cut from

---

'It's true, we did do something so advanced that doesn't exist any more.'

– US businessman Raymond Pearlson, who flew Concorde more than 150 times[2]

'The Concorde is shaping up to be a stolen glimpse of the future, a technology of tomorrow that aberrationally appeared in our lifetimes. Imagine if Nokia had distributed functional cell phones to a select, wealthy few in 1932 but withdrawn them in 1959 because they'd proved to be commercially unviable – and then re-introduced the phones successfully in the 1990s, by which time most of the original customers were dead. That's what the history and future of supersonic civil transport is looking like.'

– David Kamp, Vanity Fair, 2003

the same cloth as those who scotched the idea of its replacement in the 1990s, looked at short-term budgets rather than longer-term returns. This displays a lack of foresight that will cost us decades before there is an affordable supersonic aeroplane for ordinary people, which will save hundreds of millions of man-hours a year and make us happier, richer and more productive. But the demise of Concorde is a case study of modern European corporate barrenness mostly because the guy who killed Concorde, whoever or whatever he may be, killed a small tangible piece of the human spirit.

We'll get our cheap supersonic flight to Tokyo eventually, maybe thirty or forty years from now if we're lucky. In the meantime, though, the romance of air travel – like our dignity at the security check – is a thing of the past. Today, eighteen of the twenty Concordes originally built are still in one piece, displayed at airports and in museums in France, England, Scotland, the US, Germany and Barbados. But, just like Continental Airlines McDonnell Douglas DC10 (N13067) slowly disintegrating out in the Mojave, they no longer fly. They simply stand as slender delta memorials to the human spirit of exploration and adventure, to our desire to push the technological envelope just because we can; of a time past that was perhaps more romantic in its endeavour and certainly less *safe* than our carefully audited existence today.

So when you next glimpse Concorde 208, parked at the end of the South runway as you take off from Heathrow, or you taxi past Concorde 215 at Charles de Gaulle, think of the sensible suits who left them earthbound there. Then enjoy your flight. It's probably going to be a long one.

Rolf Harris,
Jimmy Savile & friends

Rolf Harris b. 30 March 1930
Jimmy Savile: 31 October 1926 – 29 October 2011

Once-adored television entertainers; sexual predators who used their celebritydom to abuse children; the faces of a multi-generational conspiracy of silence

THERE IS, FOR ANYONE LOOKING INTO THESE THINGS, a moment when you are forced to contrast two images. One is an image of a teenage girl called Tonya Lee. It's a blurry picture but she's a happy-looking kid, grinning from ear to ear, wearing a pretty dress and looking well set for the future.

The other image is also of Tonya Lee. In this picture she's older, in her forties now, and she is in tears. She looks exhausted. She looks exhausted and broken because of what Rolf Harris did to that 15-year-old child in the other picture. Thirty years on and the pain is as visceral as ever for Tonya Lee – you'd need to be blind to miss it – and that's because the crimes the likes of Harris and his ilk have committed are crimes that sentence their victims to a very cruel kind of torment: one of loneliness, bitter self-recrimination and crushed self-confidence. They rob these children, and the adults they become, of that thing we all desire: normality. The normality of getting to know personal intimacy, of forming average everyday human relationships, of learning to trust.

The crimes in question are the sexual abuse of children, and the rape of young men and women. Unspeakably wicked, they have only recently begun to be taken as seriously as they ought to have been. Moreover, they appear to have been rife within the seedy backrooms of entertainer celebritydom for many decades, and the exploits of Rolf Harris and his confederates seem somehow to mark a low point in the history of this most heinous betrayal of the uninitiated mind.

The Australian-born Harris, now in his late eighties, was a prominent children's entertainer in the UK, where he was seen as slightly exotic – a personification of the happy-go-lucky Aussie of the English imagination. He was a multi-talented eccentric who used to delight children with his catchy songs, his didgeridoo and his wobble board. Having emigrated to study art in the early 1950s, his art TV shows were the medium that brought his initial fame. And there's no denying his talent; he would, among other achievements, go on to paint an admirable portrait of the queen in 2005.

In the intervening years, he had become a household name to generations of young TV watchers. *Hi There, Hey Presto It's Rolf, The Rolf Harris Show, Rolf's Cartoon Club* and *Rolf Harris Cartoon Time* were all enormously popular and, indeed, enormously charming shows that aired over the course of three decades. Harris also enjoyed success with his music, initially with *Tie Me Kangaroo Down, Sport*, which became one of the best known Australian songs of all time, and especially with *Two Little Boys* (yes, really), which was the UK's bestselling single and Christmas Number One in 1969. Margaret Thatcher later picked it as her favourite song for Desert Island Discs. Harris appeared gentle and kind, and was evidently talented. His autobiography, *Can You Tell What It Is Yet?*, painted a picture of the naivety and innocence of an Aussie from Perth in the big bad city.

For almost anyone born in the Anglosphere during the 1960s through to the 1980s, Harris was massive. Massive enough for him to be awarded an MBE before the age of 40, which was, as is the way of these things for the best of society, advanced to OBE before he was 50. The CBE came in 2006. With such posh metal attached to his chest, the Aussies followed suit, making him an Officer of the Order of Australia and installing him as an Australian National Living Treasure. There were honorary degrees, patronages, memberships and chairmanships of various halls of fame, fellowships and keys to various cities… In short, this man was *loved*.

Today, following the revelations of his sordid past, his now middle-aged and once-charmed fanbase are utterly bewildered. We trusted this man and he was duping us all along – because he was ruining young lives as he put us under his spell. Harris didn't fit the picture of the pervert as imagined. This wasn't some weirdo in a park or a freak hiding in the shadows. No. It was Rolf Bloody Harris off the TV, for God's sake. Him of *Animal Hospital* and *Rolf On Saturday OK?* But a pervert is what he was – a 'sinister' one, as he was described in the 2014 trial that would lead to his conviction, with a 'demon lurking beneath the charming exterior'.[1] And he was a serial offender, active over the course of at least two decades.

Arguably Harris's most unforgivable crimes (in that initial revelatory trial, at least) were those that corrupted the teenage years of a close friend of Harris's own daughter. She was first assaulted at age 13, when she had been entrusted into his and his wife's care on holiday, and the dysfunctional relationship appears to have lasted well into her twenties, chaperoning her descent into alcoholism and destructive behaviour as a young woman. Of the twelve cases of assault for which he was found guilty in 2014, seven were against this particular girl, and she was the victim who ultimately brought long overdue justice to his door. She was also the victim that Harris at least acknowledged doing some wrong against, as evidenced by a disingenuous and calculating letter written to her father in 1997.

The others were the once-beaming Tonya Lee, who was molested at age 15 while on theatre-group tour from Australia; an unnamed waitress identified in the trial only as 'P'; and, for those who may still not grasp the extent of the evil at play here, Wendy Wild, who was assaulted when requesting an autograph – at the age of seven.

'I have been in a state of abject self-loathing. How we delude ourselves. I fondly imagined that everything that had taken place had progressed from a feeling of love and friendship – there was no rape, no physical forcing, brutality or beating that took place.

'When I came to Norfolk, [the victim] told me that she had always been terrified of me and went along with everything that I did out of fear of me. I said "Why did you never just say no?" And [the victim] said how could she say no to the great television star Rolf Harris? Until she told me that, I had no idea that she was scared of me. She laughs in a bitter way and says I must have known that she has always been scared of me. I honestly didn't know...

'She says admiring her and telling her she looked lovely in her bathing suit was just the same as physically molesting her. I didn't know. Nothing took place in a physical way until we had moved to Highlands. I think about 1983 or 84 was the first time.'

– Rolf Harris, writing to the father of one of his adolescent victims in 1997.
The letter was widely publicised during his trial, years later

Many other allegations have surfaced, from the UK to Australia and New Zealand to South Africa to Malta, spanning decades and continents and hinting at Harris's vast and insidious potential for depravity. A common refrain seems to be that he viewed his casual gropings as a bit of fun – a bit of haw-haw in exchange for a lifetime of pain and anger for the child in question. Harris, despite his convictions, refutes them all.

But Rolf Harris wasn't the only one. And he wasn't the worst of them either.

Harris is a nauseating bastard, let's be clear, and he has first billing in this entry because he was the most unexpected of the TV-star abusers, the most well-disguised snake in the grass. But he had nothing on Jimmy Savile.

Jimmy Savile was an industrial-scale paedophile and rapist who committed his crimes literally in plain sight, a man who engineered an enormous and complex machine around an invented version of himself so that it would deliver to him a steady supply of vulnerable children –

hundreds of them, and the more vulnerable the better. Today British police consider him to be one of the country's most prolific paedophiles ever.

The truth is, we'll never fully understand the scale of the harm committed by Savile. It is almost too vast to be comprehended, too ghastly to accept that this happened in a civilised country, and that he got away with it with such brazen contempt year after year. On one occasion, in 1976, he went so far as to molest an 18-year-old audience member live on *Top Of The Pops*. In the footage she tries to maintain her composure for the camera as she jumps about to fend off his wandering hands, while he laughs and exclaims, 'A fella could get used to this.'

Like Harris, Savile was regarded fondly, an entertainer with an illustrious career in both TV and radio. He was a widely travelled and prolific broadcaster, starting on Radio Luxembourg before moving on to the BBC. But, whereas Harris came across as a lovely cuddly bloke, Savile was clearly an eccentric, always absurdly dressed and issuing forth a relentless stream of inane nonsense, perhaps, in hindsight, to avoid ever having to give a straight answer to a tricky question. Looking at the career photographs of that wide-eyed half-demented stare and troglodytic underbitten grin, hindsight, that futile superpower, invites another observation: we really should have known.

It was Savile's fronting of *Top Of The Pops* and then *Jim'll Fix It* that had kids and teenagers really flocking to the man. The latter show was truly engrossing television for children, in which he answered letters from viewers asking for difficult or interesting favours. Of course, Jim always fixed it, and he fixed himself a knighthood and a battery of other honours in the process.

It is almost inconceivable. His activities were 'to the best of our knowledge unprecedented in the UK', according to the final report into his activities, so here's a vignette. Karin Ward was a boarder at Duncroft, a school for troubled teenage girls that Savile took an interest in, ostensibly as part of his charitable good works. Ward had been sexually abused by her stepfather from the age of four. In Louis Theroux's excellent and harrowing documentary *Savile*, she explains how Savile used to pick girls to take a ride in his Rolls-Royce.

'The girls he selected tended to be on the slender, less developed side,' she says. When asked to elaborate on those excursions with him in his car, she continues: 'Obviously, if you, as a child, have to fellate an adult, there's a lot of gagging and retching and quite often vomiting involved, and he flung the car door open and said, "Not in the car! Not in the car!"'

There it is, then: fellating. The words we see in reports, and find ourselves using, to describe the 'activities' of Savile and co – 'abused', 'assaulted', 'molested' – are, of course, euphemisms. What they boil down to are groping hands on breasts or buttocks or vaginas, sometimes over clothes, sometimes under them; coerced handjobs and blowjobs; and ultimately sex, most egregiously with minors, but also with adults, against their will. If it makes you uncomfortable reading the grubby reality of it, imagine what it's like living it, and living with the memory of it.

Savile encouraged compliance by promising his victims favours, including sweets, cigarettes and trips to London to appear on his variety show *Clunk Click*. While attending the filming of one episode, Ward was groped and insulted by the comedian Freddie Starr, who appeared to have acquired some of Savile's tricks of the trade. While Scotland Yard chose not to pursue cases against Starr for a lack of evidence, forty-two years later Starr took himself to court by suing Ward for libel after she mentioned the incident in an interview about Savile. He lost the case. 'It was the way men behaved back then,' Ward explained afterwards.

Such was Savile's fame and perceived power that few people complained about his behaviour, but it seems from Dame Janet Smith's 2016 report into Savile's abuse specifically at the BBC that certain people *did* know; they preferred to turn a blind eye or simply felt too disempowered to say anything. 'It is clear that a number of BBC staff had heard rumours, stories or jokes about Savile to the effect that, in some way, his sexual conduct was inappropriate,' the report held. 'No-one to whom we spoke thought that he

---

Rotten: 'I'd like to kill Jimmy Savile. He's a hypocrite. He's into all kinds of seediness that we all know about but [are] not allowed to talk about. I know some rumours. I bet none of this'll be allowed out.'

Interviewer: 'I shouldn't imagine the libellous stuff will be allowed out.'

Rotten: 'Nothing I've said is libel.'

– BBC Radio 1 interview with John Lydon, a.k.a. Sex Pistols frontman Johnny Rotten, recorded in 1978. This excerpt wasn't aired until 2015. Lydon was, he claimed, banned from BBC radio for voicing his concerns

or she ought to report such a rumour to a person in authority.' Despite the review's findings, it's hard to shake the sense that surely those at the top must have known *something* was amiss.

It is a tragic fact of history that of the seventy-two identified victims of Savile at the BBC, the first recorded incident was the rape of a 13-year-old girl in 1959, and the last an assault during a recording of *Top Of The Pops* in 2006. Yup. Forty-seven years. That's how long the BBC's staff turned its back on the abuse of children in its care. How many victims were there in total? We'll never know.

The BBC was only one part of the apparatus that Savile had fashioned around himself. Duncroft was perfect for his purposes, too, an example of the kind of charitable causes he pinned his name to because, well, it involved children and teenagers. Again, the cringing clarity of hindsight.

Savile set himself up at various hospitals. At Broadmoor, a high-security mental hospital, he had a flat on site and keys to the building acquired from senior health executives after he'd received letters of admiration from patients. They desperately wanted public perceptions of the hospital to move on from its image as a dark Victorian asylum, and Savile appeared to be the answer. Savile gratefully accepted the role, roaming the hospital corridors with a free licence from 1968 to 2004, when a new security system was fitted. The extent of his activities there will never be quantified.

At Leeds General Infirmary, Savile offered his services as a celebrity porter and an adviser to the hospital radio service. Sixty-four people came forward during the subsequent investigation, and his victims varied in age from five to 75 years old, comprising girls, boys, women, men and even staff members. The earliest case took place in 1962, the most recent in 2009, when Savile was 82. The real extent of the abuse? Again, we'll never know.

An alarming and almost inconceivably dark side of the story at Leeds Infirmary took place in the hospital morgue. An independent report described Savile's interest in the morgue as being 'not within accepted boundaries'. Different sources told the enquiry that he had removed glass eyes from corpses and that he liked to 'interfere' with the bodies and pose with them for photographs. One claimed that he performed sexual acts on the dead, an easily believable proposition if you've spent a bit of time reading up on his exploits.[2]

Savile was the driving force behind the raising millions of pounds to build the National Spinal Injuries Centre at Stoke Mandeville hospital. He

'[I]t is a profoundly uncomfortable truth. As a nation… we held Savile in our affection as a somewhat eccentric national treasure with a strong commitment to charitable causes. Today's report [shows] that in reality he was a sickening and prolific sexual abuser who repeatedly exploited the trust of a nation for his own vile purpose.'

– British Health Secretary Jeremy Hunt
apologising to Savile's victims in the House of Commons in 2014[3]

had free rein there too, including another flat on site, and seemed attracted to the vulnerability of spinal patients, which needs no further elaboration. At Stoke Mandeville he is known to have abused sixty people over a period of… By now you get the picture. Because, again, who really knows?

That, very briefly, is a review of Savile's abuses. Writing in *The Guardian* in 2014, psychologist Oliver James explained that Savile 'had what is known as the dark triad of personality characteristics: psychopathy, Machiavellianism and narcissism. These are common in famous or powerful people, and part of that mix is a strong likelihood of sexual promiscuity… He created safe environments in which he could act at will. His experiments beyond young females may have been because the buzz from them had worn off through repetition and he sought more extreme kicks. Given that inflicting distress was his primary goal, the gender and age of a victim might not matter.'

In conclusion, James notes that '[m]an hands on misery to man,' suggesting that the ripples of Savile will be felt for generations. '[I]t is all too possible that Savile drove some of his victims as crazy as him. It is horrible to contemplate the possibility that he may have spawned other abusers by his crimes.'

The great frustration here is having to exclude so many stories – so many victims passed by, invisible and voiceless. This is not a detailed report or even a complete summary of what Harris and Savile did, and we haven't got to the BBC's Stuart Hall or glam rocker Gary Glitter, both celebrity sex offenders cut from the same cloth. There is also no space for the string of sexual assaults allegedly committed by the man who represents a similar betrayal of collective childhood innocence across the Atlantic, the once-loved, now-reviled comedian Bill Cosby. But, as Solzhenitsyn observed, sometimes a mouthful of seawater is enough to know the taste of the ocean.

One silver lining to all this has been a surge in societal intolerance for the rape and abuse of children in recent years. The Catholic Church, especially in Ireland and the United States, has had to consider its own grotesque litany of abuse where, yet again, depraved and wicked men have gained access to institutions designed to care for the young and vulnerable. The scale of that particular pandemic is breathtaking – notably the deceit in concealing it so frequently and so extensively over the years – and the ocean of misery it has caused unfathomable.

The public outing of these people and practices has concomitantly made the world an openly sadder and more cynical place. In the UK the Vetting and Barring Scheme was set up to force anybody working with children in schools to register on a national database. One result was the grave offence taken by several much-loved children's authors and illustrators, including Philip Pullman, Anne Fine, Anthony Horowitz, Michael Morpurgo and Quentin Blake, who subsequently refused to visit schools. Pullman described the scheme as 'corrosive and poisonous to every kind of healthy social interaction'. And so the process of protecting future generations casts wonderful, lovely people into the role of potential rapists, emitting further ricochets of abuse. 'This reinforces the culture of suspicion, fear and mistrust that underlies a great deal of present-day society,' Pullman elaborates. 'It teaches children that they should regard every adult as a potential murderer or rapist.' [4]

It is an impossible balancing act to get right in the aftermath of such wholesale revelations, and the collateral damage that has been wrought is probably unknowable. The varied responses, often of hysterical proportions, have not only leached so much of the innocence from our children's daily existence, but have sullied the names of other prominent personalities, several now dead, who have faced public condemnation though they, most probably, never did anything wrong. Most probably.

Hyperbole is a dangerous thing, as is the appropriation of language generally. When modern university students complain that somebody else's opinion causes them 'violence', they really don't have a clue. Because the majority of the real victims will likely never even reveal themselves, let alone face closure. They will have seen that the process of justice itself is yet another trauma for them to have to overcome – the embarrassment and shame that comes with the picking apart of their damaged lives.

Harris, Savile and friends are the absolute worst of mankind, malicious and vile people, people for whom sex as a form of power and extrusion of their low self-worth, or just sex as sex, was worth the repetitive distribution of misery and pain into one life after the other. They used the new phenomenon of TV-driven stardom – something for which there was no rulebook in the 1960s and '70s – and exploited it for their own awful ends, not only to access their victims but to ensure a conspiracy of silence after the fact. They deserve nothing but our contempt, because they forced society to write its grotty little manual – one that has little choice but to presume that everybody near children just might be as much of a predator as they were, and that's not a risk worth taking.

What a bitter harvest this all is. In time, perhaps, we will get the balance right. For now, Savile is dead, unpunished in life but his many honours now rescinded and revoked, and his headstone smashed from his grave in Scarborough. Harris was released from prison in 2017, four days after a second trial for indecent assault began. The jury was unable to reach a verdict and prosecutors have since indicated that he will face no more trials. All of which means Harris is free to re-enter a society to which he has done great harm. It's really too good for you, sport.

Joseph Hazelwood

b. 24 September 1946

Captain of the Exxon Valdez; the grizzled face of environmental irresponsibility; the guy Big Corporate puts in charge when they can get away with it

IN THREE ENTRIES' TIME WE'LL DISCUSS the steady decline in tolerant discourse that the world is currently witness to *(see The Israel-Palestine letter writer)*. Before we kick that general hornet's nest, however, let's venture a proposition that many would see not so much as an opinion voiced in a free world but as an opportunity to challenge someone to a fist fight – or, at least, an anonymous social-media flaming.

Our contention is that the natural world has weathered the most awful abuse at the hands of man, but that modern technology and proper regulation will gradually reduce our dependence on fossil fuels and will limit the harm we do, eventually to such a degree that we will reverse the damage we have wrought. We believe that as humans we can live modern lives and drive cars and heat our houses and run our dishwashers without causing irreparable long-term harm. And our contention is that this is a good thing. Human lives are better, longer, more fulfilling, happier and profoundly richer in meaning principally because of how we can harness energy. It's just that we have to get better at looking after the place while we're about it, and seeing as the earth is, in practical terms, forever, and that the capitalist profit motive is a few years at best, the need for real, effective and strictly enforced regulations is critical.

Thus we have an optimistic vision for the future that acknowledges our past behaviour and our tenuous present state of affairs. But, look, if we get going on climate change we risk losing half our readership on this page alone. For one, who exactly would we blame? Thomas Edison for building the world's first usable coal power station? The flyover-state deplorable who drives a Ford F-550 instead of a Toyota Prius? Your average person who would like a working electricity supply to his house so that he might conveniently light his living room at night and watch the telly? China?

This is a most complex question that gets very ugly very quickly, and it can be impossible to adequately decipher the (always contested) facts and work out a practical and helpful way forward. As we've seen with the EU's disastrous policy to promote diesel over petrol cars *(see Ritt Bjerregaard)*, there are potential hazards when doing things for the sake of doing things. So instead let's talk about something related that we should be able to agree on and act on: direct human pollution of the natural environment.

Our track record in this field is abominable, and no incident in the history of corporate and state indifference illustrates the psychopathic carelessness of capitalism better than the catastrophic system failure that was to befall Prince William Sound in Alaska in March 1989. This was the *Exxon Valdez* disaster. Of course, the grounding of the *Exxon Valdez* was not the first and, since the *Deepwater Horizon* catastrophe in 2010, is not even the largest oil spill in the United States, but it provides some of the clearest lessons on the matter that we could hope for. The facts are straightforward and the remedies obvious in this case, and there is no contestable data to be beaten in different directions by competing agendas.

To anyone old enough to remember it, the two words 'Exxon Valdez' will summon horrific imagery of a pristine coastline coated in appallingly photogenic, glutinous, mucilaginous, toxic oil. It was unspeakable, as though the worst of humanity had been visited upon the very best of nature.

On a calm Thursday evening, shortly after 9pm, the *Exxon Valdez* departed the oil terminal at the town in southern Alaska for which the Exxon Shipping Company had named the ship. Valdez, about 150 kilometres east of Anchorage, is the nearest ice-free port to the northern oil fields of Prudhoe Bay, to which it is connected by the Trans-Alaska pipeline. The 300-metre supertanker, bound for California, was loaded with 1.3-million barrels of crude oil, which translates to more than 200-million litres' worth. It was due to pass through the Valdez arm of the Prince William Sound, bound on either side by the Shoup Bay and Sawmill Bay State Marine Parks and the Jack Bay State Marine Park, before heading due south through the sound. It's hard to imagine a worse place to install a captain who'd been on the hooch all afternoon, but hey, this was the 1980s.

Just after midnight, in the early hours of 24 March 1989 – Good Friday – the *Exxon Valdez* ran aground hard at a known navigational hazard called Bligh Reef and immediately began to leak oil. Eight of eleven compartments within the tanker's single-hull hold were ruptured, and in the days to come it would leak a fifth of its load, around 16 Olympic-sized swimming pools of crude oil, spreading towards the south and west. In the end, nearly 2,500 kilometres of pristine Alaskan coastline were oiled, equivalent to the entire coastlines of Germany or Egypt. It is notoriously difficult to put a number to the fatalities caused to local wildlife in such an incident, so let's let the Exxon Valdez Oil Spill Trustee Council summarise it for us:

> The best estimates are: 250,000 seabirds, 2,800 sea otters, 300 harbour seals, 250 bald eagles, up to 22 killer whales, and billions of salmon and herring eggs.

Nature is truly remarkable in the way that it adjusts as a dynamic system to a suddenly imposed new normal, and it is encouraging to learn that today many species of bird and fish have recovered to pre-spill levels and that Prince William Sound is once again an area of outstanding and extraordinary natural beauty. But it is equally important to acknowledge that, nearly three decades later, the area has not fully recovered. If 'recovered' means to some extent being the same place as it was before the spill, it is possible that it may never do so. There remains oil on beaches to this day, and a 2009 report concluded that it 'will take decades and possibly centuries to disappear entirely'. A sub-species of orca is considered more than likely to become extinct over the coming years as a result of the spill. Fishing stocks of certain critical species have simply never recovered, causing enormous change to a way of life for more than 30,000 local fishermen, canners and Native American populations.

How is it possible for a modern supertanker equipped with the latest equipment to run aground in fair conditions in a perfectly well-charted area with clearly defined shipping lanes? Thus begins the quest to understand a complete failure in government regulation and corporate and individual responsibility. Let's start by referring to the National Transportation Safety Board (NTSB) investigation into the accident, which determined five probable causes of the grounding:

The third mate failed to properly maneuver the vessel, possibly due to fatigue and excessive workload; The master failed to provide a proper navigation watch, possibly due to impairment from alcohol; Exxon Shipping Company failed to supervise the master and provide a rested and sufficient crew for the Exxon Valdez; The US Coast Guard failed to provide an effective vessel traffic system; Effective pilot and escort services were lacking.

Now, as you might expect from the dry language of an official report, this doesn't quite express what a gigantically embarrassing stuff-up on all fronts the *Exxon Valdez* disaster was. If there was an agency or individual who could bugger things up, then the chances are they pretty much did.

The ship itself was short on crew, that crew was exhausted and they were under pressure to get to California as quickly as possible. The captain – the 'master' referred to above – was a fellow by the name of Joseph Hazelwood, who came with something of a mixed reputation. There was the spectre of alcohol-related incidents in his past, but he had a clean captaincy history and one of some renown. In 1985, commanding another vessel, the *Exxon Chester*, Hazelwood had endured a storm that snapped the ship's mast and ripped out the radar and other electronics. The crew was ready to abandon ship, but he rallied them, rigged up a temporary antenna and guided the damaged ship to New York, where instead of receiving the thanks of Exxon he was initially criticised for not making port on time – which offers some insight into the guiding principles of the oil-shipping industry and a measure of understanding of what might contribute to a catastrophe like this.

With icebergs reported in the area, it was Hazelwood who ordered the *Exxon Valdez* to detour from the regular shipping lane as a precaution, but he also gave specific orders that the ship be returned to its lane at the appropriate point. For reasons that were never really understood, this wasn't done, but it's a fact of history that the third mate who he had put in charge of the boat before it ran aground, one Gregory Cousins, was unlicensed to take this role in the area. (At Hazelwood's trial, Cousins transferred the blame to the helmsman who was doing the actual steering of the ship at the time. Neither Cousins nor the helmsman faced censure for their roles.)

But back to the booze, because it is likewise a fact of history that the captain had been seen drinking alcohol prior to departure – 'two or three vodkas', by his own admission, between 4.30pm and 6.30pm. We hasten to add at this point that Hazelwood has always denied being intoxicated at the time of the accident, and indeed was found not guilty of operating a vessel while under the influence of alcohol after witnesses essentially said he'd sobered up by the time it occurred – and the US Coast Guard bungled his blood tests. What we can say is that he had been drinking hard tack prior to departure and was in his cabin when the accident happened. And his driver's licence was suspended at the time for an alcohol violation, his third such suspension. And he had been given ninety days' leave in 1985 to attend an Alcoholics Anonymous course at a rehab centre. And in 1987, a former second mate brought a civil case against Exxon and claimed in a pre-trial deposition that he often suspected Hazelwood of being drunk, stating that he frequently 'appeared to be intoxicated' while in command of his vessels. The accusation doesn't appear to have been proven, but it resurfaced in reports, quite unsurprisingly, shortly after the *Exxon* spill.

> 'There's a bad joke in the fleet that it's Captain Hazelwood and his chief mate, Jack Daniels, that run the ship.'
> *– pre-trial deposition by Bruce Amero filed in 1987[1]*

Whatever the unknowable details of the night in question, the picture we're getting – like an aerial view of Prince William Sound in late March of 1989 – was not a pretty one. This guy had form.

The National Oceanic and Atmospheric Administration's official report looking back at the incident on its 25th anniversary goes on to describe the reaction in the immediate aftermath of the grounding as 'a nightmare of poor preparedness and execution'. It's a description validated by the Coast Guard's own timeline which illustrates the sheer inter-galactic scales of its own buffoonery once the ship's situation had became known.

At the height of the clean-up, there were around 10,000 workers, a thousand ships and a hundred aircraft of various kinds involved. But it was mostly futile. Human endeavour was responsible for the clean-up of less than 10 percent of the spill, with natural washing and storm waves ultimately doing the bulk of the work – and still with plenty of work to do to this day.

As is the way in the US when there's an enormous cock-up that costs lots of money to go away, everybody started sharpening their lawyers. Exxon

'Initial response efforts at the Port of Valdez under Alyeska's control are hampered by equipment casualties and holiday personnel shortages... Alyeska is unable to comply with the response timeliness provision in its own contingency plan that calls for initial response at the vessel within five hours of first notification.

'Alyeska's only containment barge is tied up at Valdez Terminal, stripped for repairs. Barge was not certified by the CG to receive oil, but it could carry recovery bladders. Alaska's state contingency plan requires Alyeska to notify the state when response equipment is taken out of service. Satisfied the barge was seaworthy without repairs, Alyeska had not done so.

'Before barge could be used, pollution gear had to be loaded. Crane riggers called at 0330. By this time, [Coast Guard] estimates 5.8 million gallons already discharged from the tanks.'

– Coast Guard description of events after the grounding of the Exxon Valdez

spent $2 billion on the clean-up and ended up settling around $1.4-billion in civil damages cases and other fines. The United States pursued Exxon through the courts for nearly twenty years, initially winning a $5-billion payout.* But after endless rounds of appeals and counter-appeals, and having been found by the court to be 'worse than negligent but less than malicious', Exxon eventually gave over not much more than $500-million, a tenth of the original award, in 2008. Using the previous financial year as a guide, this would have been paid in four days' worth of profits.

And Hazelwood? Is there a better exemplar of humanity's outrageous entitlement and disregard for the environment than this man? It's true that he was acquitted of felony charges and found guilty only of a misdemeanour – he was fired, fined $50,000 and sentenced to a thousand hours of community service – but how on God's blue ocean was he allowed to captain a ship carrying enough oil to power the entire world for twelve

---

* In response to this ruling, Exxon opened a line of credit for $4.8 billion with its bank. To avoid tying up too much capital as reserve for this huge loan, the bank came up with the idea of selling the credit risk on, which they did to the European Bank of Reconstruction and Development. This was the invention of the 'credit default swap', which would later become a principal cause of the financial crisis and Great Recession. *(See Bill & Hillary Clinton.)* So, if we're being harsh here – as we feel obliged to be – Exxon helped cause the Great Recession. And the bank in question? JP Morgan, of course.

minutes in the first place*? Here was a guy who had been busted for drunk driving on no less than three occasions and liked to drink vodka at five o'clock in the afternoon before heading off into the wilderness with his cargo. Is it not staggeringly obvious that this was the wrong man for the job at hand?

Amazingly, though he struggled to find work afterwards, Hazelwood's licence was never revoked.

The *Exxon Valdez* oil spill offers important insights into a practical understanding of the way the world works. For one, what is obvious to so many is often not obvious to – or at the very least, is often not prioritised by – those who watch the bottom line and make the decisions. Whereas we are of the opinion that hands-off governance tends to be for the best, this incident offers all the evidence needed for strong and reasonable regulations in matters of such grave and undisputed environmental consequence. The philosophical questions of our rights to the earth's resources are complex and nuanced. It is in the nature of capital to seek lower costs and higher returns, and that's okay, because it's a system that has brought more wealth and happiness to humanity than any other. But given that capital will not and cannot seek justice or concern itself with environmental long-term thinking, that's where the state must step in.

The incredible truth – it seems to us in hindsight, though it was simply the way things rolled back then – is that the *Exxon Valdez* spill was just the one that was big enough and terrible enough to make the news. In the twelve years that the Trans-Alaska pipeline had been operational at Valdez to that point there were more than four hundred separate oil spills in the Bay of Alaska. That's one every ten days or so.

As with most catastrophic accidents, for the *Exxon Valdez* spill to occur many little things had to go wrong, which simple properly enforced regulations would have prevented. Mandatory crew rest. No drinking before shifts (duh). Knowledgeable pilots and/or the appropriate people on deck during transits. Better navigation technology. Double-hulled tankers. It's a long and often obvious list.

---

* Based on world primary energy consumption data for 1989, from the US Energy Information Administration.

> 'We tend to think of environmental catastrophes – such as the recent Exxon Valdez oil-spill disaster in the Bay of Alaska – as "accidents": isolated phenomena that erupt without notice or warning. But when does the word accident become inappropriate? When are such occurrences inevitable rather than accidental? And when does a consistent pattern of inevitable disasters point to a deep-seated crisis that is not only environmental but profoundly social?'
>
> *– social ecologist Murray Bookchin, 1989*[2]

Regulations like these, any one of which might have saved Prince William Sound in 1989, were introduced in the US the following year with the Oil Pollution Act, which was expedited by the disaster. They have made an enormous difference in preventing further spills and so prove the value of government enforcement of corporate responsibilities.

In the end, however, as with so much in life, it ultimately boils down to individual responsibility. We're not asking a lot here – just a basic appreciation and respect for the earth we inhabit. In choosing Joe Hazelwood as the cautionary tale of someone who has messed up the world in the most literal and unequivocally wrong way – by sailing a ship onto the land, which is the opposite of what the captain of a ship should do – we are hoping to extrapolate some working guidelines for anyone interacting with the environment (which is to say, everyone) to avoid such incidents in the future.

When you finish your cigarette on the beach (or anywhere) don't leave it stubbed out in the sand.

When you walk up your local mountain (or anywhere) don't leave your water bottle and crisp packets at the top.

When you're in charge of a 1,000-foot supertanker carrying a shit ton of crude oil passing through a pristine natural wilderness (or anywhere) stay off the liquor beforehand and make sure the guy driving the boat knows what he's doing.

Extrapolated up the scale to those who manage oil shipping conglomerates, and those who regulate the transportation of oil and other pollutants around the world, and those who make industrial-scale decisions that relate to the use of our finite natural resources, we believe this would be a good start to messing up our physical world less than we do.

Adolf Hitler

20 April 1889 – 30 April 1945

Führer of the Third Reich; original Nazi; starter of the greatest war in human history; murderer of Jews; the Hitler of genocidal tyrants; poster boy for a book like this; lucky bastard

So, to Hitler. First choice of Captain Obvious. Literally the guy at the top of the list when you think of fifty people who messed up the world, be it the modern age or eras past.

History is always complicated. Seldom are there definitive moral judgements of right and wrong to be made. And of course the life and times of Hitler were, in their detail, complex and nuanced. But history's definitively evil character, the guy who was indisputably wrong, will always be Hitler. A man filled with rage and racist hate, who had no valid claims to war and no excuses for what he did other than madness, who in a very particular manner committed the grossest, most calculating genocide possible, and who rendered fascism forever discredited.

So, to recap, Hitler was prime evil.

More than that, however, he was a prime cause.

In most of the great wars of history the first shot might have come from (or on the orders of) any number of leaders or activists, usually great men, sometimes small. World War I, for instance, was kicked off by a 19-year-old Yugoslavist conspirator in Sarajevo *(see Gavrilo Princip)* but it was a war that could have been ignited by any number of people or incidents, most likely in the Balkans, but possibly in Austria-Hungary, Russia, France, Germany or even the colonies. Historians these days are generally in agreement, however, that without Hitler, World War II would not have happened. And they are certainly in agreement with the title of Milton Himmelfarb's 1984 essay, 'No Hitler, no Holocaust'. He may not have been the only requirement in both cases, but he was a necessary one.

So, what can we say about Hitler that hasn't been said already? Even the bored Harvard undergrads that Niall Ferguson pities still learn about him *(see Hugo Chávez & Nicolás Maduro)*. Their knowledge of the French revolution, Marx and life in communist Russia may be shaky, but they'll know the rudimentaries of Hitler, one of the most significant figures in all of human history.* How he was born in Austria and may have turned out as Adolf Schicklgruber under slightly different circumstances. How he found himself in Munich in the 1920s, where he transformed into a political agitator, turned the German Workers' Party into the populist National Socialist German Workers' Party and invented the Nazi. How he laughed off appeasement, invaded Poland in 1939 and started the greatest and deadliest war in history. How he loathed the Jews and sought to exterminate them entirely as a race, in pursuit of his Aryan utopia.

---

* A widely publicised 2013 book, *Who's Bigger? Where historical figures really rank* by computer scientist Steven Skiena and Google engineer Charles Ward, which used data analysis of famous figures' presence on Wikipedia and Google Books Ngram Viewer to rank them by historical significance, placed Hitler in seventh position behind Jesus, Napoleon, Muhammad, Shakespeare, Lincoln and Washington. Stalin (18) and Einstein (19) were the only other people from the 20th century or later on the list. Similar lists usually rank Hitler as first or second (behind Einstein) on the list of 20th century individuals.

Most people know the Hitler basics so we're not going to rehash all that here; and it's difficult to misinterpret what he was all about so we see little point in reviewing his inspiration or intentions. Instead, let's take a look at the rise of Hitler – to be the most destructive man of all time – through the lens of chance. Why? Because sometimes dumb luck is the difference between a nation of pleasant and civilised human beings and a mob that has allowed evil to run riot in its midst – and, you know, that's worth bearing in mind.

> **'Historians are, rightly, nearly unanimous that…
> the causes of the Second World War were the
> personality and the aims of Adolf Hitler.'**
>
> *– historian FH Hinsley* [1]

Entire academic careers have been constructed to understand just how the wonderfully educated German people, a virtual archetype of human civilisation and accomplishment, could be seduced by Hitler's rhetoric to do the things they did – which, as we'll see with Mengele in ten entries' time, were about the lowest evils humanity has ever plumbed. Social psychologists, most famously Stanley Milgram, spent many years after the war studying the dynamics of group compliance and acquiescence to work out how supposedly respectable societies can come to follow the ideology of a lunatic leadership and end up committing atrocities. The famous Milgram experiments of the 1960s suggested that people are more likely to violate their personal code of ethics and do unconscionable things to other people when under the control of an authority figure. So, if your commanding officer tells you to shoot an unarmed civilian or load the Zyklon B canisters, you do it because you're following orders.

But how do evil authority figures come into power?

In his book *Outliers* Malcolm Gladwell argued, with best-selling ability, that pretty much all you need for professional success is ten thousand hours of practice, a modicum of talent and the luck to be in the right place at the right time. We would imagine that a similar formula could be applied for political success, just with less emphasis on the practice and a lot more on the luck. Most obviously, the fortune of the politician relates to his personal proclivities complementing the spirit of the time – the political zeitgeist, to use an appropriately Germanic term. The likes of Hitler – racist ethnophobes with a thirst for power and a crystal-clear vision for their future – have existed since that first monkey beat the monkey from the tribe next door on the head and stole his nuts. But there has surely never been such an age of discontent among a noble, ambitious people as the Germans for a populist demagogue to sow his seeds of anarchy as that which existed in the Weimar Republic in the 1920s. After the world-changing horrors of the Great War, Germany was awash with unemployment, hyperinflation and a general feeling of having been screwed by the Treaty of Versailles, which saw it losing great tracts of territory while being shouldered with war reparations of outrageous proportions – the perfect breeding ground for extreme left- and right-wing reactionary politics. Just as the post-colonial politics and socio-economics of Africa in the 1960s gave tyrants like Amin and Bokassa their gap, and the social-media economics of today have given Trump and Corbyn theirs, so the state of Germany in the 1920s gave fringe madmen the opportunity to be heard. At the end of World War I, one US dollar was worth about eight German marks; by 1924 it was worth more than four billion marks. When people are using their money as kindling, a man like Hitler has more room to manoeuvre.

Hitler's personal luck was, however, far more mundane than this, a succession of life events strung together like Christmas lights that would guide him along an unlikely path from poorly educated Austrian villager and almost-artist to starter of World War II and exterminator of the Jews. In almost any other time the landscape to achieve this would not have existed, and in almost every parallel universe imaginable he would have fallen down – often dead – many times before he did. You might conclude it was as if Providence herself was looking out for him and nudging him towards his grotesque Nazi destiny.

Let's breeze over the early days of the future Führer's fortune: Adolphus Hitler was born in a small town in Austria-Hungary, and thus was not technically German; he was one of six children, of whom three died in infancy and another later of measles; he did poorly in school and eventually dropped out at age sixteen. Legend has it that he fell through ice as a four-year-old and was rescued from sure death by a young priest. There's no need to read too much into all this. The concept of national identities was nascent and fluid then – Germany itself had only come into existence as a united country in 1871, eighteen years before his birth – and the fact that he was an outsider may have made the concept of German nationalism a more appealing prospect, as it did to many Austro-Hungarians. Either way he identified strongly as German from an early age and he lived in southern Germany for several years as a boy. As for surviving childhood in the 19th century, well, some kids had to, and we can only wonder at the potential Hitlers (and Churchills) who didn't.

Even before he was born, though, small things were falling in his favour. That surname he might have had, for instance: Schicklgruber. Or even Hiedler.

Adolf's father, Alois, who was born out of wedlock, had changed his surname from his mother's maiden name, Schicklgruber, to his stepfather's name, Hiedler, at the relatively mature age of 39. This may have been to secure an inheritance, though the details are sketchy and the identity of his father, Adolf's grandfather, remains unconfirmed and controversial to this day. (It may have been the stepfather, the stepfather's brother or, as one theory has it, an unrelated Jew who his mother worked for, which would of course be a rather pointed irony.) It seems that Alois had his name changed in front of a provincial parish priest, but when the change was registered in a government office a hundred kilometres away in Mistelbach, Hiedler was recorded as Hitler. Again, the reason is unknown but it was probably just a case of alternate spellings, as Hiedler, Hüttler and, as it happens, Hitler, were variations of the same name, just as Smith, Smythe and Smit are.

The importance of the Hitler surname has been the source of interesting historical speculation. The phrase 'Heil Hitler!' would by the 1930s be popularised in the Nazi salute as a declaration of commitment to Hitler and his party, and later serve as a daily greeting between citizens and a common way to sign off letters, in every such instance affirming his status and authority – rituals that may all have contributed to the notion of 'just following orders'. *Hitler* was clipped, striking and decisive, the name of a man with a vision. Would Adolf Schicklgruber have been interpreted by those who heard him speak as the man of action that Adolf Hitler was? Would Adolf Hiedler have conveyed quite the same command as Adolf Hitler did?

Having lived briefly in Bavaria and then been shunted around what is today Upper Austria, where he cobbled together an undistinguished school career characterised by laziness and contempt for authority, Hitler made his way to Vienna where he twice applied to the Academy of Fine Arts in his grand ambition to be a painter, and was twice rejected. How history might have unravelled had he encountered an examiner a little more forgiving of his human form drawings…* As it turned out, he squandered his small inheritance and bummed around the city, living in shelters and hostels and occasionally sleeping on park benches, and scraping together money by shovelling snow and selling landmark scenes to tourists. His only friend at the time, August Kubizek, remembered him as an unstable layabout with a temper, obsessed with architecture and Wagnerian opera. Even at this early stage his extreme intolerance for dissenting opinions was noteworthy.

Hitler left Vienna, aged 24, to avoid conscription to the Austro-Hungarian army, but was tracked down to Munich by Austrian officials in early 1914. He then faced the humiliation of being hauled back to Salzburg and rejected from service in the army for being physically feeble. Later that year, after the outbreak of war, he signed up for the German army in the Bavarian regiment and was admitted through some or other clerical error; as an Austrian citizen he should have been ineligible.

World War I made Hitler in several ways. As a dispatch runner in Belgium and France, he witnessed some of the greatest battles ever known: at Ypres, the Somme, Passchendaele. He wasn't involved in much actual fighting but there were many dangers to be faced shuttling between command headquarters and the front lines, and he appears to have led a charmed existence, avoiding injuries for the most of it and severe injury or death when his fellow soldiers were being obliterated by artillery and machine gun. At Ypres he was one of 600 out of his regiment of 3,600 to survive uninjured. At the Somme, after two years on the front lines, he was wounded by a shell and spent two months recovering, but he returned to the front later and won a second Iron Cross. A month before the war's end

---

* Hitler wasn't an entirely terrible artist, and his work periodically goes on auction. In 2014 a painting of the Munich town hall sold for €130,000. By comparison, a Churchill painting, 'The Goldfish Pool at Chartwell', sold for £1.8 million that same year.

he was temporarily blinded in a mustard gas attack. He received numerous war medals and was noted for his bravery, but he wasn't considered serious officer material because of his shoddy appearance and, so his superiors thought, lack of authority and leadership skills.

Nevertheless, the war was a hugely formative experience. Not only would it lay the political foundations for his rise to power, it also shaped him as an individual. After years of unsatisfactory, friendless drifting he found comrades and purpose; he forged a respectable military career that would later be enhanced to bolster his political reputation by the Goebbels propaganda machine; he acquired on-the-job military knowledge after years working from his regiment's headquarters; and he ultimately focused his developing political viewpoint into a hatred for the backstabbing political traitors who had betrayed the German cause in its surrender. And, through it all and quite critically, he didn't die.

His luck rolled on after the war. He remained in the army and, having been sent for training in political indoctrination, his most singular skill was identified: public speaking. It turned out that capturing an audience's attention and swaying it to his point of view – for example, that noble Germany had been sold out by devious Jews – was the thing at which he excelled. Hitler was born for rhetoric and oratory.

After a chance – yet again – assignment in late 1919 to monitor a small gathering of the German Workers' Party in Munich, Hitler was drawn into politics, and the idea of building a strongly nationalist anti-Semitic pro-military movement that would rebuild the great German nation and avenge the injustices of Versailles. Whoever or whatever was pulling the strings of history had made her move.

As the staging post for his political career, Munich offered a particular advantage: it was in Bavaria, which liked to see itself as a bit special and essentially detached from the rest of Germany. Officially known as Freistaat Bayern – the Free State of Bavaria – this sense of separatism likely played an important role in Hitler's rise, offering its population the necessary excuse to rebuff Berlin's (failing) governance.

As a speculative aside, might the very beer-hall politics of Munich in itself have provided an element of the luck Hitler needed to gain a following and rise to prominence? Those who have attended Munich's annual Oktoberfest, the world's largest beer festival, will be familiar with the process of finding oneself in a gargantuan carnival overwhelmed by children and families and then fighting into one of the various giant beer tents, once more thronging with people but now mostly in lederhosen or other such puerile outfits, and, with the realisation that oompah music may be the worst music in the world, thought, 'Is this not a vision of hell?' Then, after two litres of pils, suddenly it all makes sense and a man can be pleased about his place in the world and prospects for the future. *Prost!*

Might the same process have taken place in the Hofbrauhaus beer hall in downtown Munich in February 1920, when Hitler was top billing at a meeting of the newly named National Socialist German Workers' Party? A disillusioned young war veteran would have found himself surrounded by two thousand people pushing and shoving, including Communist extremists there to pick a fight, and then Hitler would have come on stage speaking ever more furiously of the injustices of Versailles, and calling for *Lebensraum*, and for his audience to beat up the reds in attendance, and for the rejection of the Jews from Germany, and for the confiscation of capital without compensation – he was anti-Semite, anti-Marxist *and* anti-capitalist – and the wonders of eugenics and for the promotion of the Aryan race. Hitler himself was a famous teetotaller, but one imagines that a night of Hitlerian hysteria would have made a lot more sense on the back of several steins.

Hitler was an unashamed populist extremist. Though he loathed communists for their internationalist lack of discernment in embracing people of any race into their movement, he was a real socialist, as specified in the new name of his party. Effectively gunning for the same neck of the political market as the commies, he roused rabble and he did it well, surrounding himself with men of violence who enforced his will. It took him a year and half to have the party committee dissolved and himself instated as Führer, and by 1923, with hyperinflation running rampant, the party had more than fifty thousand members. In November of that year he made his move with the Beer Hall Putsch, an attempt to kidnap prominent Bavarian leaders, overthrow the local government and bring about a nationwide uprising from Munich. It was briefly promising but ultimately proved a disaster, culminating in a clash between Nazi marchers and police that saw an exchange of gunfire and twenty people killed, including the man marching arm-in-arm with Hitler. Hitler's bodyguard, Ulrich Graf, was shot several times while covering him, probably saving his life.

Hitler contemplated suicide, was eventually arrested and should have been hanged for treason, but his trial was moved by influential friends from

Leipzig back to the more sympathetic Munich. Again, things worked in his favour, with the trial receiving nationwide coverage and offering the ideal platform to present the Nazis' political vision to a wider audience. In the end, he swayed the presiding judges to such a degree that he was given an embarrassingly lenient prison sentence, subsequently reduced to nine months – just sufficient to add another layer to his struggle credentials. Moreover, he was accommodated in relative comfort in Landsberg prison along with Rudolf Hess, who conveniently could act as his private secretary and get to work transcribing his notorious memoir, *Mein Kampf*.

After his release in late 1924 Hitler bided his time and his luck, as the German socio-economic situation stabilised. This was the extended break Hitler needed to formulate a workable strategy for the future, welcome the likes of arch propagandist Joseph Goebbels to the party and complete both volumes of *Mein Kampf*. It was five relatively low-profile years well spent, and when the 1929 Wall Street Crash hit, followed by the Great Depression, Hitler finally had the right moment and movement to propel him into a real and legitimate position of power. He just needed to survive one more near-death experience. In March 1930 a heavy truck hit his Mercedes from behind. In an age without air bags and seat belts one might have hoped for a little more damage – even a six-month layup in hospital might have changed the course of history – but he was left disappointingly unscathed.

Amid the political chaos before the elections of September 1930, Hitler and Goebbels conducted a visionary election campaign that would compare well to the politics of today (noticeably, the way it offered something to everyone while remaining light on the details). Together, they understood the power of modern technology, such as radio and effective sound amplification, as well as personal and party branding. The Nazi swastika and flag, the camp outfits, the hair and moustache – these apparent affectations played a key role in creating a memorable impression on the German voting public. Hitler emerged from relative Bavarian obscurity, scoured the land and, almost overnight, turned the Nazis into the second most popular party in Germany, with nearly a fifth of the vote.

The early 1930s saw constant squabbling in the minority government, little getting done and, when it did, a tendency to government by decree, an ominous trend. In 1932 Hitler ran against the ageing President Hindenburg, the final pillar of stability and respectability holding up the Weimar Republic, for the presidency of the country. Moderate sense prevailed, but

Hitler was now a political force to be reckoned with – and it wasn't long before the final chips started falling in his favour.

In February 1933 the Reichstag building was set alight, officially by communists though some suggest that the Nazis were in fact responsible. This allowed for a convenient issuing of emergency legislation, the Reichstag Fire Decree. Hitler could thus suppress political opponents in the runup to elections the following month, with the Nazis eventually taking 44 percent of the vote – still no majority, but the largest democratic endorsement they would receive. More critically, it gave Hitler a back door to assuming control of the country. By using the legislation to prevent communist and social democrat representatives from voting in parliament, he was able to force through the Enabling Act, allowing him to rule as chancellor by decree.

By July 1933 the Nazis were the only legal party in the country, and when Hindenburg died a year later the presidency and chancellorship were merged. Adolf Hitler was now head of state and head of government, effectively the dictator of Germany. He would need no further political luck to mould the shape of the world in unprecedented ways.

It was now just a matter of staying alive. Over the next ten years the Führer survived as many as two-dozen assassination attempts. Most were desperate and ill-conceived, but one in particular, just two months after the start of World War II, came agonisingly close to saving millions of lives and changing the course of history.

This attempt was planned meticulously for more than a year by a lone individual, Johann Georg Elser, a disgruntled carpenter by trade, who loathed Hitler and all he stood for, and seemed to have sensed his potential for destructive evil. Hitler was known for keeping a fastidiously Teutonic schedule, appearing at the same events at the same time year after a year, and Elser recognised the potential therein. In November 1938 he attended the 15th anniversary of the Beer Hall Putsch at the Bürgerbräukeller Hall in Munich, where Hitler spoke, as usual, from 8.30pm for two hours. Elser thus worked out where and how best to place a bomb that would kill the person standing at the podium in one year's time. He realised the bomb required would likely cause much damage and loss of life, but believed (with some understatement) that eliminating Hitler would be for the greater good.

Elser had previously taken a job in an armaments factory so he could learn how to make the bomb, and later while working as a labourer at a quarry he incrementally stole detonators and explosives. He then travelled to Munich – arriving in the weeks before Germany invaded Poland – and spent two clandestine months working quietly in the dead of night to hollow out a space for his bomb in a pillar behind the speaker's podium in the Bürgerbräukeller Hall. Following Hitler's usual schedule for the putsch anniversary, he set the timer to detonate at 9.20pm. But, of course, fate chose to intervene, casting a fog over Munich airport that day and necessitating Hitler's early departure by train so that he might make it back to Berlin to continue running the war. The speech was moved to 8pm, and he left the stage at 9.07pm. The bomb detonated thirteen minutes later, as planned, killing eight people and injuring scores.

Hitler had not only survived death by the narrowest margin, he had in fact had his reputation enhanced in the process. The Nazi mouthpiece *Volkischer Beobachter* described the event as 'the miraculous salvation of the Führer'. It was one of many. Other assassination attempts were foiled or spoiled in regular time. In one instance, in 1943, a bomb smuggled onto Hitler's plane failed to detonate. In another, the following year, he was saved by the heavy wooden leg of a conference table, which absorbed a bomb blast at the Wolf's Lair headquarters on the Eastern Front – this was the '20 July Plot', subject of the 2008 Tom Cruise film *Valkyrie*. Even then Hitler's death would doubtless have saved many lives, probably millions of them, but the bulk of the damage had been done.

Meanwhile, the brave and moral Elser had been captured trying to cross the border on the night of the Beer Hall bombing with incriminating evidence in his bag, detained by the Gestapo and imprisoned in Dachau concentration camp. Eventually, with Germany's defeat inevitable, Hitler gave specific orders for his execution in April 1945. He was shot several weeks before Hitler committed suicide.

Suicide, as it turns out, was the only way Hitler would go. Not by childhood accident or disease; not by shell, shot or mustard gas in World War I; not in political violence as his fascist comrades fell next to and on top of him in the 1920s; not by the justice of the state; not by car crash; and not at the hands of any number of would-be assassins.

Surveying the world in the ruins of the Great War in, say, 1920 it would have been difficult to cast your eyes twenty-five years into the future and paint a picture half as ghastly as that which Hitler delivered. Short of a nuclear exchange between superpowers – notwithstanding the fact that the concept of nuclear weaponry didn't exist in 1920 – it seems almost impossible to have conceived of a worse outcome. Six continents at war and more than 65 million people killed by the end of it; some estimates make it 80 million. For context, the first figure is the entire population of the UK in 2017; the second is the population of Germany. Either way, it was the deadliest event in human history.

This was the legacy of the unlikeliest but luckiest of tyrants, a man who taught us that fascism and radical socialism are in so many ways the same thing; a man who became the historical embodiment of why fascism, nationalism, authoritarian rule, eugenics and the formation of political policy around racial identity (what we might call identity politics today) are all wrong and should be rejected as such. Hitler taught the world that extreme politics lead to extreme repercussions and that evil lurks in the hearts of all men given the right conditions, from 'civilised' German to jungle-indoctrinated Cambodian – but also that it takes incredible fortune for a man with such fringe views to co-opt an entire democratic nation into his way of thinking.

Today, looking to the right – but also the left – we are seeing the revival of loud-mouthed lunatics lighting torches and banging populist drums. Let us hope that the Devil's luck runs with none of them.

J Bruce Ismay

12 December 1862 – 17 October 1937

President of the White Star Line; cause (arguable) and survivor (inarguable) of the sinking of the Titanic; symbol of corporate capitalism's pursuit of profit and indifference for ordinary people (often its own customers and employees)

15 APRIL 1912. THE NORTH ATLANTIC.

RMS Titanic, the largest moveable object in the world, considered 'practically unsinkable' up to this point, sinks. Or, as *The Onion* records many caustic moons later, 'World's Largest Metaphor Hits Ice-Berg'.

More than a century later and the metaphor – now cliché – remains relevant, though *The Onion'*s emphasis on it as a 'representation of man's hubris' in light of his 'mortality and vulnerability' is perhaps overshadowed today by the lessons in corporate governance it provides.

It was, as every teenager learns in school or from James Cameron, the magnificent ship's maiden voyage, an opportunity for society's elite to revel in the finest First Class luxuries of the day. The foie gras and lobster in the splendiferous à la carte restaurant; the Parlour Suites for the millionaires' millionaires; the famous Grand Staircase – it was all that and more. Of course, James Cameron (and Julian Fellowes and others) would also have you know that there were hordes of sooty-faced peasants in steerage several decks below the black-tie extravaganzas, and while their treatment and the state of their accommodation during the voyage has been just a little sensationalised in popular imagination, the fact of the matter is that a significantly higher percentage of Third Class passengers died than those from First or Second Class.

Of the 2,220 or so passengers and crew on board, more than 1,500 went down with the ship. Women and children were given priority, so a lot more men died than were saved, no matter the class, but the overall breakdown tells a story: nearly 40 percent of First Class passengers were lost, compared to nearly 60 percent of Second Class and 75 percent of Third Class passengers. (Not forgetting the bulk of the oft-forgotten crew.)

The problem, as history knows so well, was the lack of lifeboats, which moves us swiftly to the crux of the matter and this chapter's headliner, J Bruce Ismay. As chairman of the White Star Line, Ismay is credited as the man who had come up with the idea for the *Titanic* and her two sister ships, *RMS Olympic* and *RMS Britannic*, several years prior. In consultation with JP Morgan*, owner of White Star's parent company, he conceptualised the largest, finest ocean liners of their day, competing against Cunard's *Mauretania* and *Lusitania* (also doomed to a tragic and controversial end).

Ismay was, in fact, on board the *Titanic* on the night in question, travelling in one of the four kingly Parlour Suites mentioned above, and – to widespread public fury and quite possibly his regret – he survived. He was pilloried afterwards, especially in the American media, as a 'skulking coward', 'J Brute Ismay', 'one of those human hogs whose animal desires swallow up all finer feelings... whose heart is atrophied by selfishness'.[1] The assumed view was that he practically tossed helpless women and young babes into the inky black Atlantic in his effort to secure his spot on the lifeboat, and in most mainstream movies of the sinking, including the Cameron version, he is portrayed as encouraging the ship's captain, Edward

---

* Here's JP Morgan again, appearing in this entry in human form rather than as the eponymous bank he founded in 1864. He has been described by *The Economist* as 'America's greatest banker'. Given his numerous appearances in these pages, he certainly was influential.

Smith, to sail recklessly fast in hazardous waters. Both suggestions are probably unfounded, or at least overplayed. (The newspapers of William Randolph Hearst drove his vilification as partial payback for an old feud.)

The action for which Ismay will always be defined, however, came with his decision, during the build, to reduce the number of lifeboats on board. *Titanic* was designed to hold 64 lifeboats, but this was ultimately reduced to 20, which was four more than the outdated minimum carrying capacity stipulated at the time. As a result, she could save a theoretical maximum of 1,178 people on board, barely a third of her capacity.

Again, the standard narrative here is often oversimplified: a matter of White Star saving money on several dozen lifeboats that they didn't *have* to carry. But the direct cost benefit was pathetically small as percentages go: reportedly a saving of $500 per raft versus the ship's $7.5 million build cost. It would be the worst form of Scrooge McDuck penny-pinching for that to be the real justification. The indirect cost, however, might have been enormous. Had the *Titanic* and her sister ships prominently carried 64 lifeboats – they would all have been visible on deck – this precedent might have led to revised regulations for all liners to follow suit. The tonnage and capacity of ocean liners had leapt enormously in recent years and safety regulations had not kept pace. The cost for the *Titanic* would not have been a deal-breaker, but that of retrofitting an entire fleet might have been.

Moreover, and here's where the class warfare gets pointed, the lifeboats were all stored on the First Class deck, and Ismay wanted more space for his premium passengers, the big spenders, to enjoy themselves in the sun. Of course he did. Hence fewer lifeboats. Because, honestly, who cares about the plebs down below, as long as the one percent – as we'd know them today – are having fun?

And with that double-whammy the corporate rationale for a decision that sent 1,500 souls to the bottom of the Atlantic comes harshly into focus.

Yes, the decision was most likely informed by the post-Victorian hubris of the day, the notion that man had conquered the elements and that a ship might be unsinkable. But it is informative that the ship's designer, Alexander Carlisle, resigned over the matter long before the *Titanic* put to sea, insisting that the regulations they were adhering to were insufficient for the enormous new liners of the day. It was – and here's another cliché – a disaster waiting to happen.

TITANIC STRUCK BY ICY REPRESENTATION OF NATURE'S SUPREMACY STOP INSUFFICIENT LIFEBOATS DUE TO POMPOUS CERTAINTY IN MAN'S INFALLIBILITY STOP MICROCOSM OF LARGER SOCIETY STOP

– satirical reportage from The Onion a century after the fact

The White Star Line's casual disdain for its passengers, particularly its less affluent ones, has been paralleled in so much of the worst forms of capitalism in the century since. That particular case led to the implementation of far more adequate lifeboat regulations, but the question still lingers, as it did two entries ago under Joseph Hazelwood: why does the ship always have to hit the damned iceberg, metaphorical or not, before sensible, humane decisions are made?

As we touched on in our introduction, we are in precipitous times. The world appears to be at an inflection point, to borrow Barack Obama's phrase, and the injustices of corporate capitalism, real and perceived, have stoked the fires of change to the point that, in response, insane dreams of socialist utopia are being proposed as a workable alternative.

The most obvious manifestation in recent times was in the financial crisis of 2007/8 and resulting Great Recession, which saw the big banks squeezing every last drop out of the brewing subprime mortgage disaster with no qualms about the consequences to the faceless investors they would soon ruin. Just as Ismay, JP Morgan and co discovered that a Titanic *could* sink, so the drivers of the crisis (where the JP Morgan name was once more prominent) realised that the banks were, in fact, not too big to fail. A year or two later, of course, and they were raking in the fat bonuses they had before. Sadly, this neglectful, inhuman and, indeed, brutish behaviour is visible wherever the definitive psychopathic corporation, which knows only profit, not moral purpose, is allowed to flourish.

The *Titanic* was a feat of modern engineering, man's ambition and never-ceasing progress made tangible with steel and rivets. And, for this, Ismay and the capitalist drive of the modern world deserve acknowledgement. But these motivations of progress will always cast aspersions on themselves when they sacrifice our very humanity in their creation.

Ismay survived the sinking of the *Titanic*, but he was forever ruined. If only such corporate practices were, too.

The Israel-Palestine letter writer

The individual entrenched on one side of the intractable Israel-Palestine problem; somewhat unexpected metaphor for modern discourse

SEGUEING FROM HITLER TWO ENTRIES AGO to Israel here – could be tricky.

J Bruce Ismay notwithstanding, this transition from one to the other is quite appropriate, given that it was Hitler's persecution and scattering of the Jews in Europe that ultimately secured the creation of a Jewish state in Palestine in 1948. But if there is some room for misinterpretation on the matter, particularly given the hyper-sensitivities that the subjects of this entry tend to manifest, let us clarify our position right away: we see no way that the deeds of Hitler might be equated with those of the Israeli state at any point in its history. In deference to Godwin's Law – the internet dictum observing that as an online discussion grows longer it becomes inevitable that someone will compare someone or something else to Hitler[1] – we believe that the enormity of Hitler's crimes to humanity stands alongside only those of Stalin or Mao in recent times, with perhaps Lenin, Pol Pot and Enver and Talat (in present company) looking on.

Caveat over, this entry is not so much about Israel the country (or its leadership) as it is about its supporters who choose to blindly defend it and its actions, no matter the facts, no matter the ethics, no matter the costs – and, concurrently, those who oppose them, the similarly blind Palestinian supporters who do the exact same thing from the diametrically opposed position. But in describing these entrenched positions, some bare-bones background info is needed.

Israel is, by area, not much larger than Fiji. It is about 420 kilometres from north to south and it varies in width from 15 to 115 kilometres. More than half the place is the Negev desert.

Why, an impartial observer might think, all the fuss about such a speck in the wilderness?

Well, it's complicated – and the more complicated it gets, the less people want to acknowledge the complications. Let's try to demonstrate by outlining the religious significance of Jerusalem and the briefest history of the modern state of Israel in the next three or four pages.

What's so important about Israel? Jerusalem, pretty much. And, if we're reducing things down, a really small, particularly contested part of the Old City of Jerusalem.

King David, the first Israelite king, conquered the town of Jerusalem and established it as the capital of the Jewish nation around 1010 BC. Given that the purveyors of Judaism, Islam and Christianity can't agree about much, there is some irony in the fact that they all deem it a supremely holy city, a place of sacred and metaphysical value – a place, as history bears witness, to be fought over again and again.

If you want to, you could narrow the contestation of Jerusalem and thus Israel right down to a few hundred metres by a few hundred metres, approximately 15 hectares. That's the size of the Temple Mount in the Old City, where King David's son, the wise and wealthy King Solomon, built the First Temple. In it, so the legend goes, was housed the Ark of the Covenant. The temple was then plundered down the ages by various occupiers, and destroyed. Its replacement, the Second Temple, followed suit, first sacked by the Romans and then finished off by earthquake.

A few centuries later, in the late 600s AD, the new Muslim occupiers of the city chose the Temple Mount – naturally – as the perfect spot for the Dome of the Rock Islamic shrine. Other buildings followed. Today, the Dome is the most recognisable building in Israel while the Mount, managed by the local Muslim population but guarded by Israeli security forces, is a UNESCO World Heritage Site.

In short, Jews would have it that, among other things, the Temple Mount is the place where the world emerged at the Creation and where God gathered the dust to create Adam. Muslims would have it that, among other things, Muhammad ascended into heaven from the Dome of the Rock. And Christians would have it that, among other things, the original Temple was literally built for Jesus, who then kicked around the spot a fair bit. (The garden of Gethsemane, where he prayed the night before his crucifixion, is literally a stone's throw to the east, and the actual site of his crucifixion would have been within walking distance. Where exactly it is, as with so much of this stuff, is contested.)

Short of 'Don't get me started', the preceding three paragraphs are about as simplified an explanation of the symbolic significance of Jerusalem as it gets and, bearing in mind that different sects, scions and subdivisions of each religion believe and prioritise different things, it could no doubt be described as inaccurate, misleading and/or heretical by those personally invested. Many have argued that the Israel-Palestine conflict is not about religion at all. It's simply a territorial dispute, they say. US interests are well served by having a heavily armed ally strategically placed in the Middle East, they note. They make valid points but that's to miss the crux of the matter: history and religion fuel this fight.

Right, now it starts getting complicated…

The dominant religion by population in the region of Palestine has shifted over the millennia from Jewish to Christian to, from the 12th century, Muslim. By the late 19th century the latter outnumbered the others by three to one. It was at this time that the Zionist movement, calling for the establishment of a Jewish state in the historic land of Israel, came about.

Following the collapse of the centuries-old Ottoman Empire during World War I, Palestine was ruled by mandate by the British, who had made a vague undertaking to assist in establishing 'a national home for the Jewish people' there. Then, after World War II, which had seen the Holocaust cut the world's entire Jewish population by more than a third – a quite incredible statistic* – the United Nations agreed to partition the area into independent Arab and Jewish states, with Jerusalem and Bethlehem to be shared and 'managed under an International Trusteeship System'. Jerusalem, critically, would fall exactly on the border between Israel and the West Bank area of the proposed Arab state. The Jews, who understandably had a large measure

---

* According to the Jewish Virtual Library, the world Jewish population in 1939 was 16,728,000, the most it's ever been. By the end of the war it was around 11,000,000, a drop of about 35 percent. As of 2017 it was approximately 15,000,000.

of international political leverage after the war, were happy to sign on the dotted line but the Arabs rejected the plan, figuring they would rather not have their land taken over by a militant religious state.

Cue the 1948 Arab-Israeli war, involving a coalition of Arab armies versus the nascent Jewish state. This was effectively a scrambling of the territories using real-world military means rather than foreign mandarins drawing lines on a map, and after a year the new borders were taking shape. Israel had consumed large portions of the proposed Arab state and perhaps 700,000 Palestinian Arabs were forced to leave, to be replaced by a similar number of immigrant Jews, many likewise expelled from other Middle Eastern countries, along with many Holocaust survivors. The Palestinian refugees mostly ended up crammed into Gaza and the West Bank, respectively a little thumbnail of territory to the south-west occupied by Egypt, and a larger area that shared a border with Jordan, which Jordan annexed.

Thus from its very first days of independence the state of Israel has been bound on all sides and riddled throughout with constant political tension and violence, if not war. Notable highlights since have been the Suez Crisis (1956), the Six Day War (1967), the Yom Kippur War (1973), the Lebanon War (1982) and the First (1987-1993) and Second Intifadas (2000-2005) or uprisings. The Six Day War saw Israel occupying Gaza and the West Bank, as well as Egypt's Sinai Peninsula and Syria's Golan Heights. Sinai was eventually handed back to Egypt, but Israel's mutable borders and its relationship with the Palestinian Authority that oversees Gaza and the West Bank remain a defining element of Arab-Israeli conflict, seemingly impossible to resolve to either side's satisfaction.

The financial and military support of the United States – ensured by its large Jewish population – was and still is central to the survival of Israel, and in itself attracts further resentment and opprobrium towards Israel by enemies of the Great Satan. Iran, in particular, has frequently declared its desire for the complete eradication of the Jewish nation, funding and supplying weapons to Hamas, the de facto governing party of Gaza today, and Hezbollah, a militant Islamist group based in Lebanon to the north. Both groups are committed to the destruction of Israel and are regarded by the US, the European Union and other bodies as terrorist organisations or as containing terrorist elements within them. Their attacks on Israeli citizens and Israel's heavy-handed reprisals, particularly in Gaza, pour regular fuel on proceedings.

Given the existential threats that surround it, Israel has taken drastic measures to secure its survival; some consider them necessary, others unconscionable. For one, it possesses nuclear weapons, officially unacknowledged but probably in existence since the 1960s. (Read Tom Clancy's *The Sum Of All Fears* to see how that might have gone wrong.) More routinely, it is seen by many as an apartheid-style ruler that embraces state-sponsored violence and cynical land grabs, and treats its Palestinian inhabitants as second-class citizens.

And with that, many readers will doubtless be misting over and defaulting to their pre-existing position on Israel-Palestine. Finding two invested parties to agree about the finer details of Temple Mount, Jerusalem and the modern state of Israel in general is, to say the least, not easy.

In response to all of this, the Israel-Palestine letter writer has been writing his letters of outrage, in some or other form, for decades now – in pen, at his typewriter, on his laptop, now from his smartphone. In so doing, the *Israel*-Palestine writer will gloss over, without scruple, the collateral damage of children's deaths and human misery wrought by Israeli military actions as though the parents of these children brought it upon them, which is to say that it was deserved. Meanwhile the Israel-*Palestine* writer is often happy to do what we have been at pains not to: equate the deeds of Hitler with those of the Israeli state (while ignoring attacks on Israeli citizens). It is, one imagines, intentional rather than ironic, a tactic to offend and enrage.

Both sides see themselves as victims, their enemies the aggressors – they simply adjust the timelines accordingly.

You've harassed us for decades; *you've* harassed us for centuries.

You mortared us; *you* bombed us.

You're a hypocrite; *you're* a hypocrite.

freshwater1985

To blunt, everybody knows its religion war especially for the Israelis, its just that the western media steer clear of referring to Israel as the 'Jewish state' and that's what Israel was created to be a 'Jewish state'

Can anyone one imagine the BBC or even the guardian describing the Israel's atrocities as 'Jewish terrorism' when for the Palestinian it's their second name?

TrueToo

What utter crap. The BBC would stop guzzling at the public trough before it would call Palestinian terrorism 'terrorism.' It would not even call it terrorism when two Palestinians went into a synagogue and slaughtered the congregants with meat cleavers.

– Israel-Palestine letter writers exchanging blows online in the comment section below an article at www.theguardian.com titled 'The Israel-Palestine conflict is not just about land. It's a bitter religious war', published in November 2014 [sic]

As the venerable historian Bernard Lewis has pointed out, if the Israel-Palestine debate is about the size of Israel then there is room for discussion, a viable solution. But if it is about whether or not Israel should exist, that's another problem altogether. And, sadly, that approach is both unacceptable (and indicative of diminished human morality) and a reflection of so much of today's discourse – this notion not that we should negotiate and compromise, but that you're wrong and I'm right and get stuffed. That any argument is a zero-sum game: no compromise, no backing down.

We've referred to the Israel-Palestine letter writer as a he, and in his original form he usually would have been. But his metaphorical offspring today – those who follow these same blinkered tactics of non-engagement in whatever it is they are discussing; basically anyone with a conviction and an internet connection – are genderless. So much so that the argument of gender itself is a good example of a topic that has been consumed in this type of warfare, noticeably on North American campuses. And, whereas religion, or at least group identity, defines the Israel-Palestine confrontation, other topics that generate this type of fervour also tend to involve faith, proxy faith and matters of intrinsic personal identity: 'Islamic terrorism' or 'violent ideology'; climate change and what to do about it; racism or perceived racism; feminism in its various guises; identity politics; politics in general, especially right versus left; welfare; immigration; abortion; gun control… Even the inanities of life, from pop music to reality TV, can be fought with this level of untrammelled emotion. And increasingly, as the battlegrounds of our arguments are confined more and more to social media, with its on-the-loo attention span and ever-decreasing complexity – from Facebook rants to YouTube comments to, of course, Twitter meltdowns – the Israel-Palestine style of letter writer thrives in whatever guise he or she takes.

You have something to say on Israel or Palestine? Someone will hate you for it (no matter what it is).

On Trump or Hillary? Same result.

On Brexit? Same result.

On why you like eating vegetarian meals occasionally? Same result.

On making a YouTube comment? Same result. As evidence, a real YouTube comments exchange:

Jonathan Stevens
This is my first comment ever on YouTube you guys should feel honored

Bryce McLin
And who the fuck are you ? 😂 😂 😂

Jonathan Stevens
Jonathan Stevens its says it right there you illiterate fuck

Just as the Israel-Palestine letter writer can never turn his antagonist's mind, so you can never win an argument on social media, whatever the topic. But without simply acquiescing to the intractability of the Israel-Palestine situation – there *is* a solution in there somewhere – the depth and complexities of the former conflict have to at least be acknowledged, which we have tried to do in this entry. For so many of our arguments today, however, it should be far simpler for those involved to find common ground – and yet we simply refuse to make the effort. This is the way of the world these days, and the world is significantly poorer as a result.

We've lost a great deal in the fire that incinerated tolerant discourse. We've lost civility and the unity of purpose. We've lost the ability to contend with arguments, and instead rage about which MRI-slice of intersectional hatred legitimises the complete disregard of anything our opponents say. We've lost the ability to listen to the quieter voices, and in doing so we've lost a good many of our compatriots and friends. Positions entrench. Nothing changes – even when stuff really needs to change.

This is a virus that now lurks in every sphere of even the most genteel contended space, it seems. A person can barely venture the most moderate opinion without incurring an enfilade of outrage, abuse and the most absurd hyperbole. To suggest, therefore, that there is great hope for humanity and our future on this planet is not so much to raise an eyebrow above the parapet, but to flounce provocatively towards the gallows of Twitter Hill.

Still, we choose optimism. It's as human a trait as one-eyed victimhood.

The Israel-Palestine conflict is a vexed and convoluted situation. We are not proposing any easy solutions or writing it off as simply a failure to listen from leadership. The key players know what's going on, and the distinction between the Israeli and Palestinian people and their respective governments or those who purport to speak on their behalf must be recognised. But it seems undeniable to us that the way in which the supporters of either side react like a dog to a bell, and can be made to react by those leaders when necessary, lubricates this unending human catastrophe.

How to stop it? Well, there's a great quandary of our time.

When the next Mandela or Gandhi or Jesus (who knows?) cloaks the region of Israel-Palestine in rational engagement and peace – the one necessarily preceding the other, we would think – then perhaps the world will exhale a sigh of relief and we will be able, once more, to talk to each other like civilised human beings.

Alex Jones

b. 11 February 1974

Ultra-conservative American radio host; founder of InfoWars.com; conspiracy theorist; 'media provocateur'; right-wing troll feeder; attacker and proponent of fake news; Donald Trump's useful idiot

ALEX JONES IS A TEXAN TALK SHOW HOST with right-wing proclivities. That is probably something that he, his supporters and his detractors can all agree on. Beyond that, the truth gets a little trickier to discern, which is probably appropriate given that he is the man behind InfoWars, tagline: 'There's a war on for your mind!'

Jones describes himself as a paleoconservative, so let's start there.

Paleoconservatives really are a gas. They've done so much of the work for us just in naming their philosophy (no, it's not a diet) in a way that powerfully underlines its backwardness – 'Heritage!' they would shout – by harking back to prehistoric times. But paleoconservatism is, in some ways, so very modern. It's a modern American philosophy with a very modern name; a name cooked up in the 1980s (to describe a conservative movement with serious aspirations) but seemingly designed for dissemination in the 21st century. You can't call your political movement the *Backwards-Assed Douchebags For A Return To Racial And Sexual Subjugation And Nationalist Economic Bullshit* – that simply won't fly online or on air. But in our modern digital ghettos, to some, paleoconservatism sounds clever enough to just about do.

Paleoconservatives tend to be rather rigid in their beliefs and are happy to argue anything that doesn't conform to their narrow world view. Traditionally, when one-time presidential candidate Pat Buchanan was its leading light, that would've been something like nationalism, traditionalism and free markets. Translated today, that quickly becomes bigotry, intolerance and fuck you. (Despite his avowed aversion for 'cussing', Alex Jones certainly knows his way around a potty-mouthed tantrum.) Whereas we, as authors, may be eager to point out, for example, some of the pitfalls of snowflake millennial naivety, paleoconservatives generally want everyone left of centre to die, immediately. This is only a slight exaggeration.

That this is the first era in human history in which almost all that we read is completely unedited is hopefully something else that we all, even the paleos and snowflakes, can agree on. In our technologically advanced and mostly free societies, anyone with an internet connection has access to the other end of the media machine. 'Democratisation of information' is the thing, and there are many reasons why this is a happy phenomenon. It has encouraged transparency. It has made organising grassroots movements a cinch. It has persuaded mainstream media to sit up and try harder – to listen as much as they proselytise – and, perhaps most powerfully, it has made it more difficult for media monoliths to manipulate mass thought and action.

Ironically, however, it hasn't done this by cutting through the bluster, by separating the wheat from the chaff; it's done it by highlighting just how much bluster there is out there. In the title to his website, Alex Jones makes a very good point: there is indeed a war of information going on. It's a truism that Donald Trump, for one, has used to enormous strategic gain: it's all fake news, people! This is why, he says, he tweets so regularly: it's not because he's a big ol' crybaby looking for attention; it's so that you, the average Joe out there, can get the news directly from him, no censors, no filters, no interpretation. (Because obviously *he's* telling the truth…)

And so the problem of the democratisation of information reveals itself: in what is one of the free world's greatest challenges, we need to learn how to read again – critically and without prejudice. We've been so comfortable and safe in these post-Cold War times that we haven't learnt to protect ourselves from terrible ideas by engaging with them sufficiently in schools and universities. In fact, most scarily, we're actively banning ideas from campuses altogether. We have lost the means to see a terrible idea for what it is and to dismiss it as horse manure, because out there on the web every kind of lunacy is available at the touch of an app. And all this while the most biddable, naive and yet unequivocally certain generation in history steps out into the voting world, educated by digital echo-chambers and protected from challenging ideas by craven university administrators.

As a result, most of the world reads for the purposes of confirmation bias and little else. We have our social and informational milieu and we seek it out. We use the LIKE button as much as we hammer the BLOCK function. We create a digital world of certainty, unaware that it shapes us as much as we shape it, a terrifying co-dependency. *(See Mark Zuckerberg.)*

No matter how he may protest, Alex Jones is, it's fair to say, not just a paleoconservative. He is, in old-fashioned language, a right-wing conspiracy nut who gives air to the kind of stuff that used to come straight from the loony bin. He spends hours a day on air, usually speaking without script, with a team of 'researchers' in the background feeding him tenuous but on-message nuggets of 'information' that they've plucked from cyberspace. Some of it's harmless stuff, like the moon landings were faked and there's a colony of child slaves on Mars. Some is less so, like the US government is turning people gay 'with chemicals' to discourage population growth, and Governments and Big Business have combined to create a new world order. (InfoWars has a thing for gate-crashing Bilderberg Group conferences.) And some is simply vile and grossly offensive, like the US government was behind the 9/11 attacks, the Oklahoma City bombing and the Sandy Hook massacre, or actually that last one might have been a hoax and all the grieving parents were actors.

The real harm comes in Jones's huge following: he has made claims that his 'media operation' reaches 70 million people a week. Now, given the fake-news landscape in which we're operating, that may or may not be true, but the seemingly verifiable figures are still disturbingly high. As of mid-2017 InfoWars.com received as many as 7.5 million visitors a month and had 1.5 million Facebook likes and more than 670,000 Twitter followers; Jones's YouTube channel had 2.1-million subscribers and his radio show was broadcast on about 150 channels to millions of listeners daily. What he says has consequences. In the case of the Sandy Hook Elementary School shooting in Newtown, Connecticut, in which twenty children and six

'We're the most bona fide, hardcore, Real McCoy thing there is!'

– Alex Jones, discussing InfoWars

teachers and staff were shot dead in December 2012 by a lone gunman, his speculation that the events were a deliberate false-flag operation or that they possibly didn't happen at all led to parents of some of the victims receiving death threats from his followers. Only a truly vile individual creates such a situation.

Moreover, Jones is said to have the ear of Donald Trump, a man who is savvy enough to chase an easy and compliant fanbase when he spots one. As a Republican candidate, Trump was interviewed by Jones in 2015, an almost unprecedented move for a prominent politician. The relationship between the two was described as 'symbiotic' by *The Washington Post*, and President Trump and his team have kept the Jones love brewing, embracing his news feeds when convenient and keeping him on the hook, it would seem, to be used as needed.

> 'Listen, Alex, I just talked to the kings and queens of the world – world leaders, you name it. It doesn't matter, I wanted to talk to you to thank your audience.'
>
> *– Donald Trump talking to Alex Jones*
> *after his US presidential election victory (as Jones recalls the conversation)*

Alex Jones is a loathsome snake-oil salesman for a certain buyer. To the American far right he sells their biggest fears and, boy, do they lap it up. They buy it because they hear it from somebody famous on the radio – which makes it legit, bro – and it supports a vaguely formed narrative they already enjoy. They buy it because nobody ever taught them to look for answers they don't like the sound of.

Jones is an extreme example of a modern breed of shock-jocks, film-makers and online scavengers who have capitalised on the notion of fake news – in his case often married to ludicrous *National Enquirer*-style stories – and now specialise in it. He bangs on about globalists and the Jewish mafia and other vague notions. Tune into his radio show, if you must (we had to), and you may find him discussing how government controls the weather or how out-of-control fungi are attacking fish and, ultimately, our bodies, turning into 'literal fungus tumours' in our brains.

Really.

'Media provocateurs like Jones... present themselves out on the fringes because they know that passion sells and they are far more interested with lining their own pockets and getting people to pay attention to their websites and their AM talk radio shows and cable television programmes than they are [with] bringing about good governance. Their business model is built on tumult, on division, on fomenting dissent... Sadly, what may be performance art to him is real to his listeners and his viewers, and therein lies the danger: the conflation of news and entertainment.'

– CNN host Michael Smerconish
(Alex Jones would be mortified if he knew we used a CNN quote)

As much as we would like to, however, it's difficult to laugh at Alex Jones. He's more dangerous than that.

Only people who have been taught to read with discernment and a solid dose of cynicism in an unedited world are able to see the new media purveyors for what they are: activists, not journalists; niche operators feeding a targeted audience what they want to hear. In Jones's case, he is a fantasist savant with delusions of insight and a scary amount of political influence in the United States. (The jury is out as to what degree he actually believes his own tales.)

Almost all 'news' sites, whether they were invented last year or they've been around for a century, transmit their stories through some kind of ideological lens: from *InfoWars* to *Breitbart News* to *Fox* to *CNN** to *The New York Times* to Jones's diametric opposite ultra-left news disseminator *The Huffington Post*. Okay, that was a little joke to make fun of the lefties. *HuffPost* doesn't believe in slave children on Mars, and if you want real millennial left fervour – which hates on the neo-liberal left even more so than it does the right, because they should've known better – check out the *Chapo Trap House* podcast.

Thing is: ideological lenses in themselves are actually fine, and to be expected in the real world. But the genuine fake news, the stuff that turns votes and swings elections, isn't. So remember, the people putting out this stuff may be terrible in their own special ways, but *they* are not the fools.

---

* Clinton News Network, according to Jones.

Kim Kardashian

b. 21 October 1980

World-famous reality TV and porn star; social media colossus; possibly the most famous woman in the world; probably the most self-involved person in the world; avatar of modern materialism and narcissism; very, very bad role model

HOW DID KIM KARDASHIAN STUFF UP THE WORLD? She just did. And we don't want to talk about it. And if we have to explain this one, you're possibly reading the wrong book.

The end.

Okay, so we need a little more here. Well, then, if we must, here's an exercise. Take out your phone and type the two words 'Kim Kardashian' into Google. Doing so towards the middle of 2017 we get:

KIM KARDASHIAN SHARES INTIMATE PICTURES FROM TRIP TO JAPAN.

KIM KARDASHIAN WEST SPENDS $379,000 ON JACKIE KENNEDY'S CARTIER WATCH.

KIM KARDASHIAN WEST THANKS 'GOOD DAD' KANYE WEST.

Now, to the uninitiated, this would appear to be a series of news stories about somebody important, somebody who had presumably achieved something of quite notable significance or, perhaps, been born into some great purpose. But no, in this case don't go looking for it. Save yourself the baffling rabbit hole of inexplicable, pointless banality, a distant and strange culturally interstellar vacuum of absence – neither here nor there, when both here and there account for naught.

There is less than nothing that should matter about Kim Kardashian. Her family and some of her friends probably quite like her, and we imagine her children love her a great deal. But if your test is artistic or political or literary or philosophical, or indeed any of the usual measures by which society lifts onto pedestals those who have contributed positively to the human condition, then she doesn't move the needle. Not a wobble. Kim Kardashian is a great deal of nothing, an enormously celebrated irrelevance, a storm that leaves the trees unmoved.

Kim Kardashian, therefore, is a very modern phenomenon, a living example of the power of media – in her case, first internet pornography then reality TV and today increasingly social media – to deliver news without newsworthiness, to create copy without a story and to summon consequence from the headlines you read above. It is nigh-on miraculous.

It began, in 2007, with that egregious modern addition to the PR repertoire for those who have the talent to produce little else: a sex tape, in which our daughters' future role model had sex on camera with a rapper of passing consequence known as Ray J. This particular route to stardom had been successfully forged by Paris Hilton and others, and the speculation has long been that it was carefully managed to launch the Kim Kardashian career. Even as her mother Kris Jenner vehemently denied this on the ten-year anniversary of the tape's release – 200 million views and counting – the sense that she doth-protest-too-much-as-she-clutcheth-her-designer-jewellery-to-her-fake-bosom is hard to shake. Whatever the sordid details, Kim was reported to have secured a multimillion-dollar deal for the tape and by year-end her new-found fame had ballooned into *Keeping Up With The Kardashians*, a humourless show that had to be pitched as 'reality TV' because a soap opera would not have been able to accommodate the ludicrous plotlines.

Fast-forward a decade and there's a megabucks business empire driven by the ongoing TV show and its spin-offs and the Kardashians' enormous following on social media. Kim alone has more than 100 million followers on Instagram and 50 million on Twitter, and if there is a sine qua non of having made it in the millennial age it is, tragically, probably that. In the meantime, she managed, to no-one's surprise, to marry a very famous person (Kanye West), who could afford to buy her not one but two engagement rings, valued at a combined $6 million, which she can show off on Snapchat.

Before you dry-heave onto the page while considering your sisters', daughters' and granddaughters' future prospects, we are obliged to present the argument *for* Kim. Apparently, it goes something like this. In a world in which women must still battle prejudice and the odds to rise to the top, Kim is a hugely successful businesswoman – a self-made entrepreneur, no less – who has created her own dedicated fanbase by keeping herself interesting, on trend and desirable…

Jesus wept.

Not only is that the sum of what's positive about the carefully curated my-perfect-life image that she projects, but there are people who find great inspiration in her success, who admire it and watch it closely. Not in an ironic, car-crash kind of way, but as something wonderful to aspire to – as a role model. And not just any old role model; she is, as the marketers put it, an *influencer*, someone who moulds the behaviour and opinions of others. That is, someone who can get them to buy whatever she's shilling – at $500,000 for a single Instagram post – and behave the way she behaves.

To be fair to Kim, she's just the most successful of the Kardashian clan and we can point fingers at various others in her immediate circle. *Vanity Fair*'s Graydon Carter, for instance, has described Kim together with her sisters Kourtney and Khloé as 'the three horsewomen of the apocalypse', so perhaps they are equally worthy of our ridicule. Knowing observers convincingly argue that their grasping 'momager' mother Kris Jenner is the real devil behind them all, while others blame that damn Ray J for getting out the camera in the first place. And then there's the late father Robert Kardashian, who played an important cameo in the trial and acquittal of OJ Simpson, in the process nudging the Kardashian name sufficiently towards the limelight to open this family's eyes to the riches that lay in the disposable reality-media future... (*See OJ Simpson.*)

For those admiring the self-made-ness of Kim and her sisters, Robert was estimated to be worth $30 million when he died in 2003, having himself inherited a fortune from his parents. So, no, Kim overcame no overwhelming prejudice or hardship en route to the top.*

More pertinently, Kim Kardashian is a real live idol for hundreds of millions of people in America and across the planet. It is no exaggeration to describe her as one of the most famous women in the world. So let's consider what the average Kim Kardashian follower – who, according to Instagram and Twitter analytics, is likely a white or Hispanic Millennial female – might learn from her influencer idol:

- Having sex on camera and distributing it to the world is a desirable way to find fame and fortune.
- Fame in and of itself is desirable.
- Self-obsession, to the point of publishing a book unironically titled *Selfish*, including nearly 500 selfies of yourself, is your route to the top...
- ... with boobs and butt hanging out at all times, of course.
- The rank narcissism that accompanies the above is of course fine.
- Conspicuously spending money in a manner almost as revolting as the way it was earned defines a well-lived life.
- Obsessive pouting on Instagram (as long as you can airbrush the pictures just right) is an indicator of self-fulfillment.

Now, it's critical to be clear here: what a person does in the privacy of their own home or, indeed, on the internet for all to see, shouldn't be a big deal. There are people who do far worse things than Kim and her clan, and if reality TV escapism is your guilty pleasure then, you know, sure, fine, we accept that. Really, we're all adults here.

Well, except that we're not actually. Many of us – many of the Kardashian fans, that is – are in fact children, or were children not too long ago, and

---

* That honour, in fact, belongs to her great- and great great-grandparents who separately fled persecution in the Russian and Ottoman empires around the turn of the 20th century, thus avoiding the Armenian genocide. Finally, an interesting Kardashian story! (*See Enver & Talat.*)

'If aliens came down here and we had to explain human culture, what would be the most confusing thing to explain? Kim Kardashian... If you went to Harvard Business School and said listen I'm thinking of starting a business. I want to make about fifty times more than the [US] president and here's my plan: I'm going to fuck an R&B singer with a giant dick and I'm gonna film it. And that's it. They would be, like, get the fuck out of our office, you don't know shit about business. But they're wrong and she's right. A woman with a fake ass makes fifty times more than the Commander in Chief of the greatest army the world has ever known.'

– comedian Joe Rogan[1]

have been groomed by their aspirational ideals into accepting a new understanding of what are good and desirable human traits to cherish and aim for. To the Kardashian fans, positive human traits such as talent, hard work and awareness of the world around you are subservient to the new indicators in the race of life: self-obsession, narcissism, materialism, *me*.

Many observers have dismissed the superficialities of reality TV culture and all that comes with it – this is the default position of anyone with a halfway healthy perspective on life, we'd think. But in the end it was Ray J who outlined it best for those for whom the Kardashian way may be a temptation. In *Famous,* an appropriately charmless 2016 release, he sang:

> *She fucked me for fame, look in her eyes,*
> *She was the first one to sign on the line,*
> *She was the real one to plan it all out,*
> *Look at the family, they walk around proud,*
> *All because she had my dick in her mouth.*

All of which seems, on balance, to be fair, reasonable and accurate (if crude) criticism. What Kim Kardashian is famous for is something that comes naturally to stray dogs. Keeping up with the Kardashians? Nothing could be easier. It's ascribing value to it with which we can't keep up, let alone buying the goddamn Kardashian Beauty Lip Plumping Shimmer Gloss.

Look, she may only be the fourth-worst Kim in this book *(see next page),* but still, what's wrong with people?

THE KIMs

Kim Il-sung: 15 April 1912 – 8 July 1994
Kim Jong-il: 16 February 1942 – 17 December 2011
Kim Jong-un: b. 8 January 1984 (or maybe 5 July 1984)

Mass-murdering cult-leaders who have controlled a nation for 75 years and committed unimaginable crimes in the process; possible cause of next nuclear showdown; possessors of terrible haircuts

A PHENOMENON AS SORDID AND DEPRAVED as North Korea doesn't grow out of the fertile ground of freedom and light. To understand why something is broken you need to understand how it was built – and both Koreas, North and South, were fashioned from a half-century so unimaginably brutal that, perversely, it is the North that seems to makes sense and the South that looks like some kind of aberration, even a miraculous one. There is surely no better way to illustrate the value of freedom than the comparative plights of the two Koreas since their partition after World War II, and specifically since the end of the Korean War in 1953. Studying them today is the geopolitical equivalent of studying identical twins separated at birth, one now a prominent member of society, the other a pathological monster.

Between 1910 and 1945 the Korean Peninsula as a whole was a colony of a truly savage master, imperial Japan, its neighbour to the south and east across the narrow Korea Strait. During World War II Japan made a contemptible name for itself in the Western world with its surprise invasion of Pearl Harbour, its kamikaze fighting tactics and the appalling mistreatment of prisoners of war. Today it is seen as redeemed, a paragon of civilisation and progressiveness. But to its East Asian neighbours, Japan's behaviour both during the war and before is remembered with enduring grievance and anger, largely informed by the appalling treatment of occupied civilian populations. Most notable was the mass abduction of tens of thousands, perhaps hundreds of thousands, of girls and women for use in 'comfort stations', essentially rape camps for the Imperial Japanese Army. According to a UN report, 'the rationale behind the establishment of a formal system of comfort stations was that such an institutionalised and, therefore, controlled prostitution service would reduce the number of rape reports in areas where the army was based.' That progressiveness was not always admirable.

As a result, there is a long-lingering legacy of bitterness that still shapes the geopolitics of the region. In 2015 a deal was signed between Japan and South Korea in which Prime Minister Shinzo Abe offered his 'most sincere apologies and remorse'. A ¥1 billion fund (about $8.3 million at the time) was donated by the Japanese for the care of surviving comfort women, and the two countries agreed to stop 'criticising and blaming each other in international society'. It was their first deal on the matter since 1965, but within a year it was already on troubled ground after a statue of a comfort woman was erected outside a Japanese embassy in South Korea, and Tokyo withdrew two diplomats. In June 2017 new South Korean president Moon Jae-in cast doubt on the agreement.

The mass rape of Korean women was, we must grimly report, but one of the examples of Japanese abuses in the area. During the Japanese annexation of the peninsula and into the 1930s, Japanese rule became increasingly malevolent, as the occupying forces attempted to eliminate Korean culture, names, religion and language. Then came the war – and things got even worse. The awfulness of the comfort stations, for example, saw girls being forced to 'service' 40 soldiers a day and executed if they became infected with diseases.

The dropping of the atom bombs on Hiroshima and Nagasaki, both barely 250 kilometres from Korea itself, brought a decisive end to the reign of Japanese atrocity in the region. With the Soviets advancing from Manchuria, to the north of the country, down as far as the 38th Parallel, and the Americans accepting Japanese surrender in the south, Korea suddenly found itself in an uneasy state of peace.

Thus the Korea of 1945 has some quite telling context.

In communist and other totalitarian states history isn't there for interpretation and learning, but for rampant abuse in order to buttress the status quo. So what we do know is that the Union of Soviet Socialist Republics invaded Korea to oust the Japanese in 1945, and that Russian soldiers were welcomed with open arms by the abused, starved and brutalised Koreans. That's worth a pause, isn't it?

Life had been so bad that they welcomed the invasion of Stalin's soldiers…

Anyway, legend then has it that there was a frisson of excitement in the 100,000-strong crowd that had gathered in Pyongyang that October day. A heroic anti-Japanese guerrilla leader, the man who had so bravely fought the colonisers in Korea and in Manchuria with such success, would appear before them.

'Now is the moment,' a Russian general said from the platform, 'to introduce you to the new leader of your country, Comrade Kim Il-sung.'

And with that, the crowd was perhaps surprised with the presentation of a chubby little thirty-something guy – not exactly the vision of a hardened war veteran.

Ah yes. Kim Il-sung: 'Kim becomes the sun.'

Real name Kim Song-ju, the first Kim was a lie literally from the moment he appeared in front of the Korean people. His new name may have been appropriated from a genuine Korean freedom fighter to boost his credentials – we can't be sure. Either way, he was a reinvention for a purpose. He had been born into a comfortable Presbyterian family near Pyongyang, and his parents, Kim Hyong-jik and Kang Pan-sok, had fled to Manchuria to avoid famine like many Koreans. Russian propaganda had them taking part in various anti-Japanese activities, but the truth is likely to be far less exciting. It appears that Kim may indeed have involved himself in certain paramilitary activities against the Japanese in Manchuria, but the idea that he was in any way a most successful Korean military leader was likely, to use a contemporary term, spin.

Kim had spent the early 1940s safely holed up in a Russian military base, where he'd made the rank of Captain, and where he'd remained for four-and-a-half years. His eldest son, Kim Jong-il, was probably born there. This is hardly the story of a swashbuckling military leader, a man who would return to his homeland triumphant ahead of a column of tanks having thrown out the vile colonialist abusers. No, indeed. He arrived in Korea on a Russian navy ship, was met by nobody and went to a local restaurant to have beer and noodles.

What Kim Il-sung really was, critically, was fluent in Russian and willing to play along, both of which are handy if you are the Soviet powers that be and happen to want a puppet president for a puppet regime. In fact, the little schooling Kim had received had been in China, and his Korean was so weak that he required assistance in pronunciation so that he could properly address his newly acquired people. By 1948, he was installed as prime minister of the Democratic People's Republic of Korea, while in the South the US-approved strongman Syngman Rhee took the reins of the Republic of Korea. Rhee instituted a bloody and brutal crackdown on communist elements in the country, and pretty much anyone else who didn't toe the line.

Both governments wanted to unite the Korean people under their respective regimes but discussions along those lines were never promising given their leaders' respective political ideologies: both tended towards the authoritarian, but Kim was a votary of Stalin, while Rhee was belligerently anti-communist. After various skirmishes along the 38th Parallel, and much to the chagrin of their sponsor superpowers (who were more focused on possible conflict in Europe), the North invaded the South in 1950, igniting the Korean War. It was the first major engagement of the Cold War, and would see the armies of the United States, United Kingdom, Australia, France and other countries fighting under the auspices of the United Nations on the side of the South, and Soviet and Chinese forces supporting Kim's North.

As the battle lines surged south on the initial invasion, then north once the UN got their act into gear, then south again after the Chinese became involved, civilian massacres were committed by the thousands by both Korean armies. The North rooted out anti-communist class enemies, the South purged leftist collaborators. After a year, fighting stalled on the 38th Parallel, but it took a further two years of negotiations before an armistice was signed, in July 1953. By then, there were, by some estimates, up to 3 million people left dead, perhaps two-thirds of them civilian casualties of famine and disease.

It was all fruitless, and the Korean peninsula remains split to this day. Technically the two countries are still at war, with a large US troop contingent – 28,500 since the mid-2000s – permanently stationed there.

After the war, Rhee remained as president of South Korea until he was forced out and went into exile in 1960. The economic revival of the country – the Miracle on the Han River, as it came to be known – proceeded apace from the 1960s onwards, and in 1987 the country embraced democratic presidential elections. It has subsequently hosted the 1988 Olympic Games and the 2002 Football World Cup, been accepted into the G20 group of nations in 2010, and become one of the most technically advanced and industrialised nations on earth – a model case for transforming a Third World disaster zone into a vision of First World progress.

The North, however, remains the talentless twin, representing the very opposite of what the South has achieved. Together they make for the most compelling illustration of the power of good and bad politics: the same people, constrained by the same seas and neighbours, weather and geography, with a shared history – with diametrically opposed results. (If anything, the North had something of an advantage to start: it was more industrialised than the rural South, though the South had better farmland.)

Today the difference between North and South Korea can be measured in many ways – by income, health and freedom of information, for instance.

GDP per capita? North: $1,700 v South $38,000*
Infant mortality per 1,000 live births? North: 22.0 v South 2.9†
Internet access per 100 people? North: less than 0.1 v South: 85.7

Lightly unpacking that last fact offers some insight into what we're dealing with. South Korea has, quite famously, become a hi-tech hub and has, not only widespread access to the web, but the fastest average internet connection speed in the world by country by some margin (over the likes of Japan, Sweden and Ireland). Meanwhile, exact North Korean internet usage is unknown in the West, though it's estimated that barely a few thousand users have access to the actual worldwide web, as opposed to the country's rudimentary local intranet which carries a handful of censored sites mostly for bureaucrats and university workers. There are three categories of North Koreans who can really go online: government-controlled hackers, government-controlled propagandists and, of course, the elite (who live like kings, which is to say, people in the First World). The great majority of the population isn't aware of the internet and needs governmental authorisation to own a computer or even send a fax.

Thus we see the vast chasm between the two countries and the reason is obvious to all: their politics. Because while North Korea started off as a wobbly Stalinist outpost led by some loser who'd spent the war hiding and whose Korean was so bad he had to get his Soviet masters to teach him how to speak it properly, what it has become is almost unbelievable.

After Stalin died, a few months before the end of the Korean War, his successor Nikita Khrushchev denounced the worst aspects of Comrade Joe's ideologies. He was by comparison a raging liberal. Kim responded by doubling down and fashioning a parallel universe, one that he claimed, literally, to have created. He was the 'creator of the world', the man who could control the weather, and his people lived in a real-life *1984* so perfectly wrought you have to wonder whether Kim had read the book and thought it a manual, not a dystopian warning. Kim was by this stage no longer the puppet of the Soviets; he was very much his own Stalin, just with less to constrain him. He had licence now to do a lot of doubleplus ungood things.

In time, Kim created something that is not really describable in normal political language. There have been collectivised farms and starvation

---

* About equivalent to South Sudan or Sierra Leone v Japan or New Zealand, according to the CIA's World Factbook.

† About equivalent to Palestine or Guatemala v Sweden or Germany. This information is from the United Nations five-yearly table for 2010-2015. Tellingly, according to this data, the North (122.82) and South (138.12) were both at astronomically high levels in the 1950-1955 period. No country in the world today rates above 100, with five African countries in the 90s.

around the world, of course, but vehement racial nationalism is at the heart of the North Korean regime's thinking, which makes it more far right than far left. It is now also overtly a cult of dynasty, in which the supreme leaders are without fault and require actual worship, as opposed to the supposed atheist collectivism of communist states in which, in theory at least, all are equal. Kim crystallised his religion-ideology from his Marxist-warped idea of *Juche* – roughly 'self-reliance' – which he introduced in the mid-1950s. If Juche is to be considered a religion today, which seems accurate, then there are more Juche believers in the world than Jews or Spiritists because, of course, all 25 million North Koreans are by definition Juche believers. Except perhaps those in the labour camps.

However we categorise these things, Kim used Juche to develop his Hermit Kingdom, which has become more insane as it has become more isolated with the passing of the years. Despite its internal pretensions of grandeur, which seem so comical from the outside, North Korea has in its entire existence never been independent of aid and relief in terms of energy and food. Initially it was the Soviets who propped up the regime, and when they fell away China took their place. But even the Chinese, having discovered the powers of their hybrid capitalism, have backed off, leaving North Korea ever more isolated.

Following the post-Soviet collapse of communism in the mid-1990s, North Korea faced ever-worsening economic disaster. Given the cult of personality and terror that surrounded Kim, it's not clear if he knew this and didn't care, or whether the yes-men who coalesced about him simply assured him everything was okay for fear of their lives – because, historically, if your views didn't correspond with those of the Great Leader you ended up in a labour camp or firing line. What is clear is that as the original Kim began to ail, his son Kim Jong-il took over more and more of the operation of the state, and the opportunity for a change of strategy, for some kind of easing of the totalitarian nightmare began to present itself. This Kim, the international thinking went, was a bit of a non-entity – he was obsessed with making movies, and had even abducted a South Korean director and film star to assist him in his endeavours – and might be open to some sensible negotiation. To facilitate the process, South Korea adopted a 'Sunshine Policy' of engagement, while Bill Clinton's US administration was hopeful of opening a new chapter in its dealings with the country.

Kim Il-sung died in July 1994. The empty sock-puppet of no particular military talent or political courage had outlived his Soviet masters beyond their wildest dreams, and in doing so had taken a Soviet ideal and extrapolated it to its maddest conclusion. Scenes of wailing and lamentation were prepared for local and international TV cameras, and Kim's body was embalmed and put on display. You can still go and check him out if you wish. Kim Jong-il declared a three-year mourning period and changed the country's constitution (for what it's worth) to leave the presidency 'permanently vacant'; as such, his father is now the 'Eternal Leader', a dead man in charge of his country to this day.

Would Kim Jong-il take this gilt-edged opportunity to revitalise his nation, to drag it from its antediluvial backwardness? If you've ever watched *Team America* – and even if you haven't – you'll know the answer. The new Kim was simply the old Kim by another name. He was now the Great Leader Of Our Party And Nation – later to be the Glorious General Who Descended From Heaven and the Highest Incarnation Of The Revolutionary Comradeship, among 1,200 titles to be bestowed on him – and he cracked down on perceived opposition, kept the labour camps stocked to the brim, and murdered those who needed murdering. Most worryingly for the rest of the world, he continued a stand-off with the US over his country's nuclear weapons programme, which appears to have been in development since the early 1980s.

Meanwhile, with the economy in tatters and almost all food and energy imports squeezed to a trickle, it took just two seasons of heavy rains and flooding to wreak havoc on the North Korean populace. By the mid-1990s the resulting famine was at apocalyptic proportions. It's virtually an identifying trait of totalitarian communist states that we can never know just how many people die in the propagandist-obscured mayhem that invariably arises, so the numbers are difficult to tally, but in an action replay of what had happened in parts of the Soviet Union, China, Cambodia and

'North Korea [is] exactly like a *1984* state. It is as if it was modelled on *1984*, rather than *1984* on it. It is extraordinary, the leader worship, the terror, the uniformity, the misery, the squalor.'

– Christopher Hitchens

elsewhere, rural populations were left to starve to death. Recent academic investigations measure the toll at something like 600,000 souls, but some estimates put it as high as five times that. The one positive result, if it can be considered as much, was that the US could use Kim's desperate need for food aid to, at least temporarily, curtail his nuclear weapons programme.

As the years passed, the descent into the Kim Cult hysteria only deepened. The Kims, whether dead or alive, are seen to be protecting their people from rapacious and vicious enemies that are the United States and South Korea, despite the fact that these enemies have been two of its three principal food importers, along with China, since the mid-1990s. All of this would merely be something you'd file under 'horrifying' were it not for the increasingly sophisticated nuclear tomfoolery that North Korea has engaged in over the last decade, and the decreasingly sophisticated US leadership as of 2017.

In 2006, North Korea tested its first device, which was presumed to be a failure, delivering an amusingly small yield. Further tests in 2009, 2013 and 2016 were more successful, and by the time of its sixth detonation in 2017 the news wasn't so funny: the country appeared to have engineered a thermonuclear weapon five or ten times more powerful than the bombs that destroyed Hiroshima and Nagasaki.

By now Kim Jong-il had become the Eternal General Secretary of the Party – that is, he'd died – and, as of 2011, the third iteration of Kim was in command. This new Dear Leader, Kim Jong-un, was fatter of face and more interested in video games than his father and grandfather before him, and yet the apple, it turns out, had fallen directly below the pathological tree. For one, he appears partial to a showy execution, reportedly dispatching his minister of defence Hyon Yong-Chol and several other luckless lackeys in 2015 with ZPU-4 anti-aircraft guns, each consisting of four 14.5mm machine guns, positioned 30 metres from their targets. In the words of a South Korean security specialist, 'It would be hard to find the body after firing it once. It's really gruesome.' Kim's other preferred methods of execution include mortar and flamethrower. He is presumed to be behind the February 2017 assassination of his own half brother in Kuala Lumpur International Airport using VX nerve agent, which the UN classifies as a weapon of mass destruction.

So, of course, he also enjoys his atomic bomb chicken with the United States of America.

Let's take stock. North Korea is a national experiment in cultist brutality and insanity run by a psychopath who makes the average Eastern European commie dictator circa 1975 look like a choirboy and who has a terrible haircut. (At one point everyone else had to have his haircut, by the way. There is now a selection of state-approved styles.) And the United States is a prosperous and spectacularly wealthy nation with the world's biggest military by far that has, on balance (note, please, 'on balance') been a force for good in the world. Unfortunately it has in a lashing-out at its own political elite elected a wealthy businessman of doubtful talent and little political nuance as president. President Trump, in an apparent coincidence, also has terrible hair.

The signs are very, very not good.

In April 2017 Kim complained about Trump's 'maniacal military provocations'. Trump in return blustered that 'all options are on the table'. To the North Koreans, masters of 1940s high-communist hyperbole, this phrase must seem laughable. The thing about hyperbole, the linguistic version of going nuclear, is that all you have left is more of the same, so the North says stuff that is terrifying only if we take it seriously. And we're now getting to the point where we have to take it very seriously indeed because Kim's engineers have working nuclear bombs and working long-range ballistic missiles. Put the two together – which is complicated but they seem on track to do this ominously soon – and Kim, if he were having

'These days, the South Korean authorities let reptile media run the whole gamut of vituperation, hurting the dignity of the supreme leadership of the DPRK. This is an unpardonable, hideous provocation hurting the dignity of the supreme leadership of the DPRK and thrice-cursed crime which can be committed only by the confrontation maniacs.'

– KCNA, North Korea's state-run news agency, responding to reports that Kim had ordered the execution of his mistress and twelve other members of a pop band after they were found to have been appearing in pornographic movies, September 2013

a bad hair day, say, would be able to drop an atom bomb on Anchorage, Seattle or Los Angeles. The easier option, however, is much closer to home.

Pyongyang, the capital of North Korea, is less than 200 kilometres from its South Korean counterpart, Seoul. It's only 1,200 kilometres from Tokyo, a metropolis of 38 million people, the most populous in the world – and let's not forget the Japanese and Korean past if we're looking for some added motivation to target them (besides vicinity and self-destructive lunacy).

Here's the scary thing: in a nuclear showdown, the north would be obliterated by American weapons, but the Kims, including the current version, have all known this and yet they keep walking this particular path. In the original Cold War, due to human mistakes, technological errors and sheer goddamn happenstance, the world stood, without knowing it at the time, on the edge of a nuclear precipice on a dozen or so occasions. This despite the fact that the people in charge were, in fact, desperate to avoid war. In one instance there were literally three people arguing about pressing the button and two of them were *For. (See Robert Oppenheimer.)* If that happens now, the guys with their fingers on the trigger are Kim and Trump.

While the potential is globally less terrifying than that of a Soviet-American nuclear exchange, the consequences for the people of Japan and Korea are unimaginable: quite possibly the largest loss of life in a day in human history.* And those for the rest of the world are hugely

---

* Currently probably the Shaanxi earthquake in China, about 1,000 kilometres to the west of Korea, which killed an estimated 830,000 people on 23 January 1556. Second on the list is the Indian Ocean Tsunami of 26 December 2004, which killed at least 230,000 people.

unpredictable. There would be enormous economic fallout, with all the political ramifications that follow, and with enough nuclear weapons deployed there could even be effects on global weather patterns.

How do we fix this? It's hard to know and the tools at the hands of the US and other actively involved parties – South Korea, Japan, China and Russia mainly – are limited. The US, especially under Trump, is fond of 'shows of force', sending fighter squadrons and aircraft carrier task groups into the area whenever a rocket or bomb is tested. They've also tried cyber warfare which appears to have significantly, but not irreparably, slowed the pace of Kim's missile development; when you read of one of his Musudan missiles blowing up in flight, it's probably cyber sabotage. Otherwise, it's bog standard sanctions and bribery with food aid.

In a generally depressing article on the matter for *The Atlantic* in July 2017, author Mark Bowden outlined four strategic options for the Trump administration. 'Prevention' is a major pre-emptive military strike that eliminates North Korean leadership, its entire nuclear arsenal and the effectiveness of its military before the country gains the capacity to strike the US mainland. 'Turning the screws' is a more focused strike to cause significant damage to Kim's nuclear programme and make a point that the soft negotiations up to now have failed in making. 'Decapitation' is the assassination of Kim and his elite leadership, to be replaced by a more compliant regime. And 'Acceptance' involves continuing the anodyne negotiation tactics that have stuttered along to date and hoping that, once Kim has a nice stock of bombs and intercontinental missiles squirrelled away, everything will just work out okay, as it did in the Cold War.

In Bowden's estimation, every option is bad, if not terrible, and all could conceivably lead to nuclear war or a major military exchange – a second

> **'Unless Kim Jong-un is killed and replaced by someone better, or some miracle of diplomacy occurs, or some shattering peninsular conflict intervenes, North Korea will eventually build ICBMs armed with nuclear warheads.'**
>
> *– Mark Bowden, July 2017*

Korean War, which the North have been preparing for ever since the first one. Kim has the fourth largest standing army in the world at his disposal, and large supplies of chemical and biological weapons, so the latter option is only marginally more delightful than the former.

The North Korean regime seems to get madder in every generation of Kim. Decades of sanctions against the country and massive, generally positive geopolitical change in the region surrounding it have not changed a thing. It is left, we suppose somewhat hopelessly, up to the North Korean people to resolve this ongoing mess. At least a small percentage of them are indeed aware of the hell that is their lived experience.

Approximately two thousand of Kim's citizens manage to escape every year. Crossing the heavily militarised border with South Korea is not an option, so they flee into China, which will return them, if they're caught, to a dire fate of the re-education and labour camps for which the regime is famous: effectively a death sentence. Those who manage to make it 4,000 kilometres south through China, Vietnam and Laos to Bangkok are, in a great, under-reported humanitarian service, 'deported' by Thailand to South Korea, where they are taken to a place called Hanawon, the 'house of unity'. Here, the world as it is, not as it has been presented to them for their entire lives, is presented to them in what one might call a de-education camp of sorts. Interviews with those wide-eyed survivors make for difficult viewing. The extraordinary modernity of South Korea and the fate of those they love and have left behind leaves simply unimaginable scars. It is hard to conceive how such an abused people will ever have the strength to throw off the yoke of this contemptible family of fat little men, or how they will recover if they manage to do so. They will need to look South to have any hope.

So there it is. A terrifying reminder of the value of liberty and democracy. Two sets of people, essentially the same, with no major discernible cultural, ethnic or religious divisions, having taken two divergent paths: one North, the other South. If you're ever navel-gazing over the injustices of your sad life and the despicable state of your government – Trumpian or otherwise – you could do worse than spend a thought on North Korea, an entire nation subjugated by not one mad man, but three: father, son and holy grandson.

Leopold II

9 April 1835 – 17 December 1909

King of the Belgians 1865-1909; founder and owner
of the Congo Free State; merciless exploiter of central
Africa for personal gain at enormous human cost

LET'S NOT PREVARICATE HERE: colonialism in Africa was dirty and unpleasant work that involved the kind of violence and ghastliness that could put a fellow off his morning kedgeree. That's why European powers often liked to wash their hands of the administration of these colonies and hand them over to chartered companies, which could, among other things, wage wars, raise their own police forces, issue their own currencies and negotiate on behalf of the issuer with native chiefs. This reduced the treasury's exposure to risk and day-to-day administration while not limiting their usefulness in raising tax revenue. It was therefore the misfortune of swathes of Africa to be colonised by corporations such as the *Verenigde Oostindische Compagnie* (the VOC, or Dutch East India Company) and the British South Africa Company. And they really were prototypical corporates. The VOC, for example, was one of the first companies to offer shares in order to collectivise risk and reward among shareholders.

The Congo Free State, however, was different, because it was to become the largest estate owned by an individual person in the history of the world. Originally 'opened up' by the explorers Stanley and Livingstone, the vast expanse of the Congo Basin that would become the Congo Free State was agreed by the European powers at the 1885 Berlin Conference to be, vaguely, under the control of Belgium so that it might protect the natives from the rampant Zanzibari slave traders who had penetrated the region for centuries. The owner – the sole proprietor, they decided – was to be the king of the Belgians, Leopold II. To be clear, this wasn't a Belgian colony; it was private property – the world's only private colony. Into his personal ownership, then, Leopold was handed 2,600,000 square kilometres of Africa. He was the biggest landowner on earth.

If this sounds extraordinary, that's because it absolutely is. The Scramble for Africa is nothing if not aptly named. It was all done in a huge hurry at a time of bubbling tensions and puffed-up one-upmanship in Europe that would eventually explode into World War I (*see Gavrilo Princip*). As of 1870, indigenous leaders controlled about 90 percent of sub-Saharan Africa. Just 40 years later, by 1910, there was hardly a patch of the place not under the control, nominally at least, of imperial or colonial forces.

Folks didn't much like Leopold before his Congo crusade, an attitude that wouldn't change. Leopold's cousin Queen Victoria thought he was 'as unfit, idle and unpromising an heir apparent as ever was known'. British Prime Minister and novelist Benjamin Disraeli noted his undeniably impressive beak: 'such a nose as a young prince has in a fairy tale, who has been banned by a malignant fairy'. But as much as he inspired ire in those he encountered, he was cunning and ambitious. Persuading the powers in Berlin that his intentions in the Congo were humanitarian was an indication of this astuteness. Because they really weren't.

Leopold's great ambition was to match the colonial reach and power of the other European nations, but he was a late starter and he fretted terribly that his noble dreams might be jeopardised. There must have been frustration in the first few years after 1885 when his new property proved costly to maintain and bore little fruit. As an indication of the scale of the Arab slave trade in the region, consider that the private army Leopold raised there, the Force Publique, had to contend with, and ultimately routed, an army of more than 10,000 Arab traders in the Congo itself. This was supposedly Leopold's justification for being there: to end the slave trade and render

'I do not want to miss a good chance of getting us a slice of this magnificent African cake.'

– Leopold II, 1876

civilisation unto the benighted continent. But he was there, it turned out, solely for profit, which meant he would simply replace one evil with another.

Leopold wasn't interested in slaves as a commodity. He instead used labour as a form of taxation – for services that haven't been established to this day – essentially turning the Congolese into slaves on their own land. The initial focus was ivory, which was profitable but not enormously so. Then came rubber. Technological change in Europe and the United States, specifically the advance of the motorcar and the popularity of bicycles with tyres, resulted in the demand for natural rubber going through the roof. Leopold had found his market, and that's when he and his administrators embraced unimaginable cruelty on a scale we'll probably never fully know.

Leopold had invested a fortune into his African venture; it was time to reap the rewards. He had the Congo sliced up into various concessions, the largest of which he gave to himself. There was practically no judicial oversight and nobody asked or cared how these concessions were to be run; as a result, the concession holders and the Force Publique, made up principally of Congolese Africans reporting to Belgian officers, were the law. They simply impelled the Congolese to increase their rubber production, no matter the cost in human wellbeing. Standard operational procedure was for rubber traders to arrive in a village, kidnap the women and children and send the men into the jungle to harvest rubber. If the men failed to meet their targets, the traders would start torturing the children. Eventually they would just execute them. For a real sense of the brutality and horror that overwhelmed this time in the Congo there is no better place to go than Joseph Conrad's *Heart of Darkness* – a more succinctly and accurately titled work of literature is yet to be published. (Conrad had worked on a steamer on the Congo River in the early 1890s. He knew his subject.)

The effects of Leopold's approach still evoke *the horror* today. Many of the women and children held in captivity starved to death. The men, in the jungles and away from sources of food and safety, were often worked to illness or death themselves. To avoid Leopold's press gangs, entire villages decamped into the jungles and the bush, but with almost the same result: dire consequences for health, food and security. Hundreds of thousands died in the jungles. Additionally, tens – possibly hundreds – of thousands were executed in various, ultimately unsuccessful, rebellions against the 20,000-strong Force Publique. A particularly grisly practice was the use of amputations, which remains a common terror tool in the region to this day. Senior administrators wanted to see evidence that bullets were being used to kill people, not animals for food. As recorded in *Encyclopaedia Britannica*:

> To prove that he had not wasted bullets – or, worse yet, saved them for use in a mutiny – for each bullet expended, a Congolese soldier of the Force Publique had to present to his white officer the severed hand of a rebel killed. Baskets of severed hands thus resulted from expeditions against rebels. If a soldier fired at someone and missed, or used a bullet to shoot game, he then sometimes cut off the hand of a living victim to be able to show it to his officer.

As awful as these atrocities were, executions and deaths caused by amputations were only a small percentage of the carnage wrought in the Congo. Rampaging diseases brought in by the colonists or exacerbated by their practices went completely unchecked, having an impact not dissimilar to that the South American native people suffered under the *conquistadors*. African sleeping sickness, swine flu, dysentery and smallpox swept through native populations, wiping them out in enormous numbers.

The scale, in terms of outright numbers, is not something we will ever know – and statistics like these are always political. There are those who would have Leopold morally equated with Adolf Hitler. But it seems that the Congolese disaster should technically not be considered genocide because it was not intended as a deliberate eradication of a people; it was simply a gross and barbaric exploitation of those people and their surrounds by the most brutal and savagely extractive colonising force the world has ever known. The death toll has been estimated at anywhere between one and fifteen million, with some sources simply explaining that half the native population was killed.

When stories emanating from missionaries eventually began to circulate, even the Brits – who were causing their own problems elsewhere in Africa – were appalled. Mark Twain and Arthur Conan-Doyle, among others, wrote furiously about what was happening, and Conrad published *Heart of Darkness*, originally as a serial, in 1899. Eventually, in 1908, Leopold was forced to allow the country of which he was king, Belgium, to annex the Congo. Leopold was furious, and had the Congo Free State archive set alight. 'They do not have the right to know what I did there,' he said bitterly of his Parliament's decision. Belgium paid more than 215 million francs for this pleasure, a gargantuan sum of money at the time, 50 million of which

'Anything approaching the change that came over his features I have never seen before, and hope never to see again. Oh, I wasn't touched. I was fascinated. It was as though a veil had been rent. I saw on that ivory face the expression of sombre pride, of ruthless power, of craven terror – of an intense and hopeless despair. Did he live his life again in every detail of desire, temptation, and surrender during that supreme moment of complete knowledge? He cried in a whisper at some image, at some vision – he cried out twice, a cry that was no more than a breath: "The horror! The horror!"'

The ivory trader Kurtz considering the extent of his own evil, and that of African imperialism in central Africa, in his dying words, from Heart of Darkness *by Joseph Conrad*

went to Leopold's various pet development projects around Brussels, and a further 50 million of which went directly to the king. Leopold died the following year at Christmas, and Belgians at last had the opportunity to boo his funeral cortege, which they did.

For our purposes, a review of distress-causing personalities in the modern age, Leopold stands (as does Rhodes later) at the hazy end of our statute of limitations, as earlier defined. He may well have escaped inclusion on a technicality. But as the worst of the colonists, he gains his place here, a man whose legacy has long reverberated throughout the Congo and Zaire and the DRC, different names for the same place in Africa that has seen recurring horrific violence in the century since his death.

Leopold never actually ventured into Africa himself and yet he was intent on draining its very life force in the pursuit of profit and vanity. His version of colonialism was, in some ways at least, the most honest. Unlike where the British held sway, for example, there was no pretence about God or religion, no development agenda, no public works medical outreach, no attempt to build a great nation under an imperial flag – not even the most racist, patrician attempts at bringing 'civilisation'. But even in his own time Leopold was regarded with grave contempt. His creation was a savage extractive machine that regarded the Congolese as unworthy even of genocide. What a vile and sadly influential man he turned out to be.

See Idi Amin and Cecil John Rhodes.

Bernie Madoff

b. 29 April 1938

*Pioneering stockbroker and investor; past chairman
of the NASDAQ; perpetrator of the largest fraud by
an individual and largest pyramid scheme in history;
hate figure of Wall Street banksterism*

HOW MUCH IS RICH ENOUGH? The answer, of course, is different for everyone. Us? If money were no object we'd probably go for a nice house in town, a holiday property somewhere, security for the kids' future, good holidays in business class, and a small collection of cars for various purposes. And a whisky collection – to go with the wine collection obviously. Maybe some first-edition books, too. Not much more than that, really.*

Sounds good, doesn't it? Certainly, this would be the life of a wealthy person, a millionaire in any currency, and no doubt in the much-maligned one-percenter bracket. It's not that we live under some kind of Spartan rock here. It's nice to have nice things. But the pathological desire of certain men – usually men – to be rich way beyond the point that they and those near them are looked after in comfort for life, to be rich for the sake of richness alone, is hard to fathom and, let's be straight, kind of revolting.

Still, some people are just programmed that way. Wealth isn't a crime and neither should it be, because wealth doesn't have to come at a cost to your fellow man. Economists will tell you that it is possible to be spectacularly rich and have harmed nobody; indeed, that individual wealth generation makes

---

* In 2010 Nobel Prize-winning psychologist Daniel Kahneman and economist Angus Deaton calculated the average annual income per US household above which further income makes no difference to happiness; specifically 'emotional wellbeing' on a daily basis. The magic number was $75,000 – closer to $85,000 in 2018. It varies by state and, naturally, personal needs.

others wealthier too. That's Adam Smith for you. It is, however, possible to get rich at the considerable expense of other people, and those who do it are the scum of the earth, the poster boys for the dismantling of the whole capitalist system – people who take advantage of those who play by the rules with the inevitable end result of impoverishing them.

People like Bernie Madoff.

Madoff isn't included here because he's a brigand, a housebreaker, a pickpocket or any other low-grade miscreant who scaled the ramparts of the good Castle Capital and broke in through a bathroom window. He's here because he was a full-on financial courtier, a part of the system, a malignant growth in the belly of a complex, often-misunderstood machine. He was a man whose crimes showed for all to see that this was a system that wasn't policing itself properly and that as long as everyone at the top was getting ever richer, warnings would be ignored – even if some people would be impoverished for life as a result of it.

One of the saddest things about this story is just how good it should have all been. In 1960 Bernard Madoff, the New York grandson of poor Jewish immigrants, started a little trading company called Bernard L Madoff Investment Securities LLC with $5,000 saved from his sprinkler-installation business and a loan of $50,000 from his father-in-law, a popular accountant, who also punted business the firm's way from friends and family. The company traded penny stocks and, over time, was influential in the pioneering use of computer technology to disseminate its quotes, the technology that would eventually turn into the National Association of Securities Dealers Automated Quotations stock exchange, otherwise known as the NASDAQ – which Madoff helped start. Indeed, Madoff would go on to be the NASDAQ's non-executive chairman.

This was important work, heady stuff – the American Dream writ large! But while Madoff Securities had made a great name for itself as a technical trading firm, there was another part of the company, kept separate on its own floor, where employees were encouraged to keep quiet about who they worked for and what they did. This division handled asset management, and over the course of at least 30 years it perpetuated the greatest securities fraud in the history of the United States, and probably the world.

In some ways what Madoff did was straightforward. It was, simply put, a gigantic, $65-billion decades-long Ponzi or pyramid scheme, in which investors are promised good returns which are paid out, when they're called for, from the incoming funds from new investors – the change going to those operating the scam. Named for the Italian-born swindler Charles Ponzi, these rackets tend to fall apart sooner rather than later because the people running them can't maintain the flow of new investors. The moment things start looking a bit edgy and a small number of investors ask for not only their returns but their capital back too, the whole thing collapses. Ponzi himself promised Canadian and US investors inordinately high profits by buying discounted international postal-reply coupons abroad and redeeming them in the United States at face value, but managed to hold out for just seven months, from January to August 1920, before it all came crashing down. He was convicted and sentenced by November.

But Madoff? Well, Madoff was different.

To start, his brokerage business was not only legitimate, but also highly regarded. Moreover, he was wily. He chose to operate mainly with charities, which had different rules and softer requirements in terms of mandated payouts. And he sat on the board of National Association of Securities Dealers and advised the United States Securities and Exchange Commission (SEC), the institution that regulates the country's securities industry and enforces its laws. The SEC sent its interns to Madoff Securities for training, for heaven's sake – the equivalent of the fox helping to set the fox traps.

In short, Madoff's qualifications and financial skills, unlike the usual shysters and confidence tricksters, were entirely real. His deception was the investment fraud equivalent of a straight-A student studying hard for his exams and then still using crib notes simply because he'd worked out a neat system – and, fox that he is, he couldn't help himself.

Madoff also avoided the usual Ponzi temptation of offering wildly unlikely profits with some kind of miracle formula. He just offered good, steady returns that would beat the market, usually around 10 percent. And if anyone ever asked for their money, they'd get it, mainly because most people stayed invested, enjoying the power of compound interest – even if it only existed in their imaginations and the fantasy world of Bernie Madoff.

Madoff felt no shame in working his Jewish heritage, which when it tends towards the illegal is known as affinity fraud: when people are taken in by people from their own ethnicity or community. Add this to the mysteriously successful sense of exclusivity – investors were advised not to announce their privileged status as Madoff investors – and people and organisations were sucked in, billions of dollars at a time.

'He moved in some of the best social circles in New York. He worked the best country clubs. He was utterly charming. He was a master at meeting people and creating this aura. People looked at him as a superhero. People didn't want to know what he was doing. If it's too good to be true, it isn't true. But people didn't care. They were greedy.'

– a widely quoted 2008 estimation of Madoff from Jerry Reisman, lawyer for investors who lost a combined $150 million

Those taken in by Madoff have struggled to explain how brilliantly persuasive he was. Writing in *The Atlantic* about Madoff some years later, two prosecutors from the time, Gordon Mehler and Larry Krantz, supplied this vignette of how impressive he was:

> Two years before his scheme collapsed, Madoff was subpoenaed to testify before regulators. Disarmingly, he showed up at the SEC without any lawyers, and proceeded to thread his way through a minefield of questions from its attorneys, discoursing with great élan on a hopelessly convoluted investment model, one he called "MA.206", that didn't even exist. He assured the regulators that he obeyed all SEC rules, because of course anyone who didn't would quickly be caught. It was a stellar performance that apparently captivated the SEC lawyers, who asked few follow-up questions.

The confidence trick that kept it all going for so long is still, after years of review, astounding. During his trial Madoff admitted that he hadn't traded since the 1990s, and some prosecutors believe he had never actually traded at all, making it the crudest imaginable Ponzi scheme. He'd just sat there taking the money.

In the end, it took the 2007/8 financial crisis, a once-in-an-era receding of the tide, to reveal Madoff as the most naked of financial investors. To cover their losses elsewhere, his clients asked for their money back – a lot of it – and he couldn't cough up. In December 2008 he admitted to his sons that it was all 'just one big lie', and the three-decade fraud was revealed.

While you may harbour an irritating and persistent sense of admiration for a man who played the system so very thoroughly and for so very long, this isn't a movie*. This isn't a meme. The victims were very real indeed.

First, there's the scale of it all. The month before it all came to a head, in November 2008, Madoff wrote to his investors to update them on the value of their investments. All in, the scheme was worth, according to Madoff, just under $65 billion. David Sheehan, the liquidator's chief counsel, agreed on *60 Minutes* that this was a 'total lie'. At the time, Sheehan said he reckoned Madoff had taken $36 billion in 'investments' and that of that around $18 billion was missing.

Now it's a supposedly mitigating fact of history that more than half of Madoff's investors got out more than they put in – but two points here. First, these were investments designed mostly to provide for a comfortable retirement, so getting your capital back perhaps with a bit of change was a disaster in itself. Second, for every dollar over their investment anyone got back, somebody else was considerably more than a dollar short. Some clients lost nearly everything they'd invested, having invested almost everything they had with Madoff. All in, liquidators and investigators were able to recover $11 billion of the missing money, a sterling effort, which included the yacht and luxury properties belonging to Madoff and his wife Ruth. And yet more than $6 billion had disappeared.

Reading through the list of investors it seems impossible that the likes of HSBC, BNP Paribas and the Royal Bank of Scotland were able to fall into the Madoff web, but indeed they did. There were also the Hollywood celebrities: Steven Spielberg, Kevin Bacon and Kyra Sedgwick, John Malkovich and others. The realisation comes further down the list when you start to see charity after charity along with various family trusts, all with far smaller exposure in dollar terms than the big banks and clients, but with less to lose. As humiliating as it may have been, many of Madoff's victims could handle the hit; the real tragedy was in those smaller numbers.

There have, it appears, been four related suicides. Most famously, French aristocrat and money manager René-Thierry de la Villehuchet killed himself two weeks after the fraud emerged, his hedge fund having lost around $1.5 billion. And one of Madoff's own sons, Mark, hanged himself in 2010. (Madoff claims that neither of his sons was complicit.) This and lives

---

* Though it has been made into a movie and a mini-series, respectively *The Wizard of Lies* with Robert de Niro (2017) and *Madoff* with Richard Dreyfuss. There is also a feature-length documentary, *Chasing Madoff* (2010).

> **'I certainly wouldn't invest in the stock market. I never believed in it. Most people lose money because of the emotional difficulty involved.'**
> - Bernie Madoff, 2014, interview with Politico Magazine

unfulfilled, promises not kept and plans never acted out, universities never attended and all the immeasurable good this money would have done but didn't, because of what Madoff did, is the real tragedy. Let's not forget that.

But a broader point also remains. During his trial, Madoff marvelled at the incompetence of the SEC. He said he was amazed by an SEC 'blowhard' investigator who acted like 'Lieutenant Columbo'. And it turns out the SEC just didn't do its job properly.

Madoff himself has confirmed he should have been caught at least five years earlier, in 2003, had its investigators performed the most elementary checks. 'I was astonished,' he said. The SEC was also approached at least four times over several years and given a detailed 17-page tip-off by investigator Harry Markopolos, titled 'The world's largest hedge fund is a fraud' – but it turned out that the commission didn't investigate investment management cases at all, as a matter of habit. There appears to have been no other way to explain this than as unspoken policy. SEC whistle-blower Kathleen Furey was prominent in uncovering this disturbing reality, having been told flat by her boss that 'we do not do IM [investment management] cases'.

In a brilliant piece for *Rolling Stone* magazine, author Matt Taibbi described the SEC's total disinterest in pursuing investment management complaints as at best 'aggressively clueless', a euphemism so perfectly polished we can see our admiring smiles in the reflection, and as part of a 'broadening canvas of dysfunction and incompetence'. *Forbes*, equally, didn't pull its punches about the total failure of the SEC: 'Frankly it is hard to find a similarly lamentable instance of regulatory malfunction outside the Third World,' it concluded.

It's perhaps worth bearing in mind at this point that the first part of the SEC's stated 'three-part mission' is 'protect investors'. (The others are 'maintain fair, orderly, and efficient markets' and 'facilitate capital formation' – three fails, we'd say.)

It is this kind of thing that makes ordinary people sense that the world is stacked against them, that banks and financiers are evil, that capitalism is failing. It's already an exclusive, exclusionary place. The language of Wall Street and the global financial markets is utterly, deliberately unfathomable, and those who are masters of the language seem to the rest of us to be masters of our financial fate.

It is inevitable that people will be incandescent about this kind of thing, and that some will call into question the fairness of the entire system, even equating it with Madoff and his fraudulent ilk. According to this righteous anger there is good cause to tear it down entirely.

They're wrong, though. It is the SEC that failed. There will always be Madoffs and Ponzis and other thieves, large and small. That, sadly, is human nature. The whole sorry Madoff tale ought to stand as a case study on the necessity of proper regulation, independent overseers of the regulators from outside the world of the markets, and policing in markets generally. Any finance sharks who can't see as much – and of course still think they're the smartest guys in the room – need that notion stitched into their pinstriped bankster suits.

We cannot in one book say total government inevitably ends up in the gulag – as we will when we discuss Stalin and Lenin – and not, equally, warn that total capital inevitably ends up in all-consuming Ponzi schemes, industrial-scale theft and poverty. Both are true.

Madoff, by the way, got a 150-year sentence and will die behind bars. Nobody from the SEC was charged, let alone lost their job. Justice, then, was only partially served.

'Experience has taught us that material wants know no natural bounds, they will expand without end unless we consciously restrain them. Capitalism rests precisely on this endless expansion of wants. That is why, for all of its success, it remains so unloved. It has given us wealth beyond measure, but has taken away the chief benefit of wealth: the consciousness of having enough.'

– extract from *How Much Is Enough?* by Robert and Edward Skidelsky

Mao Zedong

26 December 1893 – 9 September 1976

Leader of China 1949-1976; communist tyrant; history's most effective mass killer; cultural vandal; China's greatest tragedy

MAO ZEDONG KILLED MORE PEOPLE than anyone else in history, and yet he is not universally loathed in the country to which he laid waste, China. To some, this fact – and the very obvious success and wealth that China has begun to enjoy in recent years – is used to suggest that what China went though was a 'process', a necessary cleansing of old ideas and structures, and only through this process has this amazing country's wealth and potential been unlocked. This is thinking so evil it cannot be left unaddressed, because if a 'process' also requires you to murder as many as 70-million people (yes, this is a credible estimate), then it must surely be worth checking whether anything else might have worked, such as, for example, not murdering them and democracy.

China's enormous wealth of late, of course, has very little to do with communism. In fact, it has everything to do with the wholesale abandonment of it in everything but name. The country is still governed by the Communist Party of China (CPC), as established by Mao, but capitalism roams free. Mao himself would surely have been spinning in his grave when in 2008 the CPC announced that it was ridding itself of the last vestiges of agrarian Marxism as imposed under Mao: farm collectivisation was swept away, and 193-million farmers were allowed to sell up their five-acre plots and use the money for something else. In other words, they were given title, the right to property – the simple idea that what's yours is yours to do with as you wish. This is the beating heart of liberty and capitalism, and China's garish and blingtastic embrace of consumerist ostentation in the 21st century would appear to exist almost as a deliberate mockery of everything Mao stood for.

As so often appears to be the case with mass-murdering tyrants, Mao grew up comfortably in a rural part of China and was radicalised at university in Beijing, where he was looked down upon by other students because of his country-bumpkin Hunanese accent. It was 1919 and the Russian Revolution had breathed Marxist excitement into the lives of young men such as Mao all around the world.

Mao's CPC would proclaim the People's Republic of China in October of 1949 after a brutal power struggle with Chinese nationalists that had been ongoing since the 1920s. This was a conflict that claimed his wife, among many others, and appears to have inured Mao to the suffering of his fellow man. Following the Japanese defeat and withdrawal at the end of World War II, China's civil war proper raged from 1945 to 1949, in which time China's competing parties fought as proxies for the Soviets and Americans, a pattern that would be repeated across so much of the Third World in years to come. Stalin's Soviets supported Mao's communists while Truman's Americans supported Chiang Kai-Shek's nationalists. In this instance the communists were victorious. Chiang Kai-Shek retreated to the island of Taiwan, along with 600,000 troops, and formed the Republic of China, and the two sides have been snarling at each other ever since.

Mao was, for a communist mass murderer, refreshingly honest. Violence and death were to him a necessary and important part of revolution.

One of Mao's first noteworthy moves was to send a supposed 'volunteer army' – distinct from the People's Liberation Army so as to avoid official war with the United States – to prop up the North Koreans in the war with South Korea, another Soviet-American proxy conflict. The north had been in retreat before Mao's intervention, so his role here to some extent confers on him a certain amount of responsibility for what the Kim dynasty has got up to in Pyongyang ever since. As we saw only three entries ago, this is an enduring legacy of great tragedy, and yet even the sorry tale of North Korea, in terms of scale, is small beer compared to what Mao wrought on China in the 1950s and 1960s.

It started, as it must with all good violent revolutions once the war has been won, with a 'campaign to suppress counter-revolutionaries'. Yes, that's actually what they called it.

> 'Revolution is not a dinner party, nor an essay, nor a painting, nor a piece of embroidery; it cannot be so refined, so leisurely and gentle, so temperate, kind, courteous, restrained and magnanimous. A revolution is an insurrection, an act of violence by which one class overthrows another.'
>
> – Mao

This is the kind of typically communist language that used to keep Orwell up at night, because it doesn't really go into too much detail as to what constitutes a 'counter-revolutionary' and what might be done to 'suppress' them. Hells bells it's easy to say – isn't it – in the heat of a political meeting in which you want to prove your devotion to the revolutionary cause, but what does it actually entail?

It turns out that 'suppressing counter-revolutionaries' means, in clearer language, murdering a couple of million people, any 'spies' or 'bandits' with tentative links to the old nationalist regime. Now, all commies love a production quota and a five-year plan, and so it was that Mao personally introduced killing quotas, requesting that once the number of executions reached one in 1,000 in rural areas and one in 2,000 in urban areas, the executions stop, lest it give the impression that the regime was perchance killing too many people.

Mao's 'humanitarian concern' that his thugs might be overdoing things was disastrous in its own absurd way because, inevitably, maximum killing quotas very quickly became interpreted as minimum 'production targets' for ambitious young communists on the make. In a big city such as Shanghai, with a population then of around four million, 2,000 executions were required to hit the killing quota. The result: on calculating that they had only disposed of 1,700, off they went to find another 300 souls for a mass public execution in a local stadium. Bad luck if you were in the wrong place at the wrong time.

In addition to the executions of business owners, intellectuals whose commitment to the revolution wasn't clear enough, and those who had worked for Western companies, a good two or so million folks were rounded up and sent off for 'reform through labour'. For many that was just as much of a death sentence.

In the countryside it was worse. Mao insisted that it was the duty and pleasure of the poor peasants to take part in the destruction of the property-owning classes and the wealthy peasants. Work teams created a frenzy in rural China, engaging entire villages in 'speak bitterness' accusations and trials. After such public humiliations, members of this class were executed – including babies, children and the elderly. Most were simply clubbed to death by a mob; others were shot, stoned or thrown down the well. Those who could fled. This was, in its most brutal form, 'classicide', a word that had to be coined in light of such 20th century horrors.

Adding fuel to the fire, Mao's official policy of 'not correcting excesses prematurely' allowed mobs to roam almost completely free to murder anyone with whom they had a historic grievance.

In this way more than two-fifths of China's land was redistributed to once-landless peasants, the consequences of which would be felt within time, but with immediate and astounding political success. The old order was destroyed, humiliated and, in so very many cases, murdered. A new regime of working-class cadres ruled the countryside, and it would be fiercely loyal to the communist regime.

Mao never wasted any time denying that mass murder was taking place, given that in his mind it was just and reasonable. He may have differed on the scale of it – by his account 'only' 700,000 landlords and 800,000 counter-revolutionaries died during the early 1950s – but he never made any bones about it, if you'll excuse the phrase. He was, however, savvy enough to use the historical opportunity presented by the Korean War, for instance, as the necessary background noise to mask what he was up to back home. As foreign attention was diverted to the Korean Peninsula – a process that was drawn out far longer than it would have been without the involvement of Mao's 'volunteer army' – he could quietly do the dirty work of wiping out all opposition to the revolution. The war, quite conveniently, also gave the Chinese propaganda machine an enemy against whom they might foment unity and anger.

'You'd better have less conscience. Some of our comrades have too much mercy, not enough brutality, which means that they are not so Marxist. On this matter, we indeed have no conscience! Marxism is that brutal.'

– Mao

Mao was obsessed with creating a unique Chinese version of communism that compared well against the Soviet Union. He wanted industrial output to outclass the United States and Britain, and so he became intent on taking China on an industrial adventure. By mobilising the sheer size of the country's population, he reckoned, he could transform China from being an agrarian society into a leading industrial power within a few years. This was a vaguely plausible theory in that it could be achieved with sensible policy decisions over the course of many years – as has come to fruition in recent decades – but under strict communist principles it was, it goes without saying, doomed to farce and failure.

This was Mao's second Five-Year Plan, which he called the Great Leap Forward, quite naturally therefore condemning it to become very much the opposite of that, a leap backwards with catastrophic results. It began in the wake of his fury at Khruschev's denunciation of Stalinism, and in full knowledge of all the good reasons why this was done: the mass killings and torture, the failure of Soviet agriculture, and so on. Starting in 1958, the country would industrialise and ramp up its agricultural production using what Mao would no doubt have described as his glorious worker-peasants, but which we would now call forced labour. Mao doubled down on collectivisation, creating 25,000 massive people's communes across the country. In the process, there was a mass destruction of property: at least 30 percent of houses were reduced to rubble in search of raw materials. Those who complained about the madness of it all didn't last long.

The story of Chinese steel illustrated the extent of the absurdity. Mao wanted production doubled in a single year, where necessary through the use of primitive backyard smelters. He distrusted experts, preferring the counsel of cranks and fantasists, and he knew nothing of metallurgy; nonetheless, he imposed catastrophic regulations. In order to meet absolutely non-negotiable targets, households melted down their woks, pots and pans, garden equipment, hair clips and doorknobs. What they produced was iron, enormous quantities of it utterly useless.

Just as officials started requisitioning ever-increasing proportions of the harvest for Mao's vast army of industrial workers, so the country began running out of food. Contributing factors were the over-reporting of food production by ambitious petty bureaucrats and the absolutely unsurprising failure of the collectivised farms. It also didn't help that many of those industrial workers were, until recently, productive farmers. The problem was then exacerbated by Mao's ignorance of agriculture and inversely proportional assuredness that he had an ingenious and inspired solution. The Chinese had been farming rice for around ten thousand years and were therefore quite competent in this skill; Mao, however, knew better. Peasant farmers were ordered to plant their seeds deeper and closer together so that some kind of cereal-esque class solidarity would cause their rice to grow stronger and more abundantly. It was obvious madness and the results were disastrous, though no-one was allowed to say as much.

A lunatic crusade against sparrows as part of the 'Four Pests Campaign' made matters worse. Parties of workers were requisitioned as sparrow-chasers, tasked with running around farmlands banging pots and pans and forcing any sparrows in the area to fly until they fell from exhaustion and could be killed. These tactics proved, perhaps surprisingly, to be effective, and the birds were pushed close to extinction in China. But the overall strategy was idiotic. Eradicating rats, cockroaches and flies made sense, but the extermination of sparrows allowed far more destructive pests to thrive: plagues of locusts and grasshoppers ate millions of tons of grain.

The country's food crisis was not helped by a drought in parts of China, but for Mao this would not be sufficient excuse to hide behind. In subsequent years, senior government officials felt emboldened enough to apportion 70 percent of the blame for the starvation that followed to government (Mao's) policy and 30 percent to natural disaster. And it was starvation on scales never before or again encountered in the history of mankind.

It is conservatively estimated that 30 million people starved to death in China's great famine. Historian Frank Dikötter believes that 'at least 45 million people died unnecessarily between 1958 and 1962', and goes on to propose a death toll of 60 million. Corpses littered the countryside unmolested by dogs or wild animals because, of course, they had all been eaten.

'If we were to add up all the landlords, rich peasants, counter-revolutionaries, bad elements and rightists, their number would reach thirty million... Of our total population of 600 million people, these thirty million are only one out of twenty. So what is there to be afraid of? ... We have so many people. We can afford to lose a few. What difference does it make?'

– Mao

The moral culpability of this tragedy was highlighted by Mao's inhumane and disconcertingly Stalinist decision to bolster China's international image while his countrymen were dying like sparrows, by exporting grain: more than four million tons of the stuff in 1959 alone.

All the while, Mao's endless revolution rolled on. The purges, beatings, executions and terror never stopped, and as many as three-million people may have committed suicide. The disaster that was the famine and the economic catastrophe that was the Great Leap Forward did, however, reduce Mao's prestige and standing within the party. He was forced by moderate elements to resign as leader in 1959 and hand over control of economic policy to a group of pragmatists, which saw the beginning of a period of high-stakes wrangling for control within the party.

It is hard to imagine the terror of living in China in these times, and it was into this environment of fear and death that Mao launched his next, extraordinarily vile campaign in 1966: the Cultural Revolution. Mao's motivation in this instance is variously recorded as being a result of concern that party functionaries were becoming increasingly detached from the life of the peasants or out of rage at those who had outmanoeuvred him and challenged him in 1959. Equally, he feared that the pragmatists, who for a brief period liberalised policy in order to stem the starvation, had abandoned strict Maoism and were allowing the revival of capitalist and bourgeois behaviours. Mao had over the years become a belligerent and heartless dictator, so the more likely explanation, it seems, is that he feared for his reputation. Having seen what Khrushchev had done for the name of Stalin, he would have seen the potential for the new head of state, Liu Shaoqi, to do the same.

In any case, Maoism's great comeback took the shape of a kind of rolling revolution in which youth gangs called Red Guards promoted the God-like personality cult of Mao and policed a strict interpretation of his vision for China. They carried his famous little red book – formerly titled *Quotations From Chairman Mao Tse-tung** – and put their youthful certainty and vigour into their work. This is how he would protect his legacy and impose his grand utopianism at all costs.

---

* Mao's Little Red Book is probably the second most printed book of all time, after the Bible. Credible estimates suggest that more than a billion copies have been distributed, possibly even several billion.

> 'When there is not enough to eat, people starve to death. It is better to let half of the people die so that the other half can eat their fill.'
>
> – *Mao Zedong*

A decade of mind-boggling violence ensued, creating economic and social chaos that historians have struggled to make sense of ever since. Warning that the party had been infiltrated by counter-revolutionary 'revisionists' who were plotting to create a 'dictatorship of the bourgeoisie', the Red Guards were summoned by the official mouthpiece of the party, the *Peking Review*. By August 1966 the bloodletting was in full swing, with the Guards ordered to attack the 'four olds': old ideas, old customs, old habits and old culture. They attacked people for wearing 'bourgeois' attire. They murdered intellectuals and party officials, or harried them into suicide. They shut down schools, universities, libraries, temples, shops and private homes. They ransacked and destroyed shrines and grave sites.

The impunity led other workers to join the fray to settle scores – and after the Great Leap Forward and the scale of the death toll there were scores aplenty. China fell into a de facto state of civil war in which there were no clear sides but enemies everywhere. There was a campaign of mass killing and industrial-scale torture in Tibet, a nation that saw its cultural history almost completely wiped out. Reports from various parts of China would later emerge of mass murder and people resorting to cannibalism.

Throughout the country the damage to China's ancient and impressive cultural fabric was incalculable. Artefacts, relics and written works of staggering cultural value were lost forever. Books were burned, Buddhist statues were smashed and the bones of long-dead princes and emperors were dug up and desecrated. It was an attempt to wipe out history as much as define a new future. And all the while the death toll was, as usual, appalling – another few million to add to the roster, and probably 100 million oppressed or attacked in some way.

By late 1968 Mao realised he'd created yet more chaos and ordered his Red Guards to be 'rusticated': sent to the countryside for 're-education' by peasants, yet another harebrained scheme with dire ends. The army was brought in to restore order, which unleashed another level of violence onto the country and essentially transformed it into a military dictatorship.

In the end, the typically communist obsession with death and cultural destruction was so widespread and damaging that, rather ironically, it took down Maoism with it too. Mao's final tragic experiment spluttered to an end and the old man was gently sidelined in the early 1970s.

Mao was a monster whose personal interactions and behaviours were at times as instructive as the great political gestures that affected those over whom he ruled. He was a typical narcissist: grandiose, desperate for admiration and attention, and without a trace of empathy – the archetypal tyrant. As his people suffered, he lived in kingly comfort, as you would expect. But he had no friends and ruined all family and personal relationships. For many years his closest confidant was his personal physician, Li Zhisui, who eventually came to despise him. Mao was, as described in Li's book *The Private Life of Chairman Mao*, 'devoid of human feeling, incapable of love, friendship, or warmth'. An insecure cliché, he was obsessed with sleeping with as many young women as possible, and was riddled with venereal disease as a result. He refused to brush his teeth and he hated washing; at one point he was rumoured not to have bathed for 25 years. He manipulated absolutely everyone he encountered, and revelled, for instance, in tormenting his longtime prime minister Zhou Enlai, to such a degree that he eventually refused his cancer treatment in that hope that Zhou would die before him. He did. Eventually, in September 1976, to his country's great benefit, Mao went too. He was 82.

Those who still support Mao today note that he reformed China's iniquitous feudal-style land ownership, unified China and created its Communist Party, which still rules the one-party state. This is true, and explains why the party has a conflicted relationship with its founder. It still encourages the swirling myth of him as the father of the People's China but, almost satirically, never mentions the Great Leap Forward, the famine or the Cultural Revolution. Deng Xiaoping, who put his country on the path to economic reform in the late 1970s and '80s with a sane (and really quite simple) policy overhaul,

> '[T] he dream of a better world holds out such a compelling attraction that some will become determined to kill everyone who stands in the way of its realization.'
>
> *– political scientist Alan Wolfe*[1]

> ## 'Kill, kill, kill! All I hear is this sound in my ears! Why are human beings so evil? Why so cruel?'
>
> *– Yang Kaihui, Mao's wife, writing to him in an unsent letter. She was executed by rivals of the CPC in 1930*

even attempted to quantify this position with a face-saving sound byte: Mao was 70 percent good and 30 percent bad, according to the official line (a neat inversion of the great famine responsibility).

We are, however, not the Communist Party of China, so let's not beat around the bush: Mao was one of the big bastards of history. He presided – knowingly and overtly acknowledging that it was all happening – over the deaths of somewhere between 40 and 70 million people. That we can have a plausible margin of error of 30 million, about 200 Hiroshimas, says rather a lot, not just about the extent of the tragedy, but also about the chaos and neglect that was cast over an entire country, one-quarter of the planet's population.

Mao's ideological crusade also ravaged the culture and collective wisdom of a society that had, for most of recorded history, been a focal point of human development. There are those who would argue that his shaking of the Chinese socio-economic tree laid the groundwork for China's rise in the last quarter of the 20th century, which continues apace today. We find this an ignoble and callous assessment, a bit like saying the Asian tsunami of 2004 was necessary for the redevelopment of Thai beachside resorts. Which is to say, they could have done it anyway, just without all the death and human misery.

What an extraordinary tragedy Mao was. Today, four decades after his death, he stands as a warning to all of us about the perils of unrestrained ideology and a veritable advertisement for the safety net of democracy.

'No famine has ever taken place in the history of the world in a functioning democracy,' explained the Indian writer Amartya Sen in his book *Development As Freedom*. Indeed. And a human tragedy as great as Mao's famine, and all that came with it, could take place only under a tyranny of complete and absolute indifference.

Diego Maradona

b. 30 October 1960

Greatest footballer of all time*; possessor of 'the Hand of God'; drug user, cheat and overindulged prima donna; harbinger of the modern footballer

*Well, maybe

IN ONE SHORT SENTENCE, what's your take on Diego Maradona?

If you're a fan you'll likely answer something along the lines of: *Argentinian footballing legend and scorer of the greatest goal ever.*

And if you don't like the guy it could be, roughly: *Cheat, drug fiend, fat little dwarf with bad hair.*

So, yes, the legacy of Maradona is a contested one.

Let us, however, imagine for a moment that we have no interest in who won the Falklands War and add an objective filter to this query. Then a viable answer might be: *Troubled and controversial sporting genius – a global superstar who has lived a roller-coaster life.*

Maradona's career is – conveniently, for our purposes – encapsulated in one unforgettable game, the 1986 World Cup quarterfinal between Argentina and England, played in front of 115,000 spectators at the Estadio Azteca in Mexico City in June 1986. Indeed, we can narrow things down to a mere five minutes of play in that particular game which epitomises the man's wizardry, in the best and worst sense of the word. After a goalless first half, two moments of Maradona magic would see Argentina take an unassailable 2-0 lead and live forever in the memories of those who saw them, either as glorious dream or shameful nightmare.

In the 51st minute of the game Maradona sets off on a typical penetrating run from about 40 metres out. Looking for a quick one-two, he nudges a pass towards his striker Jorge Valdano as he approaches the box, which is intercepted by England's Steve Hodge who in turn miscues his clearance kick, looping the ball back towards his goal. Maradona, continuing his run as if Fate beckons at the end of it, then leaps into the Mexican sky and bats the ball with a deft left hand into the net while feinting with his head in the process, an act of immaculate deceit. In the process, he out-jumps England's goalkeeper Peter Shilton, who is the taller of the two by 20 centimetres. Seldom has a more palpable case of handball gone unobserved by the referee (or linesmen), and Maradona has to sneak several furtive glances in his direction as he heads towards the packed stands to be sure that his somewhat nonplussed celebrations aren't going to waste. The goal stands and the momentum of the match now lies with the Argentinians.

As if a little discomfited by this incident – as if intent on remedying the perception that he might require undue assistance in the scoring of his goals – four minutes later Maradona runs half the field, the ball guiding him forward through a maze of English defenders, before scoring what will, with the greatest cause, become known as the Goal of the Century.

If you've never seen it, Google it. And if you have seen it, Google it again. You don't have to be a football fan to appreciate the magnificence.

After the match Maradona explained that his first goal was scored 'a little with the head of Maradona and a little with the hand of God', and in doing

'Maradona has it. Beats two, on the ball, down the right – the genius of world football – and a third [defender], looking for [teammate Jorge] Burruchaga. Still Maradona. Genius! Genius! Genius! Ta-ta-ta-ta-ta-ta! And goooaaal! Gooooooaaaall! I want to weep, Holy God! Long live football! Great gooooaaal! Diegooooo! Maradona! Forgive me for crying. Maradona, in a memorable run, in the play of all time! Cosmic Kite, what planet did you come from?'

– Victor Hugo Morales, veteran Uruguayan journalist, commenting (in Spanish) on the Goal of the Century. Maradona's most original nickname, Barrilete Cósmico *(Cosmic Kite), was bestowed in this moment*

so he showed no remorse for his actions. No apologies, no contrition, not a scruple on his cheeky Argentinian mug. Thus the infamous turning point in that infamous match would forever be known as the Hand of God.

Against the mortal enemy, in a game of utmost importance, Maradona had risen to the occasion, using both the fairest and foulest of means to secure his side victory. His team would go on to win the World Cup that year, beating West Germany in a tight final, but as one-time Argentinian captain Roberto Perfumo later explained it, 'In 1986 winning that game against England was enough. Winning the World Cup that year was secondary for us. Beating England was our real aim.'

That, in a highlights reel, was the man they called El Diego.

Diego Armando Maradona's story, once upon a time, seemed to have an ordained trajectory: from rags to riches, zero to hero. The fifth child of eight, he grew up township-poor on the outskirts of Buenos Aires, dodging ticket inspectors because he couldn't afford train fare and kicking an orange because he couldn't afford a soccer ball. He was scouted at age eight and made his international debut at age sixteen. By twenty he had won the under-20 World Cup Golden Ball and secured his first multimillion-dollar transfer, to the legendary Boca Juniors. The call to Barcelona came a year later, in 1982, for a world-record transfer fee of $7.6 million.

Maradona was the complete player: visionary, magic to watch, unstoppable on his day, technically brilliant and yet, as in life, impetuous and entirely unpredictable.

Even then, as a 21-year-old, he was building a reputation for attracting the ill and unsavoury along with the dear and divine. He clashed with his managers, he suffered injury and contracted hepatitis, and he spelt trouble. The testy 1984 Copa del Rey final between Barcelona and Athletic Bilbao, played in front of King Juan Carlos of Spain and a crowd of a 100,000, with half the country watching on television, degenerated into a mass brawl after the final whistle. By the time the dust had settled, sixty people were injured, with Maradona the focal point of the action.

After just two seasons at Barca, Maradona was transferred to Napoli. Here he would gain Messiah-like status during the mid- to late-1980s, his murals adorning buildings, and babies named for the man who would lead the club to its most successful era ever, scoring 115 goals and uplifting the entire city of Naples in the process. This was the Golden Boy's golden age, punctuated unforgettably by his stellar performance at the 1986 World Cup, where he was, it almost goes without saying, player of the tournament.

Which brings us back to those goals: the magic and the mischief. Or, if you prefer – and we do – the magic and the contemptible. Because once you strip away the artful dodging and roguish excuses, Maradona was as ugly off the field as he was beautiful on it.

The pitiful interpersonal skills, the telltale entourage, the profligate spending married to financial ineptness, the extreme hubris, the profound lack of humility – these were the elements that constituted a man who believed the world revolved around him. Because he was Diego Maradona, the greatest player on the planet. One of his many nicknames was 'D10s', a play on his legendary number 10 and the Spanish word for god – and it is no great stretch to suggest that Maradona, who was partial to referring to himself in the third person, had something of the god complex about him. As such, it's hard to imagine that the Hand of God was a coincidental name, given that it derived from his own description. It certainly wasn't an

'Who do you think you're talking to? People kill themselves to kiss these shoes.'

– Maradona addressing a bouncer
who had refused him entrance to a club for not wearing formal shoes[1]

> 'Poor old Diego. For so many years we have told him repeatedly, "You're a god", "You're a star"… that we forgot to tell him the most important thing: "You're a man".'
>
> *– former teammate Jorge Valdano[2]*

isolated incident; he remained unrepentant as time passed and, if anything, then and in the years to come, there was a sense of entitlement, of manifest destiny simply following its course.

As a result, the falls – and there were many – were epic.

By the early 1990s, Maradona's life was awash with tabloid scandal: drug abuse, weight problems, a love child, innumerable personality clashes and more. There were no surprises when he was dropped by Napoli and banned for 15 months for using cocaine in 1991 – but he wasn't yet halfway through his two-decade drug and alcohol addiction at that point. He would later describe how he snorted lines alone at home while his wife and children slept.

Having somehow got his act together to make it to the 1994 World Cup, once again as national captain, Maradona found himself ejected and later banned for a further 15 months for doping. Unsurprisingly, even years later he blamed everyone but himself: it couldn't possibly have been me, ref!

There we are again: back to the cheating, back to the evading, back to the Hand of God. In his autobiography Maradona writes of the goal, 'I got a lot of pleasure from [it]. Sometimes I think I almost enjoyed that one more.'

And that there is the first real problem with Maradona. He didn't just cheat; he enjoyed it and he excelled at it. And so he has legitimised it. He may not have invented diving, but every striker who dives in the penalty area does so in the shadow of the man who taught him to win whatever it takes. In the words of Brazilian football writer Alejandro Chacoff, 'Maradona, of course, always dived beautifully.'[3]

The second problem, one that Maradona later railed petulantly against, was his unprecedented position as global role model to every child with dreams of making it on a football pitch. So, the kids learnt, this is what it means to be a star, to have made it. When you get to the top – having pulled whatever trick you must, as the needs may be – you can do what you want. The kingdom is yours.

Ironically, perhaps, the sense of entitlement and self-aggrandisement that Maradona pioneered in the 1980s now pervades the English Premier League, the most watched sports league in the world, which claimed a viewership of 3 billion in the 2014/5 season. The average Premier League player earns nearly £50,000 per week, and if you've made it onto this particular stage, the consensus seems to be, you are now the centre of the universe and can have, if it takes your fancy, affairs with your teammate's girlfriend (various) or your brother's wife (Ryan Giggs, for eight years!) or strangers who enjoy 'dogging' (Stan Collymore), and you can beat women (Paul Gascoigne) and have group sex with teenaged girls (a trio of Sunderland players) and shag prostitutes while your wife is pregnant (Wayne Rooney) and shag prostitutes in general (too many to count) and drive badly (ditto) and behave badly (ditto) and dress like an organ-grinder monkey and be told, yeah, nice one, you look like a superstar, mate, can I have your autograph? And we haven't even got on to the vanity and the preening (special mention to Cristiano Ronaldo and David Beckham) and the indecent spending of pounds that are funnelled straight from your working-class fans' overpriced season tickets into your pockets. Blinged-out Bentley, anyone?

In the words of Giles Coren, writing in *GQ* in 2007, 'Footballers express and perpetuate everything that is vain, greedy, ignorant, witless, visceral and lumpen about the British working class, and by being rewarded for their indulgence of those values they conspire to keep the foul-mouthed, shirtless, beer-swilling, dog-faced horde in its own moral cesspool forever.'

How does this perverted cycle of life gain traction? Well, you take some working-class kids from Ely or Croxteth with the god-given ability to kick a ball and thrust them into a fantastical world of machismo, fame and excess – then give them Diego Maradona as a guiding light, and presto! And just as these young men once looked up to Maradona, so the incoming generation looks to them as the moral exemplars of the type of life to aspire to.

'In the course of time, it will be said that Maradona was to football what Rimbaud was to poetry and Mozart to music.'
    – *Eric Cantona, celebrated French and Manchester United footballer, speaking in 1995, the year he famously fly-kicked a Crystal Palace fan after being sent off*[5]

In 2000 Pelé and Maradona were named by Fifa as the joint players of the century, an honour that effectively (and unsurprisingly) anointed them as the two greatest footballers of all time. It's a fool's errand comparing players from different eras, but those who argue for Maradona make a helluva case: he won and was player of a World Cup with a team of journeymen (relative to Pelé's), he played against superior defences in Europe, he had every skill imaginable.

And yet – he is Maradona. A mad doper who hung out with Fidel Castro and Hugo Chávez and once shot four journalists with an air-rifle (for which he was given a suspended jail term); a 5ft5 freak of nature who for a time weighed a gargantuan 125 kilograms (before having gastric bypass surgery); a career addict who had a heart attack at age 43. Whereas Pelé is an ambassador. Sure, he was an ambassador for erectile dysfunction pills for a time, but there's no question who you'd want your soccer-loving kid to try to emulate.

The best of sport is Maradona scoring his second goal in that '86 quarterfinal. But there is more to sport than skill, as its adjective 'sporting' would suggest. So, we must conclude, that Maradona was never a sportsman; he was a footballer. The proto-player of the modern footballer, in fact. And the players of today are his progeny.

Josef Mengele

16 March 1911 – 7 February 1979

Auschwitz physician 1943-1945; conductor of human medical experiments; Nazi jackboot and personification of the worst deprivations of humanity

In January 1945, as the Soviet Red Army progressed west through Poland, slowly closing in on Berlin and the eventual defeat of Nazi Germany, they came to a network of concentration camps about 60 kilometres from Krakow, near the German border. This was the Auschwitz complex, consisting of Auschwitz, Auschwitz II–Birkenau and Auschwitz III–Monowitz, as well as smaller camps, spread over several square kilometres. The sight that greeted the Soviet liberators was like nothing the world had ever seen, for this wasn't just a concentration camp to hold prisoners of war; it was an extermination camp, the biggest and deadliest in history, specifically designed to murder men, women and children en masse. It would take years, decades even, before the full extent of what happened in Hitler's concentration camps came to be comprehended by people around the world. For many, it was simply unbelievable. Today we know that approximately six million Jews were killed in the 'final solution', nearly half of them Polish. About a million died at Auschwitz alone. Other victims there included ethnic Poles, Soviet prisoners of war, Roma and Sinti 'gypsies', homosexuals and the physically and mentally handicapped. Auschwitz was hell on earth, and its most famous inhabitant, the Angel of Death who presided over so much of what happened there, was the camp physician Josef Mengele.*

Ten days before the liberation of Auschwitz, Mengele and other doctors transferred west to another camp, fearful of the advancing Soviet troops. He moved on a month later and was eventually captured by the Americans, advancing eastwards, in June. Though a Schutzstaffel (SS) member with the rank of *Hauptsturmführer*, the chaos of post-war administration left him unidentified as a wanted SS officer and he was released the following month. There followed for Mengele an extraordinary three-decade run from the law, which saw him first lying low in Germany under an assumed identity until 1949, before he fled to South America. Periodically moving between Argentina, Paraguay, Brazil and possibly elsewhere, he was – despite the efforts of the German authorities, the Israeli Mossad and private Nazi hunters – to become the most notorious German war criminal to escape justice. And yet his son, Rolf Jenckel, was able to regularly communicate with him in this time, and ultimately track him down.

There's a video you can watch on YouTube in which Jenckel, a kind-eyed German lawyer who took his wife's surname to avoid publicity, describes the remarkable journey he took in 1977 to visit his father. By then, having survived a stroke, Mengele was holed up in São Paulo, where he 'looked small, old, somehow a little bit broken' but was otherwise unrepentant about his time at Auschwitz. Today in his seventies, Jenckel's life has been overshadowed by his notorious father despite having met him only twice. The first time was as a boy after the war, under the impression he was

---

* Other famous people to pass through Auschwitz were prisoners Primo Levi, Viktor Frankl and Elie Wiesel, who all wrote books on their experiences there.

meeting his 'Uncle Fritz'. In the interview – filmed in 1985 for German television – you can see a man trying and ultimately failing to understand what his father had done, in particular why he had never chosen to remove himself from the savage cruelty that took place at Auschwitz.

It is indeed incomprehensible.

A number of Hitler's lieutenants would appear at ease in a list of fifty people who messed up the world: the likes of Himmler, Goebbels, Göring, Eichmann, Heydrich. (The first two came particularly close to making the cut.) Ultimately, Josef Mengele finds himself here not because he conceived of or planned the Holocaust, but because every fascist or authoritarian movement that requires the total subservience of all in its web necessarily requires the jackboot, the men at the sharp end, the guys with the guns and the bayonets, the killers and the torturers, for the system to operate. From Japan's Imperial troops, Mao's Red Guards and Stalin's NKVD to Amin's torturers, Pol Pot's pyjama-clad thugs and apartheid's assassins, there have always been plenty of young chaps happy to use [insert glorious, just and fair cause here] as an excuse to fulfil their darkest primal urges.

Mengele was, if it's possible to judge this, about as bad as it gets anywhere in human history. Like all good Nazis, there was a grounding of civilisation in him – an endlessly fascinating moral contradiction that existed in these people. He was a good skier, he liked music and poetry, and he was educated and evidently intelligent, with doctorates in anthropology and medicine. But he was an early proponent of Nazism. By the age of 20, he was a member of the fascist *Sturmabteilung* (storm troopers), and by 27 he was a Nazi Party and SS member. He was 28 when Hitler invaded Poland. Mengele was also, of course, an avowed anti-Semite, and made no bones about the fact that in his mind, not only would the world be better off without the Jews, but that their extermination was a necessity for the advancement of

'He viewed himself as the leading edge of a new science, race science... He was 32 years old at the time he went to Auschwitz. He was at the head of his class, he was one of their darlings. He was looked at by the rest of the Nazi medical hierarchy as one of their star pupils, and Auschwitz was for him a human laboratory.'

– *Gerald Posner, author of Mengele: The complete story*

the Aryan people. (If the inhabitants of this book are anything to go by, no genocidal tyrant or his henchman has ever met a Jew he couldn't blame his people's and the world's injustices on. It is almost a qualifying trait.)

By the time the war came, Mengele was well on his way to a career in medical academia. He'd written three papers at the Institute for Hereditary Biology and Racial Hygiene in Frankfurt – yes, that is really what it was called – all largely in line with historically accepted methodology about race and genetics. In his conclusions, though, Mengele clearly co-opted the science into the service of a Nazi-friendly outcome: that the Nordic races were superior and that the German race would need to be 'cured' of mixing.

For Mengele, Hitler's war would cleave together two incredible opportunities. For the world, they were two tragedies: the Auschwitz death camp and Mengele's personal medical ambition, deviant personality and violent anti-Semitism. The former served him a practically limitless supply of victims for his human experiments. The latter gave him the ability, without compunction, to commit the crimes that he did.

In the first half of the war, Mengele appears to have served admirably, being awarded the Iron Cross twice for action on the Eastern front. After being wounded in battle, he was appointed as chief physician overseeing Auschwitz II–Birkenau in 1943, just as the Nazi machine began to ramp up the rate of exterminations. Birkenau would turn out to be the worst section of the worst concentration camp in history, and it wasn't coincidence that he found himself there; he'd requested the transfer on the advice of his Frankfurt university supervisor. Once in, he didn't waste time. Having worked on cleft palates before the war, he now became obsessed with the study of, and experimentation on, twins.

Auschwitz's German doctors had the principal role of taking part in 'selections', deciding which new arrivals would be sent to the gas chambers for immediate death and which would be retained for labour. This was a role they generally found unpleasant, but Mengele was famously jovial in his execution of it, strutting about in his immaculate uniform, smiling and joking with the mostly Jewish prisoners as they arrived in their 'transports', the cattle trains that hauled them into the extermination camps. At first he would shout out, 'Zwillinge heraus!', calling out any twins to be corralled for his research purposes. Then he would walk among the rest of the arrivals, breezily assigning them directions – 'links, links, rechts, links, rechts...' – with each word, or sometimes just the flick of a glove, deciding the fate of

> **'I do not have the slightest reason to try to justify or excuse whatever decisions, actions or behaviours of mine.'**
>
> *– Josef Mengele, in a letter to his son Rolf*

a human being. And he was there 'night and day', according to survivors, a true and dedicated fanatic of the 'work' he, and Auschwitz, was conducting.

Mengele's enjoyment of the God-like power over life and death that he commanded contrasted strangely with the kindness he often displayed to the Jewish and Roma twin children he had under his care. He would play games and give them sweets, and could be so kind, in fact, that some survivors battled to come to terms with what they discovered he'd done. As kids they had called him 'Uncle Pepi'.

It was Adolf Eichmann, another Nazi war criminal, for whom the sobriquet 'banality of evil' was created; and Mengele enjoyed a similar ability to morph into a creature of altogether different moral provenance. When the decisive moment came, his commitment to the Nazi cause would always overwhelm whatever fondness he had developed for a child under his care. He could be violently angry if the 'rules' were broken, a famous example coming during a selection, when a Jewish mother fought with an SS guard as they tried to separate her from her teenage daughter. He shot them both dead on the spot and, in a rage, sent the whole transport – including those already selected for labour – to the gas chambers. On another occasion, on learning that one of the Auschwitz blocks had a lice infestation, he had all 750 women in it gassed.

In his experiments, Mengele was looking for certainty on what was hereditary in humans and what was not. He considered himself a Nazi revolutionary, a leader in the new field of race science. This knowledge would help Germany understand how to advance the Aryan cause, and even choose its leaders on biological, not political, grounds. In particular, an understanding of how twins were formed would help speed up that process.

And so Mengele performed experiments that defy any sense of human morality and often any sense of medical purpose. He injected dyes into the eyes of living patients to see what would happen. He put people in pressure chambers. He injected material into victim's spines and into their blood. He performed bone marrow transplants; deprived babies of milk to see how long they'd live; operated on genitals and carried out castrations; experimented on pregnant women. He frequently didn't use anaesthetics.

His obsession with twins was beyond morbid. He would deliberately infect one twin with fatal diseases such as typhus to see how he or she developed, and then murder the survivor for dissection and comparative reports. He amputated limbs and removed organs to draw comparisons with the unaffected twin. He sewed together a set of twins in the hope of making them conjoined; they died days later in agony. Dissection was an important part of his work. On one night alone he murdered fourteen twins for dissection by injecting chloroform into their hearts. It is estimated that 3,000 sets of twins fell into Mengele's hands, and but a hundred or so survived.

Mengele's experiments on twins took place in the environment of broader human experimentation, including pressure chamber experiments to understand the effects of altitude, burns experiments, freezing experiments, seawater experiments, malaria and mustard gas experiments – all forcibly conducted on living, anaesthetic-free people.

Josef Mengele did all these things as a distinguished, apparently civilised man. To the average German soldier or citizen who he met outside of Auschwitz, he was simply an upstanding man of the Reich, nobly serving his country. One wonders whether his wife Irene had any inkling of what her husband was up to, what darkness lay in his heart, when he returned home to her. In 1944 she gave birth to their only child, Rolf.

It is a necessary understanding of human nature to realise that most people compelled into the German war effort in World War II would have done what the average soldier or prison guard did at the time: just follow orders. (Yes, probably us too.) In their limited understanding of things, authority would have superseded the ethical qualms of doing things they felt uncomfortable with; for instance, shooting prisoners when told to. But there were countless truly culpable individuals in the great Nazi death machine – the men with the perspective to see what was happening; the men who stretched the limits of their orders to the most evil ends. Many faced trial after the war. From Auschwitz alone, two dozen were executed, including its longest-serving camp commander Rudolf Höss, who was hanged in 1947. Mengele, however, managed to evade capture for 34 years, probably with financial assistance from his family back in Germany, and had

'I tried to make him clear that even to be in Auschwitz and not to try every day to come away from there is for me horrible and impossible. I could never understand how a human being could act like this, and it would not change in any position, if this is my father or not, it's really for me against all ethical and moral and human understanding, and nature.'
– *Rolf Jenckel, speaking in 1985 about meeting his father in 1976 in São Paulo*

the privilege of a humdrum death in 1979: he had a stroke while swimming in the sea and drowned. He was buried in Brazil under an assumed name, but his grave was discovered and his body exhumed for genetic testing. His son, Rolf Jenckel, provided the DNA that proved his identity.

Jenckel, emotional and in his broken English, eventually spoke out about meeting his father and confronting him about what he had done. Some measure of filial loyalty had prevented him from ever trying to turn him in while he was alive, perhaps because he couldn't wholly believe the charges against him. When father and son did eventually discuss his war record, Mengele evidently admitted to the 'selections' but was unrepentant about the medical experimentation that had taken place. Somehow those deeds had been erased from his consciousness, just as the lives of more than a million people were erased at Auschwitz.

Anti-Semitism is a strangely resilient disease, inexplicably immune to the demands of eradication we seek in other prejudices, and often found in people who otherwise proclaim their 'progressiveness'. But those who remain silent about anti-Semitism are only a short ethical step away from Mengele's protestations to his son that he was part of a machine over which he had no power; just following orders, just doing his duty. Auschwitz and similar places are the logical conclusion of anti-Semitism – or any extreme prejudice by group identity – and, just as decent people may allow them into existence in the wrong circumstances, so there are truly evil people, like Mengele, who actively seek them out and make them what they are.

Hitler may have held the ambition and ability to cause World War II and all the destruction that came with it, but the real horror of what he did is reflected in the deeds of Josef Mengele. There can be no man more evil and depraved to have ever walked the earth.

Thomas Midgley

18 May 1889 – 2 November 1944

Mechanical engineer; chemist; serial inventor; catastrophe magnet; double-trouble world stuffer-upper; cause-of-death innovator

THOMAS MIDGLEY WAS AN AWARD-WINNING, academically honoured mechanical engineer and chemist who came up with more than a hundred patented ideas and was revered in his time. Two of these ideas, in particular, were quite undeniably brilliant, their efficacy being clear for all to see. They had the unfortunate drawback, however, of being utterly lethal both to humans and to the environment.

Midgley can almost be excused for one of his inventions: chlorofluorocarbons (CFCs). These were gases widely used as refrigerants in devices such as fridges and air conditioners until the late 20th century. In the 1920s, General Motors sought a replacement for the ammonia, propane, sulphur dioxide and other refrigerant gases that, while effective, were also either toxic or explosive or corrosive. Midgley was prominent on the team that discovered CFCs, which did the trick. To be fair to the man, he was long-dead (more on that below) by the time the link between CFCs and damage to the ozone layer and the knock-on greenhouse effect was established. But, boy, were CFCs bad for the ozone layer, and by the time we'd worked this out – the 1970s – they were in innumerable other products, including aerosols. So every time a spotty teenage boy in London used his Lynx deodorant, somebody in Australia got skin cancer.

But let's not get too carried away just yet, because before he got to buggering up the ozone layer Midgley had already invented something that would kill hundreds of thousands of people and scar the lives of millions: leaded gasoline. And his role appears far less innocent in this case.

Readers old enough might remember a time when petrol stations suddenly started selling a new lead-free petrol. This was the 1980s in most reasonably enlightened places and, given that they'd been selling the nasty stuff for six decades, this seemed so late in the day that many wondered what the fuss was about. Was leaded petrol that bad? Short answer, yes.

The slightly longer answer reveals just how bad.

The reality of lead poisoning has been so well established that there are serious suggestions that it had a hand in the decline of the Roman Empire. Lead, so this theory went, would get into water and wine from lead pipes and containers, giving a sweet taste and rendering the Roman elite – that is, those who drank wine and had plumbed houses – infertile, mad and ridden with gout.

Lead is a multitalented neurotoxin, and using it in petrol was always a terrible idea. It reduces IQ in children, it destroys fertility, it brings on insanity and it ultimately kills. It can be absorbed into bones, teeth and blood, damaging kidneys, inhibiting growth, causing abdominal spasms and wreaking huge damage on the nervous system. It reduces growth of grey matter in the area of the brain responsible for impulse control and planning, and there are serious papers published by serious academics that appear to show that crime in the US (and therefore elsewhere presumably) surged twenty years after the introduction of lead in petrol and has declined dramatically since it was phased out. Lead in petrol, they argue, was the driving force behind a 70-year crime wave. It made the lucky ones mad, bad and sick. The rest it killed.

According to one credible estimate, by 1986, when lead was banned as a gasoline additive in the US, an estimated 5,000 Americans a year were dying of lead-induced heart disease. That adds up over the course of six decades.

So there you have it: lead bad.

Lots can be surmised about who knew what and when in the early days. What we do know is that when a General Motors employee – ahem, Midgley – first tested Tetraethyllead (TEL) to combat the automotive clatter known as engine knock in 1921, it surely had to have been a concern that igniting a known poison in an internal combustion engine could have potentially worrying consequences. It seems hard to believe that such an obviously intelligent man would miss the connection when GM's

Chemical Corporation started seeing a growing number of worker deaths and dozens of cases of lead poisoning from 1923 onwards, so much so that staff nicknamed one of its plants 'the loony gas building'. Nevertheless, by 1924 GM were driving the production and marketing of TEL as an integral element of the future of autoengineering. And unsurprisingly, Big Corporate won the day over those quite coherently and vociferously raising concerns of the long-term health effects. (Incidentally GM collaborated on this particular project with a company called Standard Oil, which is today known as ExxonMobil. Yes, that lot again…)

The flashing-sirens giveaway in all this is that Midgley himself had succumbed to bouts of lead poisoning as a result of his work, and had to take extended leave on at least two occasions. In late 1924, he inhaled TEL fuel fumes in front of a press conference for a full minute to illustrate just how wholesome his product was. He also rubbed some TEL-gasoline into his hands, explaining that he could do this every day without any bothersome health consequences at all, no siree Bob! If we are to give Midgley the benefit of the narrowest sliver of doubt, one wonders if he had simply been overwhelmed with lead-induced derangement.

For all the catastrophe of Midgley's contribution to the human story, there is a positive to be extracted from it: we eventually cottoned on to both problems he was instrumental in creating and the fixes appear to be working. The ozone hole scare first publicised in the mid-1980s led to the banning of CFCs across the globe, itself an impressive feat of international cooperation, and ozone levels are slowly recovering. Lead petrol, similarly, has been almost entirely phased out around the world – though it's still available in North Korea, Myanmar and a few other places, if you're interested – and we're healthier and, according to some, not killing each other so much as a result. Three cheers for human progress!

[Midgley possessed] 'an instinct for the regrettable that was almost uncanny.'

– Bill Bryson

Midgley's final contribution to humanity was his most unfortunate. At the age of 51, he contracted polio and was paralysed. Ever-inventive – disastrously so, in this case – he devised a contraption of ropes and pulleys that would help to lift him up off the bed. Four years later, in 1944, he became caught up in his own invention and strangled himself to death.

Today Midgley presents as something of the tragi-comic mad scientist of history. His two most famous inventions caused great harm to many people, ultimately conferring on him the dubious distinction of being the creator of not one but two of *Time* magazine's '50 Worst Inventions'. The less charitable reader might be tempted to see some form of justice in his faintly ludicrous departure from this world. We'll call it apt, rather, while we search for the meaning in all of this.

To shine a philosophically optimistic light on Thomas Midgley and his unfortunate career, we might conclude that his legacy is the collateral damage we must expect from the march of scientific progress (and capitalism), which tends to make our lives better and longer with each passing year. It's just that in his case the opposite happened.

But if there is a specific lesson to extract in every man's life, in this case it might be: listen to the voice of reasonable doubt in your mind. It is a quiet voice, usually quieter than the voice that seeks reputation and prominence. And certainly much quieter than the voices of the lead goblins jumping about in there.

Robert Oppenheimer

22 April 1904 – 18 February 1967

Coordinator of Rapid Rupture; mastermind of the Manhattan Project; father of the atomic bomb; destroyer of worlds?

J ROBERT OPPENHEIMER IS PERHAPS ONE OF THE UNLUCKIER entrants in these pages, bookended as he is by a lamentable inventor-killer and a genocidal maniac of the highest order, for Oppenheimer was a good and brilliant man, and a man without whom the notorious invention with which he will forever be associated, the atom bomb, would have come into existence anyway.

The harnessing of the power of the atom and the detonation of a nuclear weapon was one of those inevitable occurrences on the journey of human technological development – a bit like Judgement Day in the *Terminator* films, if we're looking for an overly convenient metaphor. Assuming Newton's law of universal gravitation as a starting point, the creation of the atom bomb is often described as 'the culmination of three centuries of physics'. It would seem more practical, though, to focus things down to a fifty-year process, from the accidental discovery of X-rays by Wilhelm Röntgen in a laboratory at the University of Würzburg in November 1895, to the Trinity detonation, the world's first nuclear explosion, in the New Mexican desert in July 1945, overseen by Robert Oppenheimer. From Röntgen to Oppenheimer, the dots that connect those two points represent some of the mightiest personalities of science: the likes of Rutherford, Planck, Einstein, Schrödinger and Bohr. There were countless smaller dots, too, and had fate snatched away any one of them before his work was done, even Einstein or Bohr, it's safe to assume that some other great mind would have stepped in to fill the gap. The timeline may have changed, and history with it, but the end result would have been the same: a working atom bomb with the potential to erase countless lives in an instant.

Who was the most important person in the process, the biggest dot? Impossible to say. Or, at the least, that's a rabbit hole of cause-and-effect what-iffing that only the most qualified of nuclear scientists could dare to venture down. Which is beyond our pay grade and we're not going there.

And thus Oppenheimer is here for two reasons. First, because at the end of it all he was the final dot, the man with his metaphorical finger on the button when that first nuke went off. He was the one who became known as the 'father of the atom bomb', and so he is now the embodiment of humankind's deadliest creation, a weapon that has the potential to extinguish the species that invented it.

The second reason is a more prosaic, utilitarian one. If we focus the fifty-year development of the atom bomb down even further, from the start of the Manhattan Project in August 1942 to the end of World War II three years later, then the historical consensus is both praiseworthy and damning: without Oppenheimer's guidance the bomb would not have been ready until after the war's end. In other words, without Oppenheimer Hiroshima and Nagasaki would not have been bombed. They *were* bombed, of course, with biblical results. Ironically, it's this very fact that is also the possible saviour of Oppenheimer's (and President Harry Truman's) reputation.

Robert Oppenheimer grew up in a golden age of physics. In the first decades of the 20th century Max Planck, Albert Einstein, Niels Bohr and many of their colleagues were global celebrities; they were the men who were revolutionising the way we understood the world. Ten of them mentioned in this entry alone won Nobel Prizes for Physics between 1918 and 1945 and were so famous they would be familiar to your average high-school physics student *today*.* By contrast, try naming two famous physicists from the last fifty years: Peter Higgs of the Higgs boson (Nobel 2013) comes to mind... otherwise, it's Stephen Hawking (still waiting).

---

* The ten are: Planck (1918), Einstein (1921), Bohr (1922), De Broglie (1929), Heisenberg (1932), Schrodinger and Dirac (1933), Chadwick (1935), Fermi (1938) and Pauli (1945). Other Physics winners included here were Röntgen, the discoverer of X-rays, who won the inaugural Nobel in 1901, Thomson (1906) and Born (1954). Richard Feynman, the last of the rock-star physicists and an important contributor to the Manhattan Project, won in 1965. Meanwhile Rutherford won for Chemistry in 1908.

Point is, for a man of his intelligence and proclivities, Oppenheimer was born at the right time. He was also brought up in an environment conducive to success. His father Julius, a Jewish immigrant from Germany who had built a thriving garment business from nothing, sent him to the Ethical Culture School in New York, which was as progressive as it got, something like a Montessori establishment with Richard Dawkins as headmaster. Whether or not this is a good thing is besides the point; it got results.

Oppenheimer was the type of retiring schoolboy prodigy who, aged 9, would get his older cousin to ask him questions in Latin to which he would answer in Greek. Besides the maths and science talents you'd expect from the future father of the bomb, he also studied history, English literature, English, Latin, Greek, French and German in his senior year. He got straight As and was class valedictorian. Later, he would teach himself Dutch and learn Sanskrit. You know, for shits and giggles.

After school, he made the mandatory move to Harvard, where he was odd, socially difficult, occasionally depressed, and of course brilliant. (While he was there, in the early 1920s, Harvard initiated a limit on the number of Jews permitted to the university – a sign of the times.)

Then it was off to Cambridge, where he came under the guidance of JJ Thomson, discoverer of the electron, and found himself sharing laboratories with the great Ernest Rutherford and James Chadwick. Rutherford – officially 1st Baron Rutherford of Nelson; unofficially 'the father of nuclear physics' – had in 1911 proposed a revolutionary new model of the atom (to improve on Thomson's) which saw electrons orbiting a tiny positively charged nucleus. Then he came up with the concept of the proton, before postulating the existence of neutrons, which were confirmed by Chadwick in 1932. (If you're not following, don't worry; no-one gets it by the end.)

Far from embracing his opportunity to work alongside the giants of his discipline, Oppenheimer's time at Cambridge was tumultuous and difficult. He suffered breakdowns and bouts of depression. He was poor at and particularly hated boring laboratory work, which would see him gravitating towards theoretical physics and away from the practical stuff. After an incident in which he apparently tried to poison his tutor with a chemical-laced apple, he was allowed to stay on at Cambridge only if he agreed to see a psychiatrist. The sessions proved disastrous and he was diagnosed with 'dementia praecox', not far off what we now know as schizophrenia. He was a beautiful mind in the making, it seemed, and in time he felt suicidal. He locked his mother, Ella, in a hotel room in Paris, and throttled a friend with a strap. Ella made him see a French psychoanalyst who diagnosed sexual frustration (*naturellement!*). A third shrink simply gave up, outsmarted by his patient. Eventually Oppenheimer went to Corsica with friends, argued about the literary merits of Tolstoy v Dostoyevsky and snapped himself out of his prolonged funk after reading Proust by torchlight.

Here was the perfect example of his timing. After a troubled year at Cambridge, he had finally got his act together just in time to be invited to study further at the University of Göttingen by Max Born, director of The Institute of Theoretical Physics and the man who had coined the term 'quantum physics' two years earlier. At this point, Werner Heisenberg and Erwin Schrödinger were leading a (literal) quantum shift in physics, and Göttingen, an unassuming medieval university town in central Germany, happened to be one of the key hubs in Europe, and thus the world. It was here that Born guided the work of Heisenberg, Wolfgang Pauli, Enrico Fermi and others; a better doctoral adviser in a better place at a better time didn't exist. Realising that 'great things were afoot', and with his decision to pursue theoretical physics made, Oppenheimer thrived.

The fast-developing world of quantum physics was all about the microscopic, subatomic world we cannot see. Before this point classical physics, derived from Newton's laws of motion originally published in 1687, had served us well. It still does. In almost all practical senses you can predict the way the world will work from the notion that 'for every action, there is an equal and opposite reaction' and the other rules of classical mechanics. But on a micro scale, where people like us stop caring and the physics nerds start, Newtonian physics fails. By the turn of the 20th century the nerds were hard at work solving the problem.

Following Rutherford's pioneering work, Planck, Einstein and Bohr received their Nobel prizes in 1918, 1921 and 1922 respectively. Planck had come up with the idea of quantum theory to explain the workings of the subatomic world in terms of discrete packets, or quanta, of energy. From there, Einstein's special theory of relativity gave us the immortal $E = mc^2$ – one of the crowning intellectual achievements of the 20th century – and the understanding that all mass has the potential to be converted into energy (NB: simple version). Together, the two German scientists had revolutionised our understanding of the universe. Bohr then used quantum theory to enhance Rutherford's model of the atom. Rather than electrons randomly orbiting a nucleus, he described a hydrogen atom with an electron that was confined to very specific possible orbits depending on how much electromagnetic energy had been emitted or absorbed by the atom; to move from one orbit, or energy level, to the next required a so-called quantum shift or quantum leap*.

And then, in the 1920s, things got complicated.

Louis-Victor De Broglie proposed that subatomic particles could behave both as particles *and* as waves. Schrödinger pioneered wave mechanics, inventing his famous equation in the process (his more famous hypothetical cat came later). Heisenberg came up with his uncertainty principle; Pauli invented the exclusion principle. Paul Dirac thought up quantum field theory (and anti-matter); Born worked on probability and causality; and Bohr, the guru-like Dane who was central to making Copenhagen another quantum-theory hub, guided and encouraged these young pioneering geniuses – and he invented complementarity, whatever that may be.

Taken together, this was the development of the new quantum physics or quantum mechanics, and if you can understand it in any kind of detail whatsoever you're a genius. Oppenheimer could, and by the time he had completed his doctorate, he had helped contribute to the development of a new set of laws for dealing with subatomic particles that opened up a post-Newtonian understanding of the universe.

As Kai Bird and Martin Sherwin phrase it in their definitive biography of Oppenheimer, *American Prometheus*, 'However weirdly unintelligible – today as much as then – to the average citizen, quantum physics nevertheless explains our physical world...[It] seems to study that which doesn't exist – but nevertheless proves true. It works.'

And because of it, we suddenly had the potential to invent wondrous new things, like transistors and semiconductors, which led to personal computers and other electronic devices; lasers, which led to CDs, laser-eye surgery and Jean-Michel Jarre concerts; and devices to split quantities of enriched uranium or plutonium, which led to fission reactions and nuclear bombs...

---

* The irony of the modern idiomatic use of 'quantum leap' to describe a sudden large advance or shift is that it originally described infinitesimally small, though very specific, changes.

Though a logical progression of quantum theory and the study of the atom, a functional atomic bomb was far from a foregone conclusion. It would require the world's most destructive war to inspire it and one of its greatest scientific projects to develop it. It was only in 1940, after the war had started, that two physicists working at the University of Birmingham calculated that the critical mass of uranium or plutonium needed for an atomic explosion could be measured in pounds rather than tons. The Frisch-Peierls Memorandum was highly influential; not only was a working 'super-bomb' that could 'destroy life [over] the centre of a big centre' suddenly attainable, but the knowledge to attain one was widely available, it explained, which meant the Germans could be working on it already. (They were.) The UK and US both got cracking on the idea, and the Manhattan Project emerged from Franklin Roosevelt's atomic programme two years later (before the attack on Pearl Harbour, when the US was technically not at war). Directed by Colonel Leslie Groves under the auspices of the US Army, it would employ upwards of 130,000 people across dozens of installations in the US, Canada and the UK in the four years from August 1942. It would cost more than $2 billion – worth just under $30 billion in 2017 – and it would need Robert Oppenheimer to guide it to its deadly fruition in time for it to pay off before the war's end.

Oppenheimer's appointment was far from a sure thing, as he was never the obvious choice. But there was no obvious choice. After his time studying abroad in the mid-1920s, the young physicist had returned home in 1927 and almost single-handedly launched the theoretical physics movement in the US. Previously, Europe was the absolute centre of the physics world; now he brought this new wave of thought to Caltech and Harvard, and then the University of California, Berkeley. He continued to mix with the brightest physicists of the day, and was esteemed worldwide. By the time Groves started criss-crossing the country looking for a suitable candidate, Oppenheimer was investigating fast neutrons in his role as 'Coordinator of Rapid Rupture' on the atomic programme. This all counted in his favour.

Against him were some important sticking points: he had unsavoury links to and possibly sympathies with the communist movement, and was thus a security risk; he was almost exclusively a theorist, with a pronounced dislike for practical work, in line for the most complex practical scientific job imaginable; and let's not forget he'd once tried to poison his tutor. But never mind all that; he interviewed well and the colonel was taken by him. About the first and last points, Groves was not concerned. If anything, he believed Oppenheimer's tenuous communist connections might be used to control him, and any mental problems he'd exhibited as a student had by then been exchanged for a remarkable social confidence. (If there was a crazy Oppenheimer, it was his wife Kitty. Bananas.)

As for the requirements for the job, this was a role that transcended mere hands-on skills. One of Oppenheimer's great intellectual abilities was the way he could comprehend a complex scientific problem almost instantly, often as it was being explained to him, and then quickly find a way forward from there. He was also a multi-disciplinarian – he knew a lot about a lot, rather than everything about a little. It was a trait that would probably cost him his own Nobel in time (he came close), but it meant he was aware of the challenges of mixing engineering, chemistry, metallurgy, ordnance and everything else that comes with a $2-billion budget. The Manhattan Project would provide countless opportunities for him to use and develop these skills, and he was ultimately as practically minded as any candidate. The fact that he was a natural (academic) leader and had the necessary ego for a job of this magnitude also helped. But his greatest skill, perhaps, was his ability to convince people to his way of thinking, and if you believe Malcolm Gladwell's interpretation of things, he got the job by working out Groves right at the start: he appealed to the engineer in the colonel and charmed him, suggesting a central research laboratory to find solutions to the many practical problems they would be facing.

Leslie Groves was a blunt authoritarian, famously loathed by those he encountered on the Manhattan Project, but his decision to appoint Oppenheimer as the scientific director of the Los Alamos National Laboratory, and thus the project's lead scientist, would be absolutely vindicated. (His respect for Oppenheimer was enormous, though qualified. 'Why, Oppenheimer knows about everything,' he said. 'He can talk to you about anything you bring up. Well, not exactly. I guess there are a few things he doesn't know about. He doesn't know anything about sports.')

Of the dozens of Manhattan Project sites, the three most important were the University of Chicago, where Enrico Fermi built the world's first working nuclear reactor; Oak Ridge in Tennessee, where enormous facilities were constructed to separate uranium and plutonium into fissile material; and the Los Alamos Laboratory, the business end of the project, which saw thousands of scientists developing a working bomb in the sparsely populated New Mexican wilderness. Los Alamos was Oppenheimer's baby; he suggested the site, having spent much time nearby on his horse ranch, and effectively became mayor of an instant town for three years.

Built at altitude, Los Alamos was a curious establishment. It was surrounded by great natural beauty and constructed in a rush, its semi-circular Quonset huts set amongst reels of barbed wire and billboards advising residents to HOLD YOUR TONGUE, THE JOB'S NOT DONE. The average age of Los Alamos residents was 25, and with so many young like-minded people filled with a unified sense of purpose in a time of war there was, of course, lots of… sex. Intense six-day workweeks were likely to end in Saturday-night blowouts fuelled by lab alcohol mixed with grapefruit juice, to the extent that a minor STD outbreak and sky-high monthly birth rates eventually had Groves laying an official complaint with Oppenheimer. In time, a veil of secrecy pervaded proceedings and the wives met up for afternoon drinks at ever-earlier hours.

With five or six thousand residents by war's end, the town turned out to be something of the socialist experiment – there was free medical care, domestic help was bussed in and shared according to needs, wives worked as assistants, no-one was unemployed, there were no idle rich – which is some irony considering the US army's obsession with rooting out communists and the later fate that awaited Oppenheimer, the man who would become the most high-profile victim of the McCarthy witch-hunts after the war.

Nevertheless, for all its unlikely quirks, Los Alamos – and the entire Manhattan Project – proved as astounding a success as could have been hoped. Just before sunrise on 16 July 1945, Oppenheimer, along with several hundred observers from the programme, waited nervously in the Jornada del Muerto desert of New Mexico for the culmination of three centuries of physics. Thirty kilometres from Oppenheimer's position, an implosion-design plutonium bomb, 'the Gadget', rested atop a 30-metre steel tower, primed for detonation. This was the Trinity test.

No-one could be sure what would happen at the critical moment. Would the thing go off? Might it ignite the atmosphere and 'blow up the world', as some had predicted? The VIP betting pool predicted anything from a complete dud (Norman Ramsey, future Nobel prize-winner) to 45 kilotons (Edward Teller, future father of the hydrogen bomb). Oppenheimer chose a measly 0.3 kilotons – he was being modest. As his friend and fellow physicist

'[T]he single most remarkable and defining moment of the past 500 years came at 05:29:45 on 16 July 1945. At that precise second, American scientists detonated the first atomic bomb at Alamogordo, New Mexico. From that point onward, humankind had the capability not only to change the course of history, but to end it.'

— *Yuval Noah Harari, writing in Sapiens: A brief history of humankind*

lsidor Rabi described it, 'Suddenly, there was an enormous flash of light, the brightest light I have ever seen or that I think anyone has ever seen.'

Indeed it was a light as bright as the sun, for mankind had finally harnessed the energy that powers stars. Edward Teller may have been a little keen with his prediction, but at 18 kilotons it was an explosion of such immensity that the path of humankind was instantly altered.

'We knew the world would not be the same,' Oppenheimer recalled twenty years later. 'A few people laughed. A few people cried. Most people were silent. I remembered the line from the Hindu scripture, the Bhagavad Gita. Vishnu is trying to persuade the Prince that he should do his duty and to impress him takes on his multi-armed form and says, "Now I have become Death, the destroyer of worlds." I suppose we all felt that, one way or another.'

These lines were said for the documentary *The Decision To Drop The Bomb* – which brings us to that particular moral quandary. Because, problem was, by July 1945 there were no Nazis to drop it on. The war in Europe was over. The war in the Pacific, however, was still to be calmed.

History will record 6 and 9 August 1945 as two days of infamy to trounce any that had preceded it. By then Roosevelt was dead, and it fell to Truman to approve, respectively, the dropping of the gun-type uranium-235 bomb codenamed 'Little Boy' over the Japanese city of Hiroshima, and the implosion-type plutonium bomb known as 'Fat Man' over Nagasaki.

The Hiroshima mission went according to plan. After months of analysis it was the US's primary target for nuclear annihilation, an important military city that was deemed geographically suitable and had suffered little bomb damage to date – all the better to assess the destruction. Dropped at 8.15am from the *Enola Gay*, a B-29 Superfortress custom-designed for the job, the bomb exploded close to target at an altitude of about 580 metres, razing everything within a radius of one mile and causing catastrophic damage to a huge chunk of the city. An estimated 80,000 people died, nearly a third of Hiroshima's population, in the deadliest minute in human history.

The second mission, on the other hand, was technically less successful. Had the wind blown a different direction over the island of Kyushu on that morning, the world would be a lot more aware today of the castle town of Kokura, about a hundred kilometres to the northeast of Nagasaki. Kokura, which was the site of a large munitions plant, was the primary target for Fat Man, but as fate had it, events conspired in its favour; a 15-minute rendezvous delay between *Bockscar*, the B-29 carrying the device, and its two support planes were enough to save it. By the time they arrived overhead the smoke from fires in a bombed neighbouring city were obscuring it, and the decision to switch to the secondary target was made. The bomb was eventually dropped on Nagasaki three kilometres off target, which served to confine the blast to a valley, thus protecting certain parts of the city. Approximately 40,000 people died on the day. The Japanese surrendered unconditionally six days later.

The Hiroshima and Nagasaki death tolls were both roughly doubled by year's end due to the after-effects of the bombs: radiation sickness, burns and the effects of injuries and malnutrition.

Should the United States have dropped the bomb? Twice?

This is one of the vexed questions of modern human history and it is accompanied by all manner of hypotheticals and secondary questions. The prospect of a nuclear war was not the threat then that it then became because

'We circled finally low over Hiroshima and stared in disbelief. There below was the flat level ground of what been a city, scorched red in the telltale scar. But no hundreds of planes had visited this town during a long night. One bomber and one bomb had, in the time it takes a rifle bullet to cross the city, turned a city of three hundred thousand into a burning pyre. That was the new thing.'

– *Philip Morrison, Manhattan Project physician*
who assessed the effects of both bombs a month after they were dropped

it was unprecedented and unimaginable: a team of Japanese scientists had to be dispatched to Hiroshima and report back that, yes indeed, a single bomb had annihilated an entire city and much of its population.

Could the Americans have demonstrated the bomb to key Japanese personnel without such loss of life, as many of the Manhattan Project scientists had hoped? Or perhaps dropped it an appropriate distance from Emperor Hirohito and his generals so that they might witness the effects firsthand? Military and moral considerations both had to be taken into account, and it would seem reasonable – in review, seven decades after the fact, and this is *still* contested – to suggest that the dropping of one bomb was justifiable as a result of the American (and Japanese) lives it ultimately saved, and that it should have been enough to secure surrender. Two was showing off – literally.

As it happens, Truman's administration was especially keen to demonstrate America's nuclear capabilities with an eye on the future, a world in which their archenemy would be communist Russia. The decision to drop the bomb not only allowed the US to win the Pacific war without assistance from Stalin, it gave them the opportunity to demonstrate to the world the country's awesome new military capability. In retrospect, the decision was, it seems, a foregone conclusion, and the military plan was, in fact, to drop more bombs as they became available; another seven would have been made ready over the following ten weeks.

Most of the scientists involved in the Manhattan Project had wrestled with the morals of what they were doing throughout the process (though only one quit as a result). They had been fired by the need to build the bomb before Hitler did and thus defeat Nazi fascism but they had delivered a weapon that could ultimately destroy human civilisation – and the European war was over by that stage anyway. Nevertheless, Oppenheimer himself believed that the bomb had to be demonstrated; were it to remain secret, larger-scale atomic warfare was sure to follow.

The nuclear-haunted Cold War that established itself after World War II was, inevitably, a time like no other in history: an often surreal age of existential dread and madness facing off to madness. Truman was encouraged by advisers to nuke the Russians in the late 1940s, before Stalin acquired the bomb, but (not being possessed of pure evil) he turned down the advice. The Russians went nuclear in August 1949. There followed an arms race of ludicrous proportions – despite the efforts of Oppenheimer,

General 'Buck' Turgidson: Mr President, we are rapidly approaching a moment of truth both for ourselves as human beings and for the life of our nation. Now, truth is not always a pleasant thing. But it is necessary now to make a choice, to choose between two admittedly regrettable, but nevertheless distinguishable, postwar environments: one where you got twenty million people killed, and the other where you got a hundred and fifty million people killed.

President Merkin Muffley: You're talking about mass murder, General, not war!

General 'Buck' Turgidson: Mr President, I'm not saying we wouldn't get our hair mussed. But I do say no more than ten to twenty million killed, tops. Uh, depending on the breaks.

from Dr Strangelove: Or How I learned To Stop Worrying And Love The Bomb

Einstein and others – that was best comprehended in *Dr Strangelove*-style farce. How else to make sense of the fact that the US alone built 70,000 nuclear weapons in the second half of the 20th century, spending $5.5 trillion in the process? The Soviets probably built far more, possessing an estimated 40,000 weapons of their own in the mid-1980s. Both superpowers built hydrogen bombs that were hundreds, if not thousands, of times more powerful than the Little Boy bomb. It was a time when warships carried nuclear depth charges and jet interceptors were armed with nuclear *air-to-air* missiles.

The prospect of Mutually Assured Destruction – the understanding, with its appropriate acronym, MAD, that either side pressing the button meant both sides would be destroyed – has surely altered the collective human consciousness. The Manhattan Project and the Cold War that came of it delivered a world where the end of humankind was a plausible daily reckoning, an existential threat like no other. Surely it has affected us to our primal core, in particular the Baby Boomer generation who grew up in and were moulded by the atomic age. Is it a wonder we became a popcorn world of short-term living when total annihilation was a mere Cuban missile crisis away?

There were two instances in Cold War history that we know of when a single individual made a single decision that prevented the likely start of nuclear war.* There are around ten further incidents that could well have led to nuclear strikes and counter-strikes. And yet here we are, alive and kicking, and hopefully keeping a tighter watch on those stockpiles.

So perhaps Oppenheimer is greater than we imagine. Yes, he orchestrated the vapourising and radiation of hundreds of thousands of Japanese civilians, and yes, he delivered unto the post-war generation an era of existential angst, backyard bunkers and air-raid paranoia – and he agonised over all of it and found himself unfairly ostracised by the anti-communist McCarthyists in the process, perhaps a victim of the terror he had invented. But there is a sound argument that he helped stop global-scale war altogether. Today we live during 'the long peace'. There are around 15,000 nuclear warheads in the world, shared between nine countries, and the US, for one, still spends vast sums on its programme (more, in both real and equivalent dollar terms, in 2014 than any year before). But for all our minor wars, skirmishes and even genocides, the world's most powerful nations no longer fight each other in pitched battle and haven't done so since the Korean War ended in 1953. Never in history has our rate of military deaths been this low. And one theory suggests that this is the real legacy of the bomb – because even the greatest superpowers fear the day after the ICBMs go up.

Anyone who believes that scientific endeavour in itself is the apotheosis of human achievement need only look to the creation of the atomic bomb, as orchestrated by Oppenheimer, to refute this claim. The Trinity test in the

---

* The first occurred under the Caribbean Sea during the Cuban missile crisis, on 27 October 1962, when a Soviet submarine was located and pursued by US Navy warships involved in the blockade of the island. Not knowing whether or not war had broken out and unable to monitor radio traffic, the submarine's commander chose to respond to the dropping of US depth charges with the launch of a nuclear torpedo. Soviet submarines typically required approval to release nuclear weapons from two individuals, the captain and the political officer; however, in this instance the commander of the submarine flotilla, Vasili Arkhipov, happened to be on board and his approval was also needed. Despite a heated confrontation with captain and political officer, he refused. After news of the incident emerged in the West in 2002, US historian Arthur Schlesinger described the confrontation as 'the most dangerous moment in human history'.

The second incident occurred on 26 September 1983, three weeks after a Soviet interceptor had shot down a Korean airliner, another time of heightened tension between East and West. On that occasion Lieutenant-Colonel Stanislav Petrov, the on-duty commander of Moscow's new satellite-linked Oko early warning defence system, chose to ignore system alerts indicating that the US had launched six ICBMs at the Soviet Union. Petrov suspected a false alarm due to the small number of launches recorded – he had been trained to expect hundreds of incoming missiles – and he was proved correct. The Soviet satellites had apparently been fooled by sunlight reflecting off high-altitude clouds over North Dakota.

Los Alamos desert was a magnificent technical achievement, harnessing the power of our greatest minds, but it was the harbinger of the purest hell on earth just three weeks later, and it signalled that moment in time at which humanity gained the means to end its own existence.

At the height of the US-Soviet MADness, a Full Force nuclear war might have left an immediate death toll of a billion or more, with rapid and catastrophic climate change and social armageddon to follow. But we're not out of the woods just yet. Today, a nuclear exchange of a hundred weapons between, say, India and Pakistan would kill millions locally and produce a nuclear winter and economic devastation that would affect the entire globe, probably for decades. The chances of it happening, however, are remarkably low.

So, to Robert Oppenheimer, we say thank you as well as damn you.

'What are we to make of a civilisation which has always regarded ethics as an essential part of human life [but] which has not been able to talk about the prospect of killing almost everybody except in prudential and game-theoretical terms?'

– Robert Oppenheimer, 1959

Pol Pot

19 May 1925 – 15 April 1998

Leader of Cambodia 1975-1979; communist, nationalist and racist; revolutionary, oppressor and mass murderer; the truest scum of the earth

POL POT WAS AN ESPECIALLY EVIL SON OF A BITCH, it is true, but this wasn't the only factor behind the murder of a quarter or more of Cambodia's population in the second half of the 1970s.

Harold Shipman was evil. Ted Bundy and Gary Ridgway were evil. Pol Pot was evil *and* driven by uncompromising hardline ideology. To kill millions of people you have to be both – one to be able to commit the crime, the other to excuse it.

Of history's recent ogres, Pol Pot probably possesses the most innocuous of names. Hitler punches you in the face; Stalin is the man of steel; Chairman Mao is the most ominous of all. But Pol Pot sounds something like a gentle garden gnome. It was, of course, made up – a self-ascribed nom de guerre to ensure anonymity in the battle against the Cambodian state in the 1960s and early 1970s. His party moniker, Brother Number One, was perhaps more unsettling, but it was his real name that, to the Western ear at least, inspires the appropriate cringe: Saloth Sar. If the name, possessing of itself a Tolkienesque menace, inspires visions of a dead-eyed lord of the underworld with an army of faceless soldiers at his bidding, then we're at least getting closer to the essence of the man. For the story of Pol Pot, the Khmer Rouge and Cambodia is almost unspeakably hard to digest, a descent into the darkest reaches of man's animal nature, where industrial-scale mass murder becomes justifiable as a means to achieve the most lunatic of political ideals.

The facts of the Khmer Rouge's reign of terror beggar belief. Pol Pot and his revolutionaries had emerged from the South East Asian jungle to win the Cambodian Civil War in the shadow of the bedlam in Vietnam. On his installation as head of state in 1975 the public knew almost nothing of their new leader. His personal story would only emerge in time: that he was, in fact, Saloth Sar; that he was a farmer's child of some privilege who'd been educated in Phnom Penh and later Paris of the early 1950s, where he had been seduced by the fashionable French communism of the time; that he was deeply racist and deceptively simple-minded, an academic failure.

Under Pol Pot, the calendar was reset to Year 0 and Cambodia renamed Democratic Kampuchea – but there was nothing meaningfully democratic about the new regime. Rather, the Khmer Rouge were decided to rip Cambodia apart, and to impose a strict Maoist-Stalinist approach to governance which would be adapted with a virulent Khmer racial nationalism, a 'purification' of society and a creation of a single class of revolutionary worker-peasants – though the more-equal-than-others hierarchy of in situ communism would quickly emerge.

Once Pol Pot's (entirely indoctrinated) young brother-soldiers took Phnom Penh, they immediately instituted a radical agrarian policy that required everybody to leave the city and 'return to the villages', though most had never been near one. And everybody meant everybody. Children, the elderly and the pregnant, hospital patients, the sick and the blind. Within three days a city of two million had been reduced to a husk of 50,000. Within weeks tens of thousands were dying of starvation and sickness. Targeted class enemies and those who didn't cooperate were dispatched far sooner, shot on the spot.

Unlike the policies of Hitler, Stalin and Mao, which, though despicable, were invested with some elements of cunning and at least a tenuous connection with reality, it's hard to judge Pol Pot's vision in a similar vein. It would be far too charitable to call it exceptionally idealised and naive; it was, simply, profoundly stupid.

Consider the approach to feeding the population, for instance. With trade and foreign aid outlawed – not the smartest start – the Cambodian state was immediately forced to be self-sufficient. But individualism was considered heresy, which meant that any use of a person's own labour or skills was also outlawed; this included fishing, for example, which until then supplied 80 percent of the country's protein needs. All citizens' labour now belonged to the state and so did all produce of the land. But 'collectivised farms' proved hopeless at meeting requirements because they proved to be, when the hard-left euphemisms were shelved, nothing less than slave labour gangs. The regime planned to produce three tons of rice per hectare per year, but we've seen how well centrally planned economies go, and the results would not have surprised any reasonable person. They produced a third of that, which was about par before the revolution. City dwellers had no farming experience, of course, and this didn't help. Nor did the fact that politically appropriate district leaders might be adolescents who didn't have a clue and yet reigned supreme. Nor did the fact that much of the slave labour was tasked with digging ditches and clearing forests, often with their bare hands, rather than farming.

Food supply was just the half of it. The usual communist bans came into effect immediately: no capitalism, class, religion or personal freedoms. But also: no music, sport, books, 'Western' medicine or holidays. Parents were deemed a bad idea; henceforth children would be taken into custody by the state from age seven. Love was not allowed; appropriate marriages would be arranged throughout society. And abolishing capitalism wasn't deemed sufficient; money itself was banned.

Within days of the regime change, banks, schools, offices, hospitals and industries were closed. Eventually almost all institutions of any kind ceased to function. The defining racism of the Khmer Rouge was quickly made apparent. Ethnic Chinese, Thais and Vietnamese were banned from speaking their languages on pain of death. Pol Pot loathed the Vietnamese, in particular, and in time they would be eradicated entirely. In the worst cases, Cambodian husbands would be forced to murder their Vietnamese wives. Muslim Chams, a Cambodian minority, endured a ferocious pogrom that wiped out half their population. Buddhist priests were executed and their temples burnt to the ground. Businesspeople, traders, doctors and

'If we wish to defend the fruits of the revolution there must be no let-up. We must strike while the iron is hot to build socialism. The party must exercise its leading role with the use of cutting-edge violence. This is the most important factor, the decisive factor, the power that drives things forward.'
– *Khmer Rouge resolution, 1976*

other 'parasites' and 'intellectuals' – basically anyone with an education – were targeted, often identified only by their wearing of spectacles or knowledge of another language. They were shot or simply clubbed to save ammunition, and buried in mass graves, 'the killing fields', a term made famous in the 1980s by the Oscar-winning movie of the name. Entire families were eradicated, the babies buried alive, thrown to crocodiles or tossed about on bayonets.

The Khmer Rouge wiped out the entire educated, intellectual, cultural and business elite of a country in a matter of months, and with it any hope of progress. It has been estimated that a million people died like that alone. A million. Of a population of 7 million.

When the inevitable paranoia settled over Pol Pot and the Stalinesque party purge was deemed necessary, his enemies – men, women and children – were taken to the high-school-cum-torture barracks in Phnom Penh known as S-21, where they were photographed, catalogued and tortured. The torturers who mistakenly killed their prisoners before a confession was extracted were themselves tortured. Of more than 14,000 prisoners who were processed through S-21, seven people survived; the rest were disposed of in the killing fields.

Pol Pot's racial obsessions and destructive bent were eventually his downfall. He antagonised the Vietnamese to such an extent that they eventually invaded Cambodia, routing the defenceless, enfeebled nation within two weeks and scattering the Khmer Rouge into the jungle. Pol Pot lived in the wild for two decades before the remnants of his very own party put him on trial, not for genocide, but for treason. He died under house arrest, possibly murdered, possibly having committed suicide, in 1998.

Several of his lieutenants, including Nuon Chea, a.k.a. Brother Number Two, and Kang Kek Iew, the commander of S-21 better known as Comrade Duch, were finally detained and put on trial from 2007 onwards. The Khmer Rouge Tribunal continues to this day.

It's far beyond the line in the sand we mark as 'superfluous' to make the point that Pol Pot was a bad person. His regime's total death toll was probably around 1.7 million, but anywhere up to 2.2 million is plausible, all of it barbarous, entirely avoidable or both. It's evident to us that his evil was – even in a book that features a collection of world-class, outstandingly high-quality bastards – arguably *primus inter pares*. To visit the 'stupas' of skulls at the Choeung Ek killing field and elsewhere, to read of the genocidal details of the Khmer Rouge, even to watch *The Killing Fields*, is enough to despair at man's incredible capacity for hate and self-destruction.

And when the emotion is spent, Pol Pot's legacy is a shattered country barely recovering today, its people reluctant to school their children because they are still terrified of the implications of education. It is also the understanding that repeated itself like a nauseating St Vitus Dance meme throughout the 20th century: that, to some, no crime is inexcusable in the pursuit of ideology.

> **'I want to tell you, my conscience is clear. Everything I've done is first and foremost for the nation and the people – the people of Cambodia.'**
>
> *– Pol Pot, speaking in an interview in the Cambodian jungle, 1997.*
> *He died the following year*

Gavrilo Princip

25 July 1894 – 28 April 1918

Youthful idealist; Yugoslav nationalist; assassin of Archduke Franz Ferdinand, heir to the Austro-Hungarian throne; unwitting instigator of World War I; personification of unintended consequences

WHEN THE CENTENARY OF GAVRILO PRINCIP'S ASSASSINATION of Archduke Franz Ferdinand came around on 28 June 2014, there was no consensus in Sarajevo on how to mark the occasion. This little fact goes some way to illustrating the complexity and the sometimes toxicity of Balkan politics, and the divisive nature of the memory of Princip.

Princip was a young Bosnian Serb activist who felt strongly that Croatia, Bosnia and Herzegovina ought to be free of the yoke of their Austro-Hungarian overlords and united with their Serbian neighbours as one country, a proposed Yugoslavia. At the dewy-eyed age of 19, Princip joined Young Bosnia, an activist grouping of schoolboys and university students with this same aim.

To that end Princip and his conspirators decided they should kill the Archduke, heir apparent to the Austro-Hungarian throne, in Sarajevo in June 1914. The assassination attempt would have gone down as a comically hopeless historical footnote had Princip not been blessed with the most extraordinary luck.

As Ferdinand's open-topped car drove through thronging crowds, the first two conspirators chickened out. The third would-be assassin, Nedeljko Čabrinović, threw a timed bomb, but it bounced off the folded convertible roof of Ferdinand's car and instead blew up the car driving behind him. Čabrinović then swallowed a cyanide tablet and jumped into the Miljacka

River, but the cyanide was out of date and only made him feel a bit ill, and the river was but a few inches deep – far too shallow to drown in – so he was captured.

The motorcade then drove off apace, speeding past the remaining assassins, who didn't have time to act. After making a speech at the town hall, Ferdinand decided to visit in hospital those injured in the earlier bombing, but the convoy took a wrong turn – into Franz Josef Street, named after the Archduke's uncle, the emperor – and was told to stop in order to return to the planned route. As fortune would have it, Princip had given up on his revolutionary plans for the day and had a bite to eat in a nearby deli. Lo and behold, as he walked out the door, his intended target was in a car stalled mere metres away. Princip walked up to the car, drew his pistol and fired two shots; one hit Ferdinand's wife Sophie, Duchess von Hohenberg, in the abdomen, and the other severed the Archduke's jugular. They both died within a few minutes. Princip chewed on another ineffective cyanide pill, tried and failed to shoot himself, and was captured.

With those two gunshots Princip unwittingly unleashed a hell on earth unlike anything humanity had suffered. The house of cards fell apart as follows. Austria threatened Serbia, which it saw as being behind the murder. But Serbia was supported by its ally Russia. Austria sought confirmation of its ally Germany's support, which it got. France, meanwhile, made it clear it stood with Russia. Austria sent an ultimatum to Serbia. Russia mobilised its army in response. Serbia rejected the ultimatum. Austria declared war on Serbia. Russia fully mobilised its army. Germany mobilised its army in return, declaring war on Russia and France, and invaded France via Belgium, in order to avoid a war on two fronts. By invading Belgium the British invoked a guarantee of Belgian safety from Germany and declared war on Germany. It was 4 August 1914.

Not bad for six weeks' work.

> # 'One day the great European War will come out of some damned foolish thing in the Balkans.'
>
> *– Otto von Bismarck, 1888*

The indescribable horrors that would follow, at Passchendaele and Verdun and the Somme and in Russia and Serbia and at Gallipoli, are all well known. Ultimately, 15 million people died – of whom 8.5 million were soldiers, an astonishing, unprecedented figure in human history – four empires collapsed and Europe was left devastated as a result of what became known as The Great War. And out of World War I came yet more destruction, not least its rematch in 1939.

It's obvious that Princip could not have foreseen all this – and it's not like we're making an argument for the justice of the Austro-Hungarian Empire here either – but that's exactly the point. History is a long tale of cause and effect, and had Princip known or cared about the extended implications of his actions, he might have second-guessed his righteous intentions. Princip's story is, therefore, a cautionary tale about the seductive dangers of youthful idealism and passion for violent and radical change that angry young men sometimes find irresistible. Princip thought he was doing the right thing for the Slavs of Europe. History, however, doesn't remember him like that.

Several of Princip's co-conspirators were executed for their treasonous actions, while he was sentenced to a 20-year prison term, too young by weeks to qualify for the gallows under Habsburg law. He would die, crippled by skeletal tuberculosis, four years later on 28 April 1918, mere months before the end of the war. He would have no doubt heard of the slaughter engulfing Europe from his jail cell. One wonders what he thought of it all in hindsight.

'The first of the two world wars proved the worst disaster in modern history, perhaps in all history, from which most of the subsequent problems of the twentieth century sprang, and many of which continue, fortissimo, into the twenty-first.'

– historian Paul Johnson

Cecil John Rhodes

5 July 1853 – 26 March 1902

Prime Minister of the Cape Colony 1890-1896; founder of De Beers; monopolist, megalomaniac and war monger; racist exploiter and corrupter of people – all in the name of Empire

THEY SAY, ONLY HALF-JOKINGLY, that the British climate was the greatest ever colonising force in the history of the world. In one case, certainly, it would appear to be the truth. It was the cold of Britain that dispatched, in 1870, one of the most voracious colonialists in world history to South Africa where, his parents hoped, the climate would help him overcome his asthma. Cecil John Rhodes was that man, and the decision to send him to his brother's cotton farm in the Umkomazi Valley near Durban would have tremendous implications for the subcontinent that are very much felt to this day. Rhodes's immense and enduring influence from Cape Town to Lake Tanganyika was possible because of the confluence of two important factors: his enormous fortune, gained at an early age, and his fervent belief in the rightness and necessity of English imperialism. Ultimately, the ambition and actions of this sickly man, despite its 'civilising' intentions, would be the supreme embodiment of the devastating and divisive legacy of empire.

Rhodes's wealth came from his dealings on the diamond mines in Kimberley. A motivated and street-smart operator, he networked and planned and collaborated, and by 1888 he had cajoled and bullied and persuaded major industry players that Kimberley's diamond mines ought to be controlled by a single entity. De Beers Consolidated Mines was formed in March of that year, with Rhodes declaring his intent to make it 'the richest, the greatest, and the most powerful company the world has ever seen'. Rhodes was despised by the many poor miners he had put out of work but, at the age of 35, he was in today's terms a billionaire. Business success was, however, simply a means to an end: power.

As he developed his diamond business, Rhodes found time to take regular boat trips back to Britain to study at Oriel College, Oxford, a place that impressed him greatly. He was much affected by the teachings of John Ruskin, who exhorted his undergraduates thus: 'We are still undegenerate in race; a race mingled with the best northern blood... Will you youths of England make your country again a royal throne of kings, a sceptred isle? This is what England must either do or perish; she must found colonies as fast and as far as she is able, formed of her most energetic and worthiest men; seizing every piece of fruitful waste ground she can set her foot on, and there teaching these her colonists that their chief virtue is to bear fidelity to their country, and that their first aim is to advance the power of England by land and sea.'

'Africa is still lying ready for us. It is our duty to take it.'

– Cecil John Rhodes

A political career was always integral to Rhodes's ambition.

Having been elected to the Cape Colony parliament at the age of 28, it took ten years for Rhodes to work his way, doing whatever was necessary, into the position of prime minster of the Cape Colony. He had also established the British South Africa Company, a chartered company much like the Dutch East India Company had been in the 17th and 18th centuries, which had an astonishing mandate to exert British influence over vast expanses of the African interior, and could call on its own private army to do so. On top of this, Rhodes controlled 90 percent of the world's diamond production, a quite astounding monopoly.

As prime minister, he – naturally – pursued legislation that favoured mine owners, such as laws that allowed the government to boot black people off their land if, for example, their land happened to contain diamonds and other minerals. He was also instrumental in the development of exclusively black 'native reserves' in the 1890s and other proto-apartheid legislation.

The road to Cairo is a long one and for Rhodes it led through Matabeleland in modern-day Zimbabwe. Armed with a dodgy concession, Rhodes received a charter from the UK government allowing him to prospect and to raise concessions from the Zambezi River to the Great Lakes of central Africa. In effect Rhodes annexed more than a million square miles, simply taking it from its indigenous people, using whatever chicanery was necessary to do so.

By the mid-1890s, there seemed but one genuine obstacle in Rhodes's way. The Transvaal Republic, with its newly discovered mineral wealth, remained stubbornly anti-British and protectionist under the leadership of Paul Kruger. In 1895 Rhodes supported a cynical raid on the Transvaal that ended in abject failure, causing great consternation. He was forced to resign as prime minister, and the affair ultimately proved to be a primary cause of the Anglo-Boer War four years later. As Jan Smuts phrased it in 1906, it 'was the real declaration of war'.

Rhodes died of heart failure in Muizenberg near Cape Town in 1902, three months before his fiftieth birthday. His name and marks are left across southern Africa, noticeably in Cape Town, where his prominent memorial looks down over the university. For more than eighty years he even had a country named after him, and the scholarship that bears his name has been hugely influential, sending thousands of students to Oxford (including Bill Clinton and three Australian prime ministers). But all that he bequeathed was based on the exploitation of black labour. The ramifications of his influence are widely evident in the politics of southern Africa in the past fifty years, particularly in the calamitous history of Rhodesia-Zimbabwe and in the actions of the leaders of apartheid South Africa, the fundamental basics of which he had pioneered.

Rhodes's legacy also continues to ricochet off the walls of South African universities. In 2015 a student movement against perceived anti-black racism at the University of Cape Town targeted a statue of Rhodes as symbolic of white supremacy and 'colonised' education. The 'Rhodes Must Fall' campaign was later hijacked by political opportunists and anti-Semitic racists who resorted to the old fascist playbook of burning art and harassing people trying to go about their business. Amid the chaos, university administrators caved under the pressure and the statue was removed. A similar attempt to have a statue of Rhodes dismantled at Oriel College – initiated by a black South African student on Rhodes scholarship – was rejected by Oxford.

The respective reactions to these campaigns says a lot about the way history is perceived in Britain and South Africa, the ex-coloniser and the ex-colony. The former regards Rhodes as a man of his time with an ambiguous past, whose statue deserves the same treatment as another at Oriel, that of Edward II, who was loathed by his subjects, forced to abdicate and probably murdered in prison. The latter, meanwhile, increasingly want to rid the physical and political landscape of his memory. In August 2017, for example, the process to rename Rhodes University in Grahamstown was publicised. There is perhaps some understanding of this discrepancy to be gained in comparing the financial and social capital of the average student at Oxford and that at the University of Cape Town. The former are not directly affected by the deeds of Rhodes (or Edward II) today; the latter certainly are.

'We must find new lands from which we can easily obtain raw materials and at the same time exploit the cheap slave labour that is available from the natives of the colonies. The colonies would also provide a dumping ground for the surplus goods produced in our factories.'

– *Cecil John Rhodes*

> 'I contend that we are the first race in the world, and that the more of the world we inhabit the better it is for the human race... If there be a God, I think that what he would like me to do is paint as much of the map of Africa British Red as possible.'
>
> *– Cecil John Rhodes*

Whatever your opinion on this particular matter, what cannot be denied by those who read history with an open mind is that it was Rhodes who first redistributed land along racial lines, usually with appalling violence. It was Rhodes who controlled the media and used paid mercenaries to put his opponents to the sword. It was Rhodes who encouraged a political culture of corporatist corruption and self-aggrandising power-mongering, surrounding himself with appeasers and sycophants and ignoring the wants and needs of the citizens of the land. And it was Rhodes who introduced violent land grabs in South Africa and in what would become Zimbabwe a century before its current travails began. Rhodes not only maintained a shockingly racist view of Africa and Africans; he regrettably had the money and the political clout to go a long way to achieving his ambitions.

Though there were other Rhodes-type figures throughout the continent, Cecil John was its greatest imperialist bar none. The rest of Africa is perhaps fortunate that he died when he did.

Charles Saatchi

b. 9 June 1943

Renowned adman; probably the most influential and highest-profile contemporary art collector in the world; the clothesless emperor of modern art

FOR SEVERAL WEEKS OVER THE ENGLISH SUMMER OF 2013, Charles Saatchi may well have been one of the most maligned men in Britain – nay, the world! After being photographed at Scott's restaurant in central London with his hands at the throat of his wife, celebrity chef Nigella Lawson, he was reported to have 'abused and humiliated' her for nearly half an hour.[1] The tabloids, ever excited by delicious scandal, were aghast. How could the delectable and plummy-voiced Nigella have to suffer such intolerable cruelty? Days later, Saatchi was cautioned by the police for assault.

As much as the incident diminished Saatchi's public reputation, and as messily as his third marriage fell apart in the weeks that followed, Charles Saatchi is not exhibited here for being the face of upper-class domestic abuse or even for being a nasty piece of work. He is here, rather, for being the man who has abused us all – with nasty pieces of artwork.

Though ours is a list beset (necessarily) with war, death and injustice, we must make room for the more refined elements of human evolution for it to offer a more complete picture of the messed-up elements of our modern existence. If our culture is what separates us from the beasts of the field then it is surely our duty to object when we see it failing; hence the sportsmen and women scattered about these pages, the boy-man whose music may well presage the end of days (Bieber) and the film-maker who forged the path for the dumbed-down movie schlock that we get served up as entertainment today (Spielberg). But what higher refinement can we claim than art? And what bigger load of absolute bloody balls than modern art?

In the descent from, say, Michelangelo's *David* or Bernini's *Apollo and Daphne* to Jeff Koons's *Balloon Dog (Orange)**, there are several junctures in the history of art that could mark the point at which art's acceptance as a widely admired aesthetic cultural reflection began to unravel. You might argue that it was the development of photography in the mid-19th century that set the ball rolling, tempting artists towards more abstract depictions of the world around them instead of competing with the verisimilitude of the camera. Or, specifically, that it was the French Impressionists of the late 19th century who promoted the idea of aesthetic relativism and upset the classicists with their revolutionary splodged take on life. Or, even more specifically, that it was a moment in 1917 when avante-garde artist Marcel Duchamp turned a urinal on its side, called it *Fountain*, and caused the art world to express a collective 'What the f-?' and spin off its axis.

As a prominent personality in the development of the 'readymade' and concept art, Duchamp probably came closest for our purposes, but he takes second place here to Charles Saatchi, the man most intimately associated with the branding and marketing of modern art today. In particular, Saatchi was the driver at the forefront of the emergence of the Young British Artists (or YBAs) in the late 1980s, and if there is a movement that represents the descent into farce of what art is meant to be, this has to be it. If you're not sure what we're talking about, think: *The Physical Impossibility Of Death In The Mind Of Someone Living*, which is a tiger shark preserved in formaldehyde; or *My Bed*, an unmade bed with some unappealing bedroom detritus on the floor next to it. These are the seminal works of the most celebrated of the YBAs, respectively Damien Hirst and Tracey Emin – and by seminal, it is literally so in the case of the latter installation, which includes used condoms (among other things) in it.

If the preposterous pretension of the title of Hirst's pickled shark doesn't fire the distress flares, consider the deterioration of the work: the original shark was incompetently preserved in 1991 and had to be replaced with a new specimen in 2006. Interpret that how you will.

---

* If you don't know it, it's a large stainless-steel sculpture that looks like a balloon dog. In orange. It sold on auction for $58,405,000 in 2013.

Meanwhile, Emin's 1998 artwork didn't feature a tricky technical challenge – it really is just a bed with junk next to it – but she does have to remake it whenever the installation is moved. (Or should that be 're-unmake it'? In the world of concept art, this may be a deep and meaningful question.)

When it was displayed in the Tate Liverpool in 2016, *Guardian* art critic Jonathan Jones was there to witness, in some awe, Emin in action. He wrote:

> *My Bed* has turned into a Proustian time machine. It precisely preserves the stuff of Emin's life at a very particular moment, and this means it gets ever more atmospheric, resonant and mysterious. It is gradually turning into the Pompeii object of the 1990s. There's even a yellowing copy of *The Guardian* from September 1998. All our yesterdays. It goes into the accumulating wreckage beside the bed, along with an Orangina bottle whose contents are so brown and murky I thought it was diseased piss.

There appears to be no sense of irony in any of this. In his concluding paragraph Jones writes:

> It is finished. Stuff has become art. And not some dry intellectual work of conceptual art, either. *My Bed* is a visceral monument to being alive. It is a mirror of its maker. Emin is pleased: she reckons this is the best bed she's done.

At this point it's worth noting that both artworks were nominated for the prestigious (and lucrative) Turner Prize, of which Jones has been a juror. The prize is named for JMW Turner, arguably the UK's most revered artist of all time, and for fans of the celebrated Romanticist painter it may be difficult to compare the emotional heft of, for example, Turner's *The Fighting Temeraire Tugged To Her Last Berth To Be Broken Up, 1838* with that of *The Physical Impossibility Of Death In The Mind Of Someone Living*, or admire the wonder and technical brilliance of, say, *Rain, Steam And Speed* against *My Bed*.

We don't need to explore Charles Saatchi in too much detail to gain any deeper understanding of his role in all this. He comes from a wealthy immigrant family and evidently grew up a shy and retiring type needing constant reassurance. He turned himself into one of the world's great admen, starting Saatchi & Saatchi with his brother Maurice in 1970 and growing it into the largest agency in the world. And he was obsessed with pop art from a young age.

Most damningly for our purposes, Saatchi was effectively the patron of the YBA movement, funding many of them in their early years, collecting their art and displaying it in exhibitions with names like 'Sensation' that gained global fame and recognition. In the case of the two artworks mentioned above, he was, not incidentally, their original owner. He commissioned Hirst's shark for £50,000 in 1991 and sold it for either $8 million or $12 million, depending on your source, in 2004. He bought Emin's bed for £150,000 in 2000 and sold it for £2.54 million in 2014.

Today, Charles Saatchi's great artistic legacy is represented by the Saatchi Gallery in London, self-described as 'The World's No 1 Museum On Social Media'. Housed somewhat unexpectedly in the magnificent, classically lined Duke of York Headquarters in Chelsea, the gallery boasts of more than 1.5 million visitors a year and offers free entrance – a gesture of Saatchi generosity or an indication that money in this oeuvre is not made at the gallery door?

Either way, a wander about is as enlightening as you might expect. On one particular visit you might find a couple of Hirst paintings that could be described as 'colourful' or 'child-like' depending on your point of view. (Certainly 'expensive' comes to mind, starting at £30,000.) There may be a notably abstract creation of pencil, oil stick, spray paint and oil by Christian Rosa titled *Oh Fuck*. And a five-metre-long canvas of random pen-like scribblings – *Madre Perla V-11* by José Lerma – which appears to be a collage of pen-on-paper doodles that a gloomy teenager has put together over a year's worth of boring biology lessons. The whole thing is balanced on a cheap keyboard on the one side and what appears to be a

'You needn't be a foot soldier in the "my child could have done that" brigade to wonder whether, in some cases, a blizzard of artspeak might not disguise a thin thought with complex articulation; and that far from opening the gates of self-realisation, it's a deception perpetrated on a credulous public with the connivance of a powerful elite who do very well out of it, thank you.'

– *Jonathan Beckman, UK author and journalist* [2]

fake baguette on the other and, needless to say, is aesthetically displeasing and inherently awful. But it has the redeeming feature of appearing to have taken a long time to complete – at least, you figure, the artist didn't just throw some rubbish on the floor. *That* piece is in the next room. It's called *I'd Take You There But It Doesn't Exist Anymore*, it's by Oscar Murillo, and it's literally four by five metres of actual rubbish ('mixed media') stuck to some plywood on the floor.

The point, of course, is that all you have with modern art in its current state are (potential) talking points. There is no objective beauty or inherent joy or even eye-catching intrigue in any of this. Art may well be in the eye of the beholder – the rote modern-art counter-argument – but there must surely be something to admire, at least. Where is the talent? Where is the insight and emotion? Why has my soul left the building and popped over to Partridges next door to find a jar of capers and some decent Scottish salmon? (It is, under the circumstances, as valid a question as any to ask.)

The very fact that Charles Saatchi is not an artist is probably the critical factor in all this. He is, if we might put it this way, the enabler. He is the man who has most obviously encouraged the creation of and market for the type of art that can be thrown out by the janitor by mistake*; the type of art, we'd suggest, only the deluded can convince themselves is worthy of any objective admiration. And in giving prominence to these creative frauds he has left little room for the next Matisse or Picasso or vaguely agreeable movement to emerge. (You don't have to love Matisse or Picasso, but you can at least acknowledge their aesthetics and skill.)

As with all art, however, this is merely an opinion: you, dear reader, are free to make up your mind as you see fit, just as someone who buys a £2.5 million unmade bed has made up theirs. If, however, you're still not

---

* Which has happened on at least five occasions that we are aware of. Damian Hirst, our intrepid shark bottler, was the artist affected in a 2001 incident at the Eyestorm Gallery in London, which saw one of his artworks, consisting of beer bottles, coffee cups and filled ashtrays, being cleared away. A similarly themed artwork was treated with similar results by the cleaning staff at the Museion museum in Bolzano, Italy in 2015. In 1986 a work in Dusseldorf featuring a dirty bathtub was scrubbed clean, while artworks with cardboard, paper and newspaper, which apparently looked like leftover packaging after the installations had been erected, were disposed of by mistake at the Tate Britain in London in 2004 and the Sala Murat gallery in Bari, Italy in 2014. Most appropriately for this discussion, Tracey Emin's *My Bed* was once tidied up by a museum guard who believed it had been vandalised.

> **'Modern art is a disaster area. Never in the field of human history has so much been used by so many to say so little.'**
>
> *– Banksy*

convinced that the emperors of modern art – whether they be the artists themselves, or their curators and collectors – have no clothes, we suggest looking up the opinions of legendary UK art critic Brian Sewell, who died in 2015. Sewell, known for calling a spade a spade, described Tracy Emin as 'talentless' and 'a self-regarding exhibitionist'.

Of the work of Damian Hirst, he said, 'I can sum it up as shiny shit.' And: 'fucking dreadful'.[3]

OJ Simpson

b. 9 July 1947

One-time all-American sports hero; once wealthy, now bankrupt NFL Hall-of-Famer; central figure in 'the trial of the century'; godfather of reality television

HEREWITH THE EVIDENTIAL TRAIL of Orenthal James Simpson's crimes to humanity.

First, he became exceptionally famous playing American football, otherwise known as gridiron, and starring with Leslie Nielsen in the *Naked Gun* movies.

Then, in 1994, he killed his ex-wife and her friend (sigh... legal disclaimer: still disputed; see next page).

Then, several days later after he had been charged with murder, he was pursued at low speeds in his white Ford Bronco – while holding a gun! – for a hundred kilometres around southern Los Angeles by a cavalcade of police cars and seven news helicopters. US television stations interrupted their coverage, including a key NBA championship decider, to transmit the chase live to enthralled viewers. The first live police pursuit in LA had been aired in 1992 but this one was special: it lasted two hours and was watched by an estimated 95 million people, more than had watched that year's Super Bowl.

Then, he became the focus of 'the most publicized murder case in history' and 'the trial of the century'. The criminal trial lasted nearly a year, was famously televised, made ongoing headlines around the world, and resulted in a controversial verdict that was viewed by 150 million people in the United States alone. It was reality television in the truest sense of the term (and much of it was genuinely gripping from legal and socio-cultural perspectives). In the process, OJ Simpson introduced to this enormous audience and made individually famous the members of his legal 'dream team', including a certain Robert Kardashian, his long-time friend who sat next to him throughout the trial. Kardashian's daughters Kourtney, Kim and Khloé were 16, 14 and 11 at the time, and ex-wife Kris Jenner was in the courthouse with her new husband Bruce on the day of the verdict. And so it was, to put it in biblical terms – because let's be a little dramatic about this, it seems appropriate – OJ begat the celebritydom of Robert Kardashian, and Robert Kardashian (literally and figuratively) begat the Kardashians.

OJ Simpson was, infamously, acquitted of the murders of Nicole Brown Simpson and Ron Goldman in the criminal trial in 1995 but found guilty of causing their wrongful deaths in the subsequent civil trial in 1997, and ordered to pay $33.5 million in damages. Polls show that a significant majority of Americans today believe he was guilty of murder, though at the time of the trial it was a hugely divisive racial issue.*

OJ has had numerous other brushes with the law, and in 2008 he was convicted of kidnapping, robbery and various other charges, and given a 33-year prison sentence, having held up a couple of dealers who had

---

* The notable controversy at the time was race-related: the majority of white Americans polled believed Simpson was guilty of murder, while the majority of African-Americans believed he was not guilty. Media interpretation of the results at the time was that this indicated a racial divide within the United States. Today, the controversy has faded, and the majority of both black and white Americans believe he was guilty.

'The world had followed every turn of the case so closely that the trial would permanently change the news cycle and media patterns. Americans had never been so consumed by a single news story. They were forgoing scripted television dramas and soap operas to watch months of trial developments... The trial, culminating in the verdict's broadcast from within the courtroom, created some of the most intense early demand for the current 24-hour news cycle and sowed the seeds for the reality television boom to follow.'

– *Time magazine, reviewing the OJ Simpson trial on its twentieth anniversary in 2015*

apparently stolen some of his sports memorabilia. He was granted parole in 2017.

In our broad survey of some of the people who have wrought misery, mayhem and general degeneracy on the earth, OJ Simpson does not qualify simply for being a criminal, however guilty he may or may not be. He is here as the original subject and foundational building block of modern reality TV. The genuine cultural and social significance of his trial notwithstanding, OJ is now inextricably linked to the average human being's obsession with watching famous and semi-famous and actually-not-that-famous people doing mostly unimpressive, uninteresting, everyday things: driving a car, trying on clothes, talking to a person whose surname is or was Kardashian. He popularised the live car chase. He transformed the way news is reported, in particular celebrity trials, but in fact all news. And, ultimately, he gave us *Keeping Up With The Kardashians*.

So it is thus that OJ Simpson is the First Cause, the Creator of reality TV. A most wicked and regrettable cultural legacy.

See Kim Kardashian.

Steven Spielberg

b. 18 December 1946

Acclaimed film director; pioneer of the New Hollywood era; inventor of the summer blockbuster; basically the reason why the Transformers franchise is a thing

Is STEVEN SPIELBERG OVERRATED? Is he 'crippled as an artist' and even a 'very bad director', as the critics Christopher Bray and Pauline Kael have respectively described him? [1]

Or is he, in fact, underrated? The greatest director of all time, as voted by readers of *Empire* magazine in 2005, with an unrivalled body of work and not enough recognition for his efforts?

Meh. We're on the fence on Spielberg movies. Some good, some bad.

Jaws – good. *Always* – bad.

Raiders Of The Lost Ark – fantastic. *Indiana Jones And The Kingdom Of The Crystal Skull* – a steamy pile.

And yes, if we're plotting trends we could propose that his later work is less interesting and authentic – and good – compared to the earlier stuff, perhaps due to the general fuzzy decline that comes with age or perhaps because it's tough to stay edgy when you're managing your *Forbes*-estimated $3.7-billion empire. Whatever. If that was our general drift this would be an entry on George Lucas.

So, Steven Spielberg isn't here for his artistic merit or lack thereof. He's here because of one of the movies mentioned above, his first big hit, *Jaws*.

Now, if we were philosopher-critic Slavoj Žižek we might be tempted to critically analyse *Jaws* as a mirror of fascist ideology, or dissect the transposition of Peter Benchley's 'great fish' from book to screen in terms of the American right-wing anti-immigrant agenda or Fidel Castro's leftist Marxist interpretation of the shark... Because evidently Castro was a fan.

But we're not doing that either. *Jaws* was a damn great movie any which way you interpret it, and even if it negatively affected beach tourism in the 1970s and '80s and radically depleted your average author's predisposition for wading any further than knee-deep into the ocean, its cultural effects were more fascinating than destructive.

So, to the point then.

Spielberg, by virtue of being the creator of *Jaws*, is here because he invented the summer blockbuster. And the summer blockbuster has ruined movies and movie-going for, by the looks of things, ever more.

Before 1974, when the sea and the cinema were (relatively) safe, movie blockbusters, or 'megapictures', did not exist. There were just movies – of all types and sizes and genres, some good, many bad. *Jaws* was most notably different, not because of its subject matter or story-telling approach, but because of the hoo-ha associated with it: the production budget, the marketing, the *branding*.

'The modern development of [film tie-in] revenue stream is usually seen to have begun with the marketing of the 1975 film, *Jaws*; merchandise connected with *Jaws* included a soundtrack album, T-shirts, plastic tumblers, a book about the making of the movie, the book the movie was based on, beach towels, blankets, shark costumes, toy sharks, hobby kits, iron-on transfers, games, posters, shark-tooth necklaces, sleepwear, water pistols, and many more. We have gone well beyond that today.'

– from *Film As Social Practice* by Graeme Turner

Before *Jaws*, summer in the US was assumed to be a dead time for the studios, when second-rate movies were released to die quiet deaths while everyone was outdoors having a good time. But the producers at Universal Studios, who had bought the cinematic rights to Benchley's book before it was even published, saw in Spielberg's film – set around the 4th of July weekend, the climax of US summer – the opportunity for something else: a revolution in the way movies were watched. Having given the green light to a large production budget, they were persuaded to nearly treble it to $9 million during the prolonged production process. They then doubled down on the promotion. A further $1.8 million was allocated to marketing, of which $700,000 alone went to prime TV advertising spots, an unheard-of strategy. This was all in the run-up to a 'saturation booking' release which saw the film premiering in more than 400 theatres across the country on the same day, another unprecedented move.

Thus was the blockbuster born, a 'high-concept' film with a simple premise, fast-paced action and unforgettable special effects – and an attached franchise-economy. *Jaws* lured in the crowds from their fun in the sun, and presumably the sea, and then brought them back again and again to watch the movie over the course of the summer.

You may be tempted to divert the blame for the invention of the blockbuster to the powers that be at Universal. After all, Spielberg was just a 28-year-old kid with a camera and they were the ones pushing the publicity machine, reinventing the way Hollywood did business. Don't be fooled. It was Spielberg's ability to create a believable escapist fantasy with unforgettable special effects that elevated *Jaws* to era-defining success. In making such a fuss of the movie, the studio was obliged to deliver, and their visionary young director did it for them. (The days when you could polish a movie turd with some sweatshop toys and junkfood tie-ins were yet to come.)

'What interests me more than anything else is the idea. If a person can tell me the idea in 25 words or less, it's going to be a good movie.'

– Steven Spielberg, speaking in 1978 about 'high concept' film-making

Moreover, Spielberg (along with Lucas) was savvy enough to realise that this was the future. In the years ahead he would forge on as the blockbustering pioneer of cinema. Within the decade he had added *Close Encounters Of The Third Kind, Raiders Of The Lost Ark, ET: The Extra-Terrestrial* and *Indiana Jones And The Temple Of Doom* to his CV, and today he is by some margin the highest-grossing director of all time.

Was this new formula for making and selling a movie a bad thing? Not immediately, no. Certainly not if you were a member of the *Star Wars* generation who grew up wishing you could use the Force to open doors and choke out your teachers. Or wishing you could be Indiana Jones or Marty McFly in a time-travelling DeLorean. Or, it should go without saying, a US Navy pilot flying an F-14 Tomcat into the danger zone because you're dangerous, Maverick…

Tony Scott's *Top Gun* was, of course, just an extended music video – an excuse to turn some high-octane aerial footage and homoerotic volleyball shots into a film – and if we're honest and we remove our rose-tinted Ray-Bans, we might concede that the problem here is one that is at least exacerbated by perspective. Which is to say, *Top Gun* was actually a giant crock and we liked it because we were kids. And blockbusters are, essentially, movies for kids.

Today *Jaws*'s $1.8 million marketing budget appears laughable in an age in which the major studios can spend half a billion dollars or more on marketing in a year*. The upshot is that blockbusters are now generally defined by the following criteria:

- marketing budgets that come close to matching or even exceed the production budgets;
- a better-than-average chance of being a sequel, prequel, spin-off or remake[†];
- committee-written plothole-riddled storylines that serve merely as a tenuous link between action set-pieces;
- paper-thin characters that serve merely as cyphers around which the action is based;
- wooden acting that's dialled in by overpaid stars who are basically grown-up babies;
- relentless close-ups of digital explosions, bullets in slow motion and fantastical and supposedly scary creatures;
- a high likelihood of actually being quite boring.

Ironically, Spielberg's *Jaws* was nothing like this. Though the story was improbable and clearly suspended belief, it at least made sense; the characters were complex and memorable (they developed!); the acting was decent; the movie itself wasn't beast-porn, with the shark itself only revealed in all its glory in the last act[‡] – and yes, it was gripping entertainment.

Four decades later, Steven Spielberg is in his seventies and we're all grown up.

If we're being generous and let the 1990s slide, you could say that movie-going has largely been a waste of time since the last half hour of *The Lord Of The Rings* trilogy in 2003. This is because Spielberg's successors – the Michael Bays and Brett Ratners and Gore Verbinsksis and Timur Bekmambetovs – are lazy hacks who are happy to pander to the modern world's instant gratification cravings with *More explosions! More action! More more!* So we see that Steven Spielberg's *Jaws* was the first domino on the disastrous path

---

* According to *Adweek*, the studio that made *Jaws*, Universal, spent $485 million on marketing in 2013. It was beaten into third place by Warner Brothers and Disney, which spent $582 million each.

[†] Eight of the ten highest-grossing movies in 2016 qualify according to this metric. The other two have sequels planned.

[‡] Admittedly this was an act of necessity, as the three mechanical sharks used in the film kept breaking, hence the production delays and budget overruns.

> '[T]here is no question but that movie and ad techniques are intermingling. In fact, one might argue that the New Hollywood's calculated blockbusters are themselves massive advertisements for their product lines – a notion that places a very different value on their one-dimensional characters, mechanical plots, and high-gloss style.'
>
> *– author and critic Thomas Schatz, writing in 2003* [2]

to Michael Bay's *Transformers* franchise. And if you're thinking surely he's not *that* culpable, you're wrong: Spielberg is the executive producer of the franchise.

Yep. Spielberg first made *Transformers* possible, then he actually made *Transformers*.

The real problem, however, is less about the infantile badness of the blockbusters that are being micromanaged into existence these days – you can, after all, just not watch them if you choose. It's that, because the annual studio budgets are hoovered up by the endless pursuit of smash-hit glory, there is almost nothing left over for the moviemakers who want to make films that are thoughtful and engaging and meaningful and, hey, possibly even memorable. Which is why the talented ones do TV these days.

Now that we are not children any more – and are, in fact, acknowledging the cantankerous embrace of middle age – it does get rather tiresome when, come Friday cinema night, your movie viewing options are *Transformers: Never Going Away*, a superhero flick, some or other disaster bomb and a choice of 3D cartoons.

Ah well, this not entirely unrelated quote from Neil Perryman at least provides some perspective on all this: '*Jaws 4* was so bad it made *Jaws 3* look like *Jaws 2*.' [3]

Stalin & Lenin

Vladimir Lenin: 22 April 1870 – 21 January 1924
Joseph Stalin: 18 December 1878 – 5 March 1953

Founders and leaders of the Soviet Union; tyrant and ultra-tyrant of 20th century Marxism; mass killers; solid argument for the end of communism in all forms

Stalin

IN THE LIBERAL WEST, WHEN A PERSON IS BEHOLDEN entirely to others for his livelihood and owns nothing, not even his own labour, this is known as slavery. Elsewhere it's called communism.

There are socialists and communists out there – and the one is, in practice, but a short ethical step from the other – who might accept these requirements of communism but then quibble about the notable differences between it and slavery; what not only sets it apart from the worst forms of human bondage but in fact elevates it into a blissful and desirable state of existence. Before they're tempted, let's add a further layer of common description. In both slavery and communism, an individual has heavily curtailed rights and if he doesn't do what he's told he gets punished, severely and without due process. Frequently, he will be locked up and tortured as a result, and in the worst cases he will be executed.

For those who would argue that this is an overstated charge, the obvious evidence presents itself as the life and times of Joseph Stalin, one of the most evil men of influence in recent history, even of all time – a man who killed dozens of millions of his own people, and who armed the Soviet Union with nuclear weapons in a game of international brinkmanship that might have destroyed the world. Stalin compares (un)favourably with Hitler and Mao for cruel intentions and misery bestowed, and for this reason he headlines our brief account of Soviet communism, but we would be remiss in leaving off Lenin or even in including him separately from Stalin. Because theirs is, in fact, the same story, with the same inevitable outcome.

In the 1920s and '30s the ideological stand-off between capitalism and communism expressed itself in vigorous theoretical debate, especially with the apparent failure of the former as the Great Depression took effect. Both Lenin and Stalin were seen by many prominent thinkers, including the likes of HG Wells, George Bernard Shaw and just about every French intellectual of the time, as wise and wonderful modern saviours, and any inconvenient bloodshed that came to light could, they figured, be brushed aside as a means to a glorious end. (The phrase 'useful fool' or 'useful idiot' is attributed to Lenin's view of these Western acolytes.) It was Orwell who observed that the 'morally sound have known since about 1931 that the Russian regime stinks', but it was only after Stalin's death and his own party's 'de-Stalinisation' from the 1950s onwards that his tyranny came to be universally accepted. Lenin, however, remains something of a contested figure – which is a great injustice for all those he murdered and terrorised.

So for those misguided souls who might concede that okay, yes, Stalin may have got carried away just a little and isn't perchance the best role model for an international ideology but actually Lenin was a champion of the people and his vision was corrupted by his successor, let's start with the original Russian communist revolutionary.

One of the observations you might make after reading about the surge of jingoism that flooded Britain at the start of World War I is the length of the civilian peace that preceded it. All that 'Let's tally-ho and give Jerry a jolly good wallop' nonsense that reached its bitter harvest at Ypres, Verdun and the Somme, and in the verses of Sassoon and Owen, can better be understood if one looks at what people knew. The last major war a standing army had been involved in was in the Crimea, and before that the Napoleonic wars, a century past. Colonial fighting, even the Boer War, were distant affairs and of little relevance to the average Jack. Not only had the technology of mechanised warfare changed for the horrific worse, but the institutional memory of what war actually meant had disappeared.

Are there parallels with the politics of today? When we see leaders publicly calling for the redistribution of private property in London – as, for instance, after the Grenfell Tower inferno in June 2017 – and militant hard-left movements such as the antifa groups* exploding in popularity in the United States and elsewhere, it would suggest as much. Yes, the sheer horror of the story of Soviet communism is all there to be read and understood, with far more information freely available on your smartphone than the 1914 populace would have enjoyed. But a hundred years later we find ourselves in an age of unawareness similar to that which existed in the early 20th century, not for a lack of information but due to a surfeit of it. Today we drown in hashtags and phone alerts and are overwhelmed with information, much of it sheer rubbish, and so the idea to simply expropriate the land/house/Porsche of the wealthy seems a logical idea, because why wouldn't it?

Let's be honest, most of us have Instagrammed more pictures of our breakfasts than we have read books on the fate of the Romanov family in

---

* Members of antifa, short for 'antifascist' or Anti-Fascist Action, are, nominally, opposed to fascism. This may appear to be a good idea but the historical reality suggests otherwise. The original Antifaschistische Aktion, from which the name is derived, was one of several paramilitary-style groups that evolved in Weimar Germany to counter the rise of Hitler's fascism. It can be reasonably argued that ongoing clashes between communists and fascists in fact helped normalise political violence at the time, leading to a wider acceptance and legitimisation of extreme Nazi policies. Today, antifa activists use many similar tactics to ultra-rightwing neo-Nazis and are similarly authoritarian and intolerant of dissenting viewpoints. As such they are effectively the same type of extremist, just from incompatible identity groups and with some moderate but by no means diametrically opposed differences on socio-economic policy. This is a subtler lesson of Hitler and Stalin: that fascists and hard-left socialists are cut from the same cloth, encourage the growth of each other, and are even co-dependent – they need each other to exist.

1918 or the devastating plight of the Ukraine under Soviet collectivised farms in the 1930s – or books, to use the language of preference, on the regime change of a cruel and heartless government and the expropriation of land from wealthy landowners for the benefit of the people.

For the record, seeing as it came up, the Romanov family was the imperial family of Tsar Nicholas II, the last official tsar of Russia, and they were brutally murdered by Lenin's revolutionaries. A year earlier, Lenin had returned from exile abroad after the revolution of February 1917 had seen the abdication of Nicholas. He had then marshalled the Russian Social-Democratic Workers' Party – the Bolsheviks – and taken power by coup in the October Revolution. It was a near-run thing, with a devastating five-year civil war between Red and White (and Green) armies to follow, and it was an event that was to radically shape the history of the world.

The worst of Lenin's terror would be carefully massaged into oblivion by Russian propaganda. For instance, it only emerged after the fall of communism in the early 1990s that he was directly responsible for the deaths of up to 300,000 people at the hands of his secret police, the Cheka. He himself had robbed banks to finance his party in the early days, and he embraced and used men of absolute violence to further his bidding, Stalin and Trotsky the most high-profile of the lot. A famous quote of his, 'A revolution without firing squads is meaningless,' is enlightening. For any who once doubted or (credulously) still doubt his and his revolutionaries' moral approach, the treatment of the Romanovs is even more so.

Revolutions are seldom inspired by benevolent emperors doing right by their people, so make no bones about it, Nicholas was himself an inept and tragic leader. A man from another age, he had led his country to ruin, most notably in World War I, so let's assume the harshest punishment: he would have to be sacrificed in execution. Lenin's men, however, defied any notion of moral treatment. After 16 months under house arrest the order was given, and Nicholas, his wife, five children and remaining entourage were shot, bayonetted and clubbed to death, after which their bodies were hacked apart, doused in acid, burned and buried in the forest. Afterwards the Bolsheviks announced the death of Nicholas but claimed that his family were being held securely in captivity. News of the mass murder only leaked in 1926, and the Soviet government repressed all investigation into the matter for decades. The Romanovs' remains were located by an amateur investigator in 1979 and made public ten years after that.

Now here's the thing: though it has never been confirmed, it is highly likely that Lenin gave the order. For certain, he approved of the killing and didn't punish the perpetrators. Here, then, was the nascent communist movement in action: revelling in the mutilation of women and children without even the tenuous benefit of some kind of political purpose, and suppressing news that the public would, one imagines, find important when considering their choice of political allegiance. This microcosm of the Russian Revolution was Lenin in summary.

In the harsh, but we would conclude fair, judgement of Simon Sebag Montefiore, an authority on Russian history, Lenin was the man 'who created the blood-soaked Soviet experiment that was based from the very start on random killing and flint-hearted repression, and which led to the murders of many millions of innocent people'. He 'relished the use of terror and bloodletting and was as frenziedly brutal as he was intelligent and cultured'.

In his cruel and rational wisdom, Lenin ultimately saw the potential for vast destruction in Stalin and, having elevated him to general secretary of the party, he wanted him demoted. But his rule ended prematurely: he suffered a series of strokes and died at the age of 53. Stalin would go on to win the battle for succession with Trotsky. Thus, out of Lenin came Stalin.

Born Josef Djugashvili in the Georgian town of Gori 2,000 kilometres south of Moscow, there are no naive Western interpretations of Stalin, the Man of Steel. If anything, his positive geopolitical achievements are underplayed. In particular his role in defeating Hitler, which saw the Soviets conservatively losing 20 million soldiers and civilians while inflicting 80 percent of German casualties, should probably be better appreciated. (Stalin's ruthless capacity for sacrificing his own people and cities played its part here.) He also industrialised his previously primitive country – just in time to help win World War II – and, for what it's worth, expanded Russia to its greatest territorial extent.

But he is known for his tyranny and deaths and gulags, as well he should be.

Stalin's crimes as leader of the Union of Soviet Socialist Republics are vast and altogether too well documented – if not well read – for us to make much of a dent in the list of gigantically awful things that happened to people under Soviet rule. This, then, is a mere taste.

As a boy, Josef Djugashvili was bullied at school because of his pockmarked face, caused by an attack of chicken pox. His mother had wanted him to be a priest and, indeed, he is said to have excelled at the seminary in Tiflis. His reasons for diverging from this chosen path in 1899 have not ever really been established, but it is likely that his increasingly loud politics had some part to play, specifically his rabid anti-tsarist sentiments. One imagines, on this note, that his brewing megalomania and psychopathy may not have been entirely validated in seminary school.

Staying in Tiflis, he joined the revolutionary labour movement and, apparently without self-consciousness, changed his name to Stalin, one of many aliases, and set out to establish himself as a man of action for the cause of Lenin's Bolsheviks. To do so, he would use his two God-given natural skills: thuggery and a mundane ability to organise meetings and posters and pamphlets and whatnot. It is said that Stalin wasn't much of a speaker, but he was not averse to killing those who needed to be killed and he was extremely good at robbing banks and kidnapping people for ransom, which was how fringe political parties raised money in those days. He was arrested twice and served two sentences in Siberia.

His rise as a Bolshevik operative allowed him to slowly infiltrate the revolutionary and eventually Soviet machines, and he used both his position as secretary general of the party and the Russian Civil War to build a power base that included the key generals. After Lenin's death in 1924, there was a lengthy period of manoeuvring as Stalin forged convenient partnerships to sideline Trotsky and consolidate his position. All the major players he allied with at this point would later be liquidated, as was Stalin's way. By 1929 Trotsky, now his mortal enemy, was in exile – he would wind up dead, by ice pick to the head, in Mexico City a decade later – and Stalin was the uncontested top dog. It was finally time for Stalin to assert himself, and at this point in the story we return to the Ukraine, briefly touched upon before, for his first great criminal act and the consummate example of the failure of communism in at least two distinct ways.

The standard communist move, collectivised farming, had now been implemented, and with it came the inevitable suppression of those peasants who resisted its sheer idiocy and inefficiency. Thus we see the immediate functional problem of communism: that the theory translates poorly into practice and one of the basic human needs, a reliable food supply, is put in jeopardy almost instantly.

Another necessary Marxist move, as per the theory, is the elimination of class differences, which in the Ukraine called for the eradication of the kulaks, the supposedly wealthy peasants, who had differentiated themselves from their countrymen by making a fist of things and were therefore labelled 'profiteering bloodsuckers' or similar dehumanising terms. Bear in mind that a generation earlier they had all been serfs under the tsar, and the definition of 'wealthy' might translate to a few cows more than your neighbours. The kulaks tended to be wealthier because they were more successful farmers; by exiling or murdering them Stalin effectively culled the portion of the farming population who knew what they were doing, a familiar communist refrain if you've read this far in the book, but something of a duh-revelation at the time.

The famine that resulted from all this was industrial-scale. Between 1929 and 1933, anywhere from three to ten million died, even as Stalin continued to export grain, both to avoid losing international face and also to earn foreign currency to pay for his economic plans. Timothy Snyder lays the circumstances bare in his harrowing book *Bloodlands*:

> Survival was a moral as well as a physical struggle. A woman doctor wrote to a friend in June 1933 that she had not yet become a cannibal, but was 'not sure that I shall not be one by the time my letter reaches you'. The good people died first. Those who refused to steal or to prostitute themselves died. Those who gave food to others died. Those who refused to eat corpses died. Those who refused to kill their fellow man died. Parents who resisted cannibalism died before their children did.

Stalin's regime responded not by ceasing its grain exports, but by printing posters that read To EAT YOUR OWN CHILDREN IS A BARBARIAN ACT. The Ukrainian government has since declared this period a genocide, on a par with the Holocaust, which it terms the *Holodomor*. (Since 2015 all Soviet statues in the Ukraine, including 1,320 statues of Lenin and more than a thousand miscellaneous monuments, have been taken down.)

Other than driving millions of people from serfdom (under the tsars) to slavery (in collective farms) and making them choose between the equally unappetising extremes of eating their neighbours' suppurating corpses or death, Stalin also ramped up the paranoia surrounding those who would undermine the revolution, which is to say pretty much anyone he didn't like. In 1934 he used the murder of a high-profile politician, Sergei Kirov – which he may have ordered himself – to initiate the Great Terror, a purge which lasted years and saw up to a million souls exiled, fired or executed. One-third of all army officers were shot, and mass graves were filled with thousands of bodies on the outskirts of major cities. Stalin's paranoia was almost completely boundless, and as a result Russians were driven to observe a terrified cult of personality around the man.

In time, approximately three million people died in the gulags, the *Glavnoe Upravlenie ispravitel'no-trudovykh LAGerei* or Main Administration of Corrective Labour Camps, which were strung out like a chain of islands across the Soviet Union – hence the title of Aleksandr Solzhenitsyn's book *The Gulag Archipelago*. What kind of 'correctives', you might legitimately ask, went on there? Well, these were violent corrections by the state of the thoughts, ideas and opinions of people who were found to be wrong. So, as in Solzhenitsyn's case, you might be sent to various labour camps for eight years for complaining to a friend in a private letter in 1945 that you thought Stalin could do a better job of running the war effort. Solzhenitsyn acknowledged that he was relatively lucky; he was not excessively tortured, forced to dig canals in the ice-riven earth with his hands, or indeed worked to death. Others were, and they may have been locked up simply because of their ethnicity and class, which also needed violent correction or just a plain old-fashioned bullet in the skull.

The upshot was a state of politics and being that was the closest approximation to hell on earth that could be formulated by man: a society in which daily life was steeped in a misery of lies for all – except those who were sent to the gulags, tortured and killed.

To attempt to quantify this sordid state of existence, Stalin is generally held responsible for the deaths of somewhere in the region of 20 million people, perhaps two-thirds from straight-up murder, the rest from criminal, often intentional neglect. As ever, the numbers are something of a thumb-suck, with estimates varying wildly – as high as 50 million overall at the extreme end.

But the numbers become almost meaningless after a while, don't they? Anybody who has lost a friend or a family member will know that a single life is irreducibly precious. That's why it's so critical to remember that these large numbers are made up of individual tragedies of unimaginable vastness, and that they are not diminished in any way by the reality that they were one of many, or by the supposed good intentions and unfortunate incompetence of those who implemented the policies.

This is a critical understanding. Whereas there is, at a stretch, a possible reading of Soviet history that suggests a positive idea lost its way, you need to be pretty blind to the enormous evidence available that shows the reality of it; that purges, gulags, slavery and mass executions are a necessary part of the communist state. So, equally, is war. Marxism dictates that the workers of the world will unite, that communism is stateless and thus a global, internationalist movement. So, not only do communist states send dissenting individuals for correction, they also attempt to correct external states that take a different view. They set themselves as mortal enemies and do what they can to consume them. World War II was thus a wonderful opportunity for Stalin, a chance for him to expand the Soviet empire by gobbling up great chunks of Eastern Europe in the battle against Hitler's fascism. The crimes that had to be committed along the way – such as the murder of 28,000 Polish officers in the Katyn Forest in 1939, and the complete destruction of Warsaw by the German Wehrmacht in 1944 as the Red Army watched, indifferent, from across the Vistula River – simply came with the territory, as it were. Anyone who lived through the subsequent high-stakes chill of the Cold War will not remember it with joy.

Solzhenitsyn – who had to write his book in secret and ultimately won the Nobel Prize for it – was very clear on this. The communist state cannot exist without its worst excesses, he explained. He expanded on this notion in a speech he made in the United States in 1975 while in exile:

> There is a word very commonly used these days: 'anti-communism'. It's a very stupid word, badly put together. It makes it appear as though communism were something original, something basic, something fundamental. Therefore, it is taken as the point of departure, and anti-communism is defined in relation to communism. Here is why I say that this word was poorly selected, that it was put together by people who do not understand etymology: the primary, the eternal concept is humanity. And communism is anti-humanity. Whoever says 'anti-communism' is saying, in effect, anti-anti-humanity. A poor construction. So we should say: that which is against communism is for humanity. Not to accept, to reject this inhuman communist ideology is simply to be a human being. It isn't being a member of a party.

Solzhenitsyn lived an absolutely extraordinary life, and *The Gulag Archipelago*, published illegally in the West in 1973, probably did more than any single thing to bring down the Soviet colossus's pretence of moral integrity and intellectual superiority over the messy democracies of the free world. At a critical time, *The Gulag Archipelago* made it simply impossible for a moral state to deal with the Soviet Union without contempt.

'It was a masterpiece of literary endeavour, language and polemic,' wrote Marcus Warren, a former Moscow correspondent for *The Telegraph*. 'Once read, it destroyed any argument for accommodation with the Soviet Union beyond that of realpolitik. That was all that remained until Mikhail Gorbachev ended the need for even that by presiding over the country's collapse.'

We should all read the book. If it could somehow be condensed into 140 characters the world might be a calmer and safer place. Perhaps then we might all recognise that slavery is the enemy of the people, no matter the ideology, no matter the good intentions.

'One execution away from utopia – that's the vision of the left.'

– Jordan Peterson, authority on the psychology of ideological belief and repression[2]

Margaret Thatcher

13 October 1925 – 8 April 2013

Prime minister of the UK 1979-1990; prescriber of bitter economic medicine; purveyor of cold-hearted economic liberalism; scourge of those left behind

IN THE EARLY 1980S, Margaret Thatcher gave to Britain a dose of seriously nasty, vile-tasting medicine, and – you know what? – it was an unavoidable necessity and we're sure not blaming her. The good Doctor Thatcher was convinced of the liberal* necessity of Friedrich von Hayek's economics, she gave it to the Brits by the bucketload, and it worked.

---

* For this entry, we feel it is appropriate to take back for the forces of good English the meaning of the word 'liberal', which often translates as 'progressive', 'leftie' or even 'libtard'. We prefer the 'classical liberalism' sense: the political perspective that emphasises individual freedom and limited government.

There can be no sensible opposition to the two truths that the British economy was a collectivist, corporatist mess when she inherited it, and that it was in something approaching fine health when she left. In 1976 James Callaghan's Labour government suffered the humiliation of having to take a £2.3 billion loan from the International Monetary Fund to counter an inflation rate that had reached 25 percent the year before. In 1978-79 the country was crippled by trade union strikes during 'the Winter of Discontent'. Thatcher came to power in May 1979. By the mid-1980s the mass strikes were history, unemployment was coming under control and the economy was booming.

Notably, before she died Thatcher achieved one of her own stated aims in life. 'My task will not be completed,' she once said, 'until the Labour Party has become like the Conservative Party, a party of capitalism.' By 1997 Tony Blair's New Labour – as we saw around 130 pages back – was exactly that. She had, in her own words, 'helped to make it electable'.

But Thatcherism had many victims. It was Thatcher's steeliness in the face of the Cold War that earned her the Soviet sobriquet 'Iron Lady', which she absolutely loved, and it was this iron-clad certainty that had the effect of steamrolling all who opposed her. She seemed almost inured to the human cost of being right, and unwilling to make small allowances to care for those left behind. Her callousness (combined with an economic depression) was such that 18 months into her first term her approval rating was the lowest ever recorded for a prime minister, at 23 percent. It mattered little to her.

When state-owned coal mines fell into irretrievable uncompetitiveness, the solution was simple: she started closing them down. In response, the National Union of Mineworkers, fired up on a Marxist vision of permanent employment no matter the cost, led a violent year-long strike in 1984-85. Thatcher won. During her time as prime minister the number of those employed in the coal industry would drop from around 240,000 to 60,000 or less. Today it's a couple of thousand.

Many of those who lost their jobs in South Wales and Yorkshire – along with all those who knew them – would harbour the bitterest resentment for her until the day she died, swearing to dance a jig on her grave. It's easy to see why. There was no provision for sacked miners, who must have surveyed the job market in their gutted pit towns and villages, and in their hearts known that many of them would never work again.

'To those waiting with bated breath for that favourite media catchphrase, the U-turn, I have only one thing to say. You turn if you want to. The lady's not for turning.'

— *Margaret Thatcher, 1980*

Privatisation was a fundamental element of Thatcher's mission to remedy the British economy. In selling state-owned enterprises such as British Airways, British Rail, British Telecom and Rolls-Royce, she transferred almost a million workers from the state into the private sector. Even the Post Office was let loose.

She also slashed expenditure where she could, stripping down the welfare state. Housing and education suffered, in particular, so much so that Oxford refused to give her an honorary degree, something that had been a formality for Oxford-educated prime ministers in the four decades since the war. In her desire to rekindle the fires of capitalism she slashed the top rate of income tax from a positively socialist 83 percent on entering office to 60 percent on her first budget to 40 percent by the end of her tenure.

Elsewhere, her foreign politics was similarly hard-headed. She refused to let a grotty Argentinian junta lay claim to an outcrop of rock in the south Atlantic owned by Britain, mobilising the army and the navy to have the Falklands Islands liberated. This turned out to be an extraordinary operation in difficult conditions, and a nearer-run thing than may be imagined today. She played a firm hand in the final years of the Cold War, this time on more charming terms with the major players, Reagan and Gorbachev. And she simply refused to deal with the IRA, most notably during the Irish hunger strike of 1981.

Despite being bombed herself at the Conservative Party conference in Brighton in 1984, Thatcher avoided worrying too much about the Troubles in Northern Ireland because she considered them intractable. She was much resented in Northern Ireland and Ireland for this attitude. Her Tory successor John Major's different approach, followed by Tony Blair's continuation of those discussions and eventual success, proved how wrong she had been.

And then, towards the end of her time in charge, she stopped listening altogether. A flat tax to pay for council services was forced through to the horror of constituency MPs in marginal Convervative seats. Not just property owners but all residents would pay a flat rate, irrespective of wealth. Everybody hated the 'poll tax', and by the time senior Tories rebelled against Thatcher and ousted her, her reputation as a tyrannical and hard-hearted Tory of 'Nasty Party' fame was assured for many.

Margaret Thatcher was an effective and necessary prime minister of the UK. As she had explained before her election (though not quite in these words), the problem with socialism is that sooner or later you run out of other people's money. But the problem with Thatcherism was that its suck-it-up tough love made no effort at conciliation and left entire swathes of society wishing fervently for its failure – many of them still doing so. Thus her real malefaction was her interminable divisiveness, and to this day she still inspires either breathless admiration and adoration or frothing indignation and anger. Few people find any space between the two.

Britain was in such a dire state by the time she took power that much of what she did was, it must be concluded, unavoidable – assuming, that is, that the British people didn't want their country run entirely into the ground like, say, Burma at the time, or Venezuela today. Her uncompromising manner was, her supporters would argue, a necessary part of the medicine – but was it, really? Did the animosity she entrenched in the hearts of those who had to suffer have to run so deep, so that Britain remains politically delineated along those lines decades later, divided by emotion rather than

'Monetarism, privatisation, deregulation, small government, lower taxes and free trade – all these features of the modern globalised economy were crucially promoted as a result of the policy prescriptions she employed to reverse Britain's economic decline.'

– Margaret Thatcher obituary, The Telegraph

'Margaret Thatcher [was] a political phenomenon. She was the first woman elected to lead a major Western power; the longest-serving British prime minister for 150 years; the most dominant and the most divisive force in British politics in the second half of the 20th century.'

– Margaret Thatcher obituary, The Guardian

considered thought? In a country that wealthy and progressive there ought to have been a way to try to re-skill, scoop up and help out those who fell afoul of difficult decisions. Yet there was, for many, the impression that she just did not give a damn about human beings – her own people – if they fell outside of her domain of thought.

Unpleasant as her time in office was for many working people, though, it's worth remembering that Margaret Thatcher won three elections fair and square. So, what do we learn from *that* difficult truth? Simply that broken dysfunctional economies are – technically – rather quite easy to fix. But the human pain of these reforms is often dreadful to endure, as any unionised workers in the UK in the early 1980s will tell you.

That's worth considering when you're contemplating putting your cross next to the politician who's promising you free everything with extra Bollinger without explaining where the money's coming from. Unfortunately, as it turns out, your children will pay for it in misery and shattered dreams. The pain of unyieldingly orthodox liberal economics in a recession can be avoided, but only if you don't elect to power spendthrift populists. Because then, after that, you get the Iron Lady.

And on that note, we turn our gaze across the Atlantic to a leader who, though it might once have been inconceivable, deals in politics that are more divisive than Maggie Thatcher could ever have countenanced. And unlike the tough economic sense that she espoused, this guy speaks... a lot of crazy.

Donald Trump

b. 14 June 1946

*President of the United States of America; leader of the
free world; political disrupter; symptom and abuser of
a system in crisis; complete jackass; compelling reason
to listen and not shout*

THERE MAY BE SOME POINT IN GETTING INTO A LATHER here about the
crazy stuff Donald Trump has said and done, but it would be a really small
one. Very, very small. Like, for instance, his hands.

As we type, in the first week of August 2017, here are some highlights
from a simple Google search of current news stories pertaining to the
American president.

- He has just fired his communications director Anthony Scaramucci who's been in the job for less than a fortnight. (He will later tweet that it had been 'a great day in the Whitehouse'.)
- He has apparently described the White House as 'a dump' to explain his regular visits to a local golf club. (He will later call this fake news.)
- He appears to have invented a phone call from the Boy Scouts in which they thanked the president for a speech he made to the Boy Scouts National Jamboree, describing it as 'the greatest speech that was ever made to them'.

By the time this chapter is read by the proofreader, let alone by you, the reader, these little episodes will have long been buried in an avalanche of almost relentless news and outrage surrounding the Trump administration. It is its principal product. It is the mallet that relentlessly hammers the wedge into the great chasm that is American politics, a chasm that has rendered president after president before Trump unable to get meaningful things done while in office, and which is widening at an exponential rate under Trump.

For the occupant of a position that is supposed to emanate the decorum and seriousness of the world's most powerful individual, Trump is a cartoon jackass, a *Simpsons* character made worse by the fact that he's actually *been* a *Simpsons* character. Not to mention a reality TV star who, not long ago, would have made more sense in an episode of *Keeping Up With The Kardashians* than in the White House – and, come to think of it, still would.*
A guy who we all thought was hamming it up, until we realised he wasn't. Until he was, despite all the publicly known facts about his unsuitability for the job, elected as president of the United States of America.

So, to get back to where we started, there is almost no point, therefore, in recording Donald Trump's many and various crimes, abominations and embarrassments here.

---

* In a 2000 episode of *The Simpsons*, titled 'Bart To The Future', Lisa Simpson succeeds Trump as president after he has bankrupted America. Trump, as a character, has made several *Simpsons* appearances since 2015, when the real Trump announced his decision to seek nomination to run as the Republican candidate for 2016. He's also a WWE regular – a Hall-of-Famer, in fact – having, for instance, headlined Wrestlemania XXIII in 2007, where he body-slammed Vince McMahon and shaved his head. And while he hasn't ever been on *Keeping Up With The Kardashians*, Kim Kardashian appeared on his show, *The Apprentice*, in 2010. This is the guy we're dealing with.

Oh, but we can't resist.

He has hair that defies the natural laws of the universe.

He is orange!

He is more sensitive than a millennial snowflake and gets upset when you make jokes about, among other things, his very, very small hands.

He is the leader of the free world but seemingly spends more time sending cry-baby tweets than doing any actual leading.

He has the vocabulary of a 5th grader.

There is, in fact, a plausible case to be made that he is in an advancing state of dementia, as opposed to simply being a narcissist and egomaniac. (He is the oldest US president to take office.)

His favourite word is 'I'.

He has a Golden Raspberry Award for Worst Supporting Actor for a cameo in the 1990 movie *Ghosts Can't Do It.*

He didn't realise that being president of the United States 'would be more work than in my previous life'. As Seth Meyers, Stephen Colbert and others asked of this frank admission of his: did he think that running the free world would be easier than appearing on a reality TV show and selling luxury meat?

He has reduced the presidency of the United States to a laughing stock.

'How do you put your shoes on in the morning? How do you exist and be so dumb?'

– *Howard Finkler, who was so horrified by the prospect of a Trump presidency that he wrote a novel about the man, called Pussy*

'I found much that was alarming about being a citizen during the tenures of Richard Nixon and George W Bush. But, whatever I may have seen as their limitations of character or intellect, neither was anything like as humanly impoverished as Trump is: ignorant of government, of history, of science, of philosophy, or art, incapable of expressing or recognizing subtlety or nuance, destitute of all decency, and wielding a vocabulary of seventy-seven words that is better called Jerkish than English.'

– Philip Roth, 2017[1]

Okay, we have to stop it there. We could go on for pages and pages and we haven't even got to the bad stuff. The personality defects that militate against wise leadership. The tactlessness, the divisiveness, the unfounded confidence in everything he says, the dearth of emotional intelligence, the effortless offence-causing – complemented by his own ability to take offence at almost anything in return. The fact that he has no meaningful experience as a politician whatsoever – see that luxury-meat point above.

Donald Trump's faults are manifest and they are many, and the unremittingly furious 'liberal' – by which Americans mean left-leaning – media will continue to record them in gaudy, glorious detail until his dying day. But those same newspapers and websites really ought to try harder, because ceaseless squealing about Trump isn't going to change anything. A Trump administration was just as absurd an idea before the election as it is after, which explains, as of August 2017, that while his overall approval ratings are reasonably poor, those parts of the US that voted for him remain relatively loyal. To OpEd editors sitting in LA and New York, this appears to be regarded as a kind of madness. It is perhaps easier for them to understand Trump more as a desperate act of self-harm by a section of American society in trouble than as a considered response to the status quo. This is a section of society so completely removed from the wealthy, cosmopolitan seaboard conurbations that they even have a name for it: *fly-over states*. These are the states you fly over on your way from one blue coast to the other.

Ah yes. The casual contempt with which Americans regard each other is often simply astonishing to behold. What's remarkable about the distress and pain of working class 'white trash' America is the almost complete dearth of compassion for their plight from those who are not them.

While the American dream has died in the Appalachian and Rust Belt communities, commentators have denigrated broken and impoverished white communities as hillbillies who have descended into poverty and drug abuse because, as liberal commentator Josh Marshall puts it on his *Talking Points Memo* blog, 'the stressor at work here is the perceived and real loss of the social and economic advantages of being white'.

Now, it's not a sensible idea to delve too deeply into the merits of this argument other than to say that for somebody living in a trailer park in the Midwest, unwell and crushingly poor, it just might potentially be more complicated than this, and that this entirely common analysis – great for quoting on Facebook – is more than just a little bit ungenerous. Indeed, you might go so far as to describe it as indurate callousness. For that individual – and indeed for those millions of individuals – the notion that they are regarded by wealthy New Yorkers as 'privileged' as a result of their race or gender must seem the very height of farce.

It's not as if there is overwhelming conservative sympathy for these communities. In *Hillbilly Elegy*, JD Vance's compelling and at times jaw-dropping memoir of white working-class existence in the Rust Belt, the author joins in with conservative calls for tough love for the Trump-voting poor white communities too. Conservative controversialist Kevin Williamson explains it like this:

> Nothing happened to them. There wasn't some awful disaster. There wasn't a war or a famine or a plague or a foreign occupation. Even the economic changes of the past few decades do very little to explain the dysfunction and negligence – and the incomprehensible malice – of poor white America. So the gypsum business in Garbutt ain't what it used to be. There is more to life in the 21st century than wallboard and cheap sentimentality about how the Man closed the factories down.
>
> The truth about these dysfunctional, downscale communities is that they deserve to die. Economically, they are negative assets. Morally, they are indefensible. Forget all your cheap theatrical Bruce Springsteen crap. Forget your sanctimony about struggling Rust Belt factory towns and your conspiracy theories about the wily Orientals stealing our jobs... The white American underclass is in thrall to a vicious, selfish culture whose main products are misery and used heroin needles. Donald Trump's speeches make them feel good. So does OxyContin.

So, how to vote? When the Democrats abandoned class in their very urban, very nuanced pursuit of intersectional social justice – telling niche demographics what they wanted to hear, apparently without considering a coherent strategy required to deliver on these customised promises – it abandoned poor white Americans in the process. When Chelsea Clinton, who has so obviously been 'on manoeuvres', as they say, lectures away on Twitter about how white or male or straight or Christian people have in some way contributed to the parlous state of America, it seems depressingly clear that the Democrats haven't been listening to large segments of their country, and that change won't be happening any time soon.

'White parents need to talk about racism & hate with our children throughout their lives,' Chelsea generously explains. Her mother, meanwhile, simply wrote them all off as 'deplorables'.

And the Republicans? Well, they're much more likely to simply tell people to pull up their goddamn socks and get a job, all the while trying to reduce the amount of healthcare the state might provide for them. But they've done such a poor job of fostering leadership within their own ranks that a man like Trump can parachute in and hijack their cause, to the horror of establishment Republicans across the land.

So Donald Trump does two things. One, he irritates the crap out of the liberals – which is always a win for those abandoned in the new political culture personified by the rich, white, East Coast entitled elitism of Hillary Clinton. Two, he says things that resonate about protecting the very American industries that have died out in those fly-over states, and protecting American workers from competition from illegal immigrants.

'America has cancer... On the one side, a racist, identity-politics Left dedicated to the proposition that white people are innate beneficiaries of privilege and therefore must be excised from political power; on the other side, a reactionary, racist, identity-politics alt-right dedicated to the proposition that white people are innate victims of the social-justice class and therefore must regain political power through race-group solidarity... There is a cancer in the body politic. We must cut it out, or be destroyed.'
– *conservative US commentator Ben Shapiro, August 2017*[2]

The fact that Trump couldn't deliver a pizza, let alone profound societal change, is ultimately irrelevant.

Trump is the symptom of America's culture of partisanship, of the new era of the primacy of politics over culture in the national discourse. It's become ingrained in the United States – more so every day that he's in power – and it's spreading throughout the modern world, as we've seen elsewhere in this book. Trump is the result of America's great self-imposed 21st century undertaking: to work feverishly on what divides it. He is the festering stench left in the room by the cruelty and pitilessness of this new way and, no doubt, a precursor of more of the same – until Americans can find a way to talk to each other again, instead of looking sniffily out of their Boeing as they fly over those they despise.

So what has Donald Trump done to stuff up the world? In our criticism of the failures of the American (and world) political system, we are by no means trying to deny or excuse his ongoing contributions, be they policy

'Sorry losers and hater, but my I.Q. is one of the highest – and you all know it! Please don't feel so stupid or insecure, it's not your fault'

– May 2013

| 'My use of social media is not Presidential – it's MODERN DAY PRESIDENTIAL. Make America Great Again!' *– July 2017* | 'Obama resigns from office NOW [...] – I will give him free lifetime golf at any one of my courses!.' *– September 2014* | 'It's freezing and snowing in New York- -we need global warming!' *– November 2012* |

'The W.H is functioning perfectly, focused on HealthCare, Tax Cuts/Reform & many other things. I have very little time for watching T.V.'
– July 2017

implementations or the social and cultural effects of his newsworthiness. As of the time of writing, we'd say he's tarnished just about everything he's touched as president of his country and his potential as 'an extinction-level event', as he's been described[3], is off the charts. But any major disasters are yet to be properly defined. With Putin plotting in the Kremlin, Kim in Korea going intercontinental, Europe falling to pieces, the Middle East already in pieces – well, you'd think he's going to slip on a very large banana skin at some point. And that's assuming he doesn't break America itself in some special, Trumpian way; perhaps by actually building his stupid wall or banning Muslims from existence entirely or somehow weaponising his ugly sexism. In the meantime, he is here as the symbol of the divisive and increasingly dividing modern American way; someone who has instinctively taken note of what's happening, but instead of trying to fix it, has simply taken advantage of it.

Still, let us at least try to remain upbeat. If Trump can bring about some good as leader of the United States, we would like to think that it may be as the corrective needed for those on both sides to right their respective ships – to bring some introspection, decency and respectability to mainstream politics – to realise that if they carry on in this way then next time there's an election they may just find Kim Kardashian as president.

Perhaps this, then, is the glimmer of hope in a Trump presidency. Sadly, the odds are about the same of him nuking North Korea.

'The vital and valid lesson of the Trump phenomenon is that if the elites cannot govern by compromise, someone outside will eventually try to govern by popular passion and brute force.'
– Andrew Sullivan, writing in May 2016,
before Trump had won the Republican ticket, let alone the election[4]

See The Clintons and The Kims.

Verwoerd & Malan

DF Malan: 22 May 1874 – 7 February 1959
HF Verwoerd: 8 September 1901 – 6 September 1966

Prime ministers of South Africa; champions of Afrikaner nationalism; architects of apartheid; Mandela's foes; torch-bearers for modern racism

THE CRIME OF APARTHEID may seem like a story that needs no introduction. It has, after all, come to represent one of the great scourges of modern times – racism – both in South Africa, where it was formulated, and around the globe. Apartheid may also seem like a villainy past; a government-legislated social-engineering project that violated so many principles of modern humanity (and common decency) and yet met its match in the peace-bringing, Nobel Prize-winning 20th century super-icon Nelson Mandela. As with so many human tales, much of what the greater world knows of apartheid and its aftermath is a combination of myth, fallacy and wishful thinking. And, sadly, many of the important lessons to be gleaned from its failures appear to have been discarded.

South Africa's famous road to redemption has been told in literature and film ad nauseam. The problem, however, is that it hasn't been told terribly well. From the left-leaning pages of the great liberal newspapers that played their role in its demise to the Hollywood of *Invictus*, editors and film producers have long preferred a simple narrative of good and evil in which good prevails and everything works out in the end. This is all very fuzzy and heart-warming, though it comes with a disclaimer: it's utter horseshit.

All has not been okay in the end. South Africa is still an unmitigated mess, in which the life you are likely to live is defined not by Martin Luther King's 'content of your character', but largely by the legislative depredations of two men who felt driven by a duty to the Lord above, and never failed in their convictions, to keep white and black South Africans separated.

Those men were Daniel 'DF' Malan and Hendrick 'HF' Verwoerd – Nazi sympathisers, white supremacists and Afrikaner nationalists. Today, in 2017, in South Africa, where you are born, where you go to school, what you learn, what employment you might enjoy, whom you marry, where you live, and ultimately how long you live and what eventually kills you were, on average, decided by Malan and Verwoerd in the 1950s and '60s.

It is true that South Africa should have progressed much further under successive (increasingly corrupt and incompetent) ANC-led governments since its democratic revolution in the early 1990s – a South Korean economic miracle, it most certainly has not been. It is similarly true that race-based social engineering and legislated racism were not new in the world, and that apartheid was, ultimately, the sad progression of centuries of global imperial oppression, typified in South Africa by the work of Cecil John Rhodes. Segregation or enforced 'apartness' – which is how 'apartheid' translates from Afrikaans – in supposedly civilised nations was rampant across the world deep into the 1960s. Both Rosa Parks's refusal to give up her bus seat and the last known lynching of a black man in the United States occurred in 1955, seven years *after* the Afrikaner nationalists came to power under Malan and apartheid was well under way.

So, you know, it's not like the South Africans were the only ones doing it – which was how many justified it.

And yet the questions remain.

How did South Africa morph from a standard-issue racist African colonial society into a pin-up for evil and a notorious pariah of the free world? Why was the South African experience so especially brutal and how did its policies of segregation become so detailed in their application that races could be delineated into Whites, Indians, Coloureds and Blacks – using, if necessary, the infamous 'pencil test' to do so* – with differing rights assigned to each group? And why, when the rest of the world was coming to terms with the folly and cruelty of colonialism overseas and

---

* Of the various tests to classify a person's race, this was perhaps the most absurd. Subjects of dubious classification would have a pencil slid into their hair; if it fell out easily, they were considered white; if it stuck but fell out with some shaking of the head, they were considered coloured (mixed race); if it didn't fall out after shaking of the head, they were considered black.

fascism in its own domestic politics, did South Africa stride so defiantly into Harold Macmillan's 'wind of change'? What the hell went wrong?

The answer lies not, unfortunately, in the simplistic demonisation of the white African, or in any other relativist, collectivist nonsense. The answer lies in the perfect intersection of two determined, clever and ruthless supremacists, and their reluctance to adapt to a changing world.

Though the apartheid state would never murder on the Soviet scale, Malan was to Verwoerd as Lenin was to Stalin – and so, similarly, Verwoerd must be the headline act here while Malan takes the necessary mention.

Before Malan there was Smuts. Which is a bit like saying, before Lenin there was Benjamin Franklin. South Africa's greatest statesman after Mandela, Jan Smuts is the only person to have signed the peace treaties that ended both World Wars, and he's the only one to have signed the charters to both the League of Nations, in 1919, and the United Nations, in 1945. He was a war hero, scientist, philosopher, genius; such a giant of a man that it was Churchill's desire for Smuts to govern Britain if anything happened to him during World War II. And yet in 1948, he lost a Whites-only 'democratic' election to Malan's Nationalists.

In his post-war exhaustion, Smuts had misread the great thrusting reach of the upwardly mobile, yet ideologically conservative, Afrikaner people. Once a uniter of those who'd fought against each other during the Boer War, now Smuts was gone. In his place came Malan, a man who believed fervently in the Afrikaner race's god-given rights to ownership of the South African land, and who would quite deliberately manufacture a mythology around their history of migration and battles against indigenous people that ultimately equated the Afrikaners with the people of Israel in the land of Canaan.

Such religious entitlement made up half the story. The other half was bitterness and resentment. The Boer War of 1899-1902, now known as the South African War, between mainly British and Boer armies in a bunfight over gold and diamonds had destroyed the countryside. The British policy of rounding up civilians who were supporting the Boer guerilla commandos into camps – history's first concentration camps – resulted in appalling death rates as a result of disorganisation and disease. It is a disastrously awful fact of history that half of the Afrikaner people's children died in those camps, a tragedy almost too ghastly to contemplate.

Even in the context of all this hideousness, Malan had few excuses. He was a highly educated man, apparently filled with Christian conviction, who had studied to be a minister and also gained an MA in philosophy and a doctorate in divinity at Utrecht in the Netherlands. You might expect, therefore, that Malan would have developed into a worldly, open-minded Christian. Sadly, that was not the case. Having spent the duration of the South African War in the pro-Boer Netherlands, Malan was ordained as a minister in the Dutch Reformed Church on his return to South Africa in 1905. In his work, he became increasingly concerned by the plight of poor white Afrikaners, and the move into politics came in 1915 when he was asked to edit Cape Town's new Afrikaans daily newspaper, *Die Burger*. He became head of what would become the infamous National Party in 1934 and spent the next fourteen years in opposition.

Fate was to throw Malan's party just the crowbar he required to prise power from Smuts. It arrived in the guise of South Africa's entry into World War II, which came after much political debate and which ultimately served to emphasise the resentment that Afrikaners felt towards Britain. Such sentiment among Afrikaans voters would eventually propel Malan into government three years after the war ended.

Malan was 74 when he came to power, and it was this old man, who was really from a different era, who presided paternalistically over those first years of apartheid and the beginning of the legislative assault on black South Africans. Apartheid was Malan's dream. But it was Hendrick Verwoerd who would deliver it.

During the apartheid years, white South Africans travelling abroad were regarded en masse as pariahs, presumed racists, as personified in the memorable 1980s *Spitting Image* sketch, 'I've never met a nice South African'. Many felt hard done by the judgement, and one of the long-running jokes in South Africa in the years after 1994 is that you can never find a white South African who voted for the National Party. This is a problem because they were repeatedly elected in whites-only elections, and Verwoerd came to be regarded by many of his fervent admirers as the father of the nation.

Interestingly, given his unyielding vision for the future of the country, Verwoerd was not born in South Africa. He did, however, get the next best option, the Netherlands. His family moved to South Africa a couple of years later, in 1903, in support of the Afrikaner nation after the South African War. So he was well schooled in the injustices and challenges facing the volk. Verwoerd was, it appears, something of an academic genius – an evil genius in the making, if you will – winning scholarships and achieving a *cum laude* doctorate in philosophy from Stellenbosch University before furthering his studies at various universities abroad.

Whether Verwoerd was influenced by Nazi racial ideology during his time in Germany in the mid-1920s has never been established, but he certainly showed good form before the Nats assumed power in 1948, and Hitler's hierarchies of racial supremacy clearly resonated with him. In 1936 he spoke out against the arrival in South Africa of Jews fleeing Hitler, believing they would compete directly with Afrikaner professionals. (Nothing to do with their Jewishness, you see.) Then, once war in Europe had broken out, he vehemently opposed South Africa's siding with the Allies. In an echo of Malan's path into the public eye, he also took over a newspaper, *Die Transvaler*, which was essentially a conduit for pro-Nazi propaganda under his time in charge. In 1948, delighted by the triumph of Afrikaner nationalism under Malan, Verwoerd entered the senate. A star in the making, he was in the cabinet two years later, having risen to the position of Minister of Native Affairs.

The simplest way to deal with Verwoerd is to look at his legislation. Apartheid, after all, was a collection of laws, and Verwoerd was their driving force. By the time he assumed his cabinet position in 1950, Malan had already passed the Prohibition of Mixed Marriages Act. Verwoerd quickly added the Immorality Act, which banned sexual relations between black and white people, a thought that must have horrified him and his fellow party members.

In the modern world the notion that what happens in people's bedrooms is a concern for the state is virtually inconceivable, but Verwoerd was just getting going. He believed that South Africa was not a nation, but a collection of nations defined by their race. In order to create these nations, the respective races had to be defined in law, which he did via the Population Registration Act of 1950. Suddenly, South Africa was officially a country of Whites, Indians, Coloureds and Blacks. (In cases where it was tricky to tell who was what, this was where the pencil test came in handy.) The latter category was further split up into eight ethnic subdivisions, each of which was to be assigned a 'homeland', for example KwaZulu or the Transkei, of which members of each division would then become citizens – even if they'd never been there in their lives.

The Group Areas Act, passed in the same year, then consolidated Verwoerd's official racial classifications by demarcating exactly where people could live. This was grand apartheid at its most insidious and destructive, and explains why, if you are living in South Africa today, where you live is in all likelihood still defined by your race, and was effectively decided six decades ago by Dr Verwoerd. Such was the impact of Verwoerd that geographical apartness still defines South African life, still scars its landscape and still divides its people.

And it was tough if you found yourself living in the wrong area. Entire communities were uprooted and destroyed. In Cape Town, District Six was famously cleared of all Coloured people. Blacks in Johannesburg were moved from suburbs like Sophiatown to the far-away South Western Townships, otherwise known as Soweto. Indians were forced from Fordsburg to Lenasia 25 kilometres away. In Pietermaritzburg they were corralled into Northdale. It was astonishing and appalling social re-engineering.

The vice grip of the apartheid government had been ruthlessly and systematically applied, but it wasn't yet the end of the legislative onslaught on the black people of South Africa. Political parties were banned. Mixed-race people were banned from the voting roll. Blacks were banned from

'Oh yes. You see, one does not have the problem of worrying whether one perhaps could be wrong.'

– Hendrik Verwoerd, on being asked by a reporter if he slept well at night

performing skilled work in White areas. The Minister of Native Affairs – Verwoerd – was awarded the right to boot Blacks off private or public land and establish resettlement camps. Blacks were required to carry pass books at all times, the much-loathed *dompas*, without which a black person could do little more than stay in the countryside.

Just four years into the nightmare that was the National Party government, Verwoerd had created the building blocks of a bizarre and twisted image of Malan's dream – a whites-only, Afrikaans-led republic that would one day be free of troublesome natives and meddlesome British.

In a crime of lasting and monumental proportions, he then penned and promulgated the 1953 Bantu Education Act. There is no better person than Verwoerd himself to articulate how he felt about the education of black people. 'There is no place for [Blacks] in the European community above the level of certain forms of labour,' he declared. 'What is the use of teaching the Bantu child mathematics when it cannot use it in practice? That is quite absurd. Education must train people in accordance with their opportunities in life, according to the sphere in which they live.'

Blacks were, as he put it, destined to be 'hewers of wood and drawers of water'. In a stroke, Verwoerd had stolen the opportunity of a better life from black people, and by the 1970s black schools enjoyed one-tenth, perhaps even one-fifteenth, of the funding of white schools. For all the terrible society-transforming legislation that Verwoerd passed in his time, the education system he imposed on generations of South African blacks remains, today, one of the most bitterly catastrophic aspects of his legacy. (Almost unbelievably, it has deteriorated further under ANC rule.)

Naturally, the madness of apartheid fomented anger and resentment. Offensive and discriminatory racial practices had, to a greater or lesser degree, been taking place in South Africa since the moment the Dutch set up shop in 1652 but Verwoerd's vision was all-encompassing, his laws uncompromising. He was the devil who even served the coffee cold, and he wholly redefined the way people lived in South Africa.

The *dompas*, in particular, provided a daily humiliation, an enforced subservience to the South African Police and the white boss. On 21 March 1960, two years after Verwoerd's election as prime minister, a protest against its use in the township of Sharpeville led to the gunning down of 69 people, including women and children, and injured hundreds more, many shot in the back while fleeing. It was a watershed, as Nelson Mandela would make clear during his treason trial in 1962, and it became both an event that attracted much international condemnation and served as inspiration for the soon-to-be-banned ANC's armed struggle for liberation.

Verwoerd, utterly sure in his convictions, was content simply to retreat into the laager. Later in the year, he rigged a plebiscite on the creation of a republic by lowering the voting age to include a young Afrikaner demographic. He won with a 52 percent mandate, created his republic and took South Africa out of the Commonwealth. South Africa would remain stuck in his laager until 1990.

On 6 September 1966 Hendrik Verwoerd was stabbed to death in Cape Town by a deranged parliamentary messenger who would later explain that he was obeying the orders of a giant tapeworm living in his stomach. Two-hundred-and-fifty-thousand white South Africans attended his funeral.

By the time of Verwoerd's death, Mandela and co were crushing rocks on Robben Island, the ANC was in exile and a low-grade state of civil war existed between the white and black people of South Africa. It was some legacy. Verwoerd and his mentor Malan cast the longest of shadows over South Africa, and stand as terrible testaments to the fact that oppressive politics of any flavour can, in the passing of such a few short years, condemn generation after generation to its consequences.

The sad fact is that apartheid was merely one era in a long-running history of human oppression of one group by another. Without suggesting that what was to become South Africa was a peaceful United Nations of African ethnicities, the white man, in the form of the Dutch, brought the proto-version to the Cape in the second half of the 17th century; the English refined it, most notably in its management of the new and bounteous gold mines discovered in the interior in the late 1800s; and since apartheid

> '[It] is only on the basis of apartheid in regard to residential areas that we shall be able to achieve sound relationships between the one race and the other. Only on that basis will we be able to secure justice for both sides. What justice is there for the non-European if he is in the position in which he is today? He will always have a sense of inferiority. He is unable to do justice to himself. On the basis of apartheid, however, with his own residential area, he will be in a position to do justice to himself. There he will be able to live his own life.'
>
> – DF Malan, 1950

proper was vanquished by Mandela in the early 1990s (with the help of several other less lionised great men) the country's 'economic apartheid' has in fact worsened, most notably since the mafia-infiltrated regime of Jacob Zuma assumed power in 2009. Major life quality, education and health indicators detail this unconscionable fact. Affirmative action policies, such as Broad-Based Black Economic Empowerment and sports quotas, have been introduced as necessary means to integrate the previously separate socio-economic system, but often with perversely negative effects. Through mismanagement, corruption and a catastrophic loss of skills in certain areas, they have grossly enriched a very few black people while leaving the rest behind; Malan and Verwoerd's racial apartness has simply become an exacerbated economic apartness.

In apartheid the civilised world saw a reflection of its own past and of its worst self. It saw the shame of man's unbridled tribal instincts in action and was reminded that it followed these self-same instincts until really rather recently. It came to be a defining example – probably *the* defining example – of how some people, both individuals and the nations they lead, cannot or refuse to discern the upwards arc of human civilisation and humanity itself. And so apartheid – the most formalised, legislated form of identity politics ever implemented on a national scale – represents the potential for our moral regression and even self-destruction.

The lesson of this travesty of social engineering came in understanding the moral perniciousness and social-economic effects of judging individuals by their group identity instead of the content of their character and their personal abilities. Identity politics was integral to the apartheid

> 'I mean, they just move in the neighbourhood. You just can't come in the neighbourhood. I'm for democracy and letting everybody live but you gotta have some respect. You can't just come in when people have a culture that's been laid down for generations and you come in and now shit gotta change because you're here? Get the fuck outta here. Can't do that!'
>
> *– Spike Lee, discussing gentrification in Brooklyn, 2014.*
> *He was wearing a hoodie with the words DEFEND BROOKLYN written on it [2]*

government's means of oppression; Malan, Verwoerd and their cronies were expert at the politics of divide and conquer, at classifying races and ethnicities on an imaginary hierarchy – using the pencil test, if necessary – and pitting them against each other. The end result of such policies, as we've seen recorded in various entries here and elsewhere, are genocides and 'cleansings', and as such the moral to take is seemingly obvious (viz: don't do this). It is, however, one that is increasingly worth revisiting in a world in which prejudices and intolerances have hardly disappeared, but have instead evolved in different ways. A world that is seeing aggressive movements, corralled and most obviously active on the internet, that consider those who do not indulge in identity politics to seek societal justice as criminals and – rather ironically – racists. This is the precise opposite of what Mandela taught in his shepherding of a potentially explosive South Africa into its democratic era. The sensible middle ground, which suggests that we should aim to treat people as equals with some consideration for their likely experiences of life, sadly appears to be drifting from fashion.

For the final word on the matter, a disturbingly recent one, we turn to Steve Bannon, the strategic mastermind behind the rise to power of Donald Trump, the most divisive and potentially destructive leader of our age. In August 2017, Bannon outlined his take on the matter:

> The longer [the Democrats] talk about identity politics, I got 'em. I want them to talk about racism every day. If the left is focused on race and identity, and we go with economic nationalism, we can crush the Democrats.

The women's glossy magazine editor

b. earlier than she says

Morally dubious thought-leader of the 'modern woman'; shameless purveyor of unnecessary tat; unrepentant maven of sexual impossibilities, body dysmorphic disorder and pointless gossip

HAVE YOU EVER READ a women's glossy magazine? Did you know that there's a good chance most of what you read was created at the whim of an advertiser and not of an editor? Did you know that the editors of these things are more like facilitators for puff pieces designed to primp said advertisers? Did you know that they basically hate you?

Yes, sadly this is all true. (Just about.) But before we expand on this possibly contentious thesis, let's wind it back a little.

If we are to rail against glossy women's magazines and the worst of what they represent in the second decade of the 21st century – the warped image of society they reflect back to their readers; their capture by unprincipled commercial interests – you may think it makes sense to pin the blame on a high-profile figurehead who got this particular ball rolling. A Helen Gurley Brown, say, or an Anna Wintour. Though these unique women are certainly integral to this discussion, the pioneers of the industry (as we know it) are most certainly not to blame. Because women's glossies weren't always like this. There was a time when they really did carry the torch; when they were fresh and amazing and had a profound impact on society.

Helen Gurley Brown was the 'revolutionary in stilettos' who told women they could be fun and fearless and have it all: 'love, sex and money'. Rising from Arkansas poverty in the 1920s to Manhattan prominence in the 1960s, her extraordinary contribution to what one might loosely call 'women's lib' came in its greatest force through her re-imagining of *Cosmopolitan* magazine. She took a plodding, high-minded magazine written by men for women and turned it into a monthly version of her smash bestseller *Sex And The Single Girl*, busting taboos that seem trite today – that women might have sexual desire, that sex before marriage was really okay.

Gurley Brown believed that good looks weren't a necessity for women to get ahead; smarts and attitude would do. In 1972 she put a naked Burt Reynolds on her centrespread, and sold 1.5 million copies. She campaigned for the pill, abortion and women's rights in general, utterly ground-breaking concepts when she took over as editor-in-chief of *Cosmo* in 1965. She was at the forefront of reinventing American women's magazines, transforming them from a century-long era of how-to-be-a-better-doormat domesticity to a new definition of women's identity – a vision that was then taken to the world. Under her guidance the magazine was eventually published in scores of countries, in dozens of languages for tens of millions of readers.

That, by any measure, is a cultural revolution.

Inevitably, Gurley Brown attracted controversy along the way, both from the conservative right and from what she might have referred to as 'dour feminists'. While her penchant for plastic surgery and cheerful admissions that she'd slept with 178 men before settling down (in her late thirties) made her an easy target, there is certainly room for debating the merits and drawbacks of her approach to life.

It's also worth pointing out that Gurley Brown stepped into the *Cosmo* editor's office at age 43 having already had a successful career in – you've guessed it – advertising. But the point is not to criticise her commercial smarts or her vanity. Far from it, in fact, because what she put in her magazine was driven by a real desire to offer women something better and her unqualified belief that she was doing so.

A similarly contentious and unavoidable figure in this realm is, of course, Anna Wintour, long-standing editor-in-chief of US *Vogue*, éminence grise

'She was 90, though parts of her were considerably younger.'
– *New York Times obituary of Helen Gurley Brown, August 2012*

of world fashion and persistent reminder that print can be both editorially driven and profitable. She of the severe bob and permanent sunglasses. It's difficult to overstate Wintour's influence on fashion and the magazine industry over the past three decades. She has the power, as *Time* magazine put it, to create or cripple trends on command, and her status brings her profusions of both adoration and criticism. She is said, for example, to have been responsible for the death of the grunge look in the 1990s, for which she must surely exist in a state of insurmountable forgiveness. Nonetheless, she is often portrayed as the wicked ice queen of fashion, most famously as Miranda Priestly in her depiction by a former PA in the novel and then film *The Devil Wears Prada*. So no, she's probably not an entirely delightful person to assist. But there is more to the Nuclear Wintour than a frosty demeanour and predictable haircut.

Another aspect of her character, for example, is exemplified by her first-ever cover of US *Vogue* in November 1988 which, in her words, 'broke all the rules' of the time. Previously, the trademark *Vogue* cover was a headshot photographed in studio. Wintour's inaugural cover was a girl walking down a street in a pair of faded jeans and a bejewelled Christian Lacroix top worth tens of thousands of dollars. The value of the garment aside, Wintour had hit on something: that this is how people dressed, by mixing up what they had and what they could afford. In the faded jeans and the setting, she was offering the average reader a glimpse of herself; in the Lacroix, there was a dream of what may be. It was aspirational and yet inspirational, too.

And as Arctic as Wintour's froideur may be – look, she's actually English, and now a dame, so give her a break – the fact remains that *Vogue* remains the powerhouse of fashion. It seems churlish to criticise her elitism, too. What is high fashion, if not elitist? Isn't that precisely the point?

Moreover, any attempts to smear her as commercially compromised fail by comparison, given the industry within which she works. *Vogue* is certainly not averse to looking after its advertisers; Wintour is on record as acknowledging that in the walk-off between two dresses of similar appeal she'll take the advertiser's goods each time. But she has famously fallen out with some of the biggest brands in the game, and in the showdown between an advertiser's money and editorial independence she knows where the priority lies. In an environment where so many have capitulated so completely, she acknowledges the necessity of looking after the bottom line while retaining her magazine's integrity. Ultimately she leads the advertisers, which is as it should be; not the other way around. And she does so, as Gurley Brown did, with real vision and talent. Today, after three decades in charge, she runs a profitable print magazine that remains cutting edge, uncompromised and reader-focused, which is, frankly, a hell of a thing in the digital era – and an exception to the rule.

So if not these two, then who's to blame for the state of women's glossies today? The answer is their weak and biddable successor manqués who, far from rising to the challenge of what Gurley Brown, Wintour and their forward-thinking contemporaries of the 1970s, '80s and '90s bequeathed them, have taken the low road of personal enrichment in a steadily imploding industry. Whereas the pioneering women's editors uncovered and publicised the truth about the likes of breast cancer, domestic abuse, workplace inequality and, of course, sex, this lot adds nothing new. Instead of reinventing, they rehash to increasingly diminished effect; instead of taking a stand, they bow fawningly to the pressure of the advertising dollar; instead of prioritising their reader, they consider her a fool to be duped.

Here, then, is the formula to the average women's glossy magazine on racks around the world today (give or take):

- Highlight the various insecurities and struggles in your readers' lives.
- Provide them with 'solutions' to these problems.
- Source these solutions from advertisers.
- Rinse and repeat.

The essence of this pernicious approach to editing is to prey on the insecurities of your customers based on the trust your brand has built up in years past, and the key to its ongoing success is the offering of quack solutions good for a coverline rather than actual solutions that work and are sustainable: quick fixes, temporary fixes, fixes that will be out of date next season, or simply fixes that fix fuck-all (and they really do know it in the editorial meeting). Given the intention, they've worked out that it makes sense to cut out the editorial middle man and go straight to the advertisers, the guys who came up with this unholy cycle in the first place.

Effectively, the reader finds herself in an abusive relationship with her monthly magazine, and the principal abuser of all is the editor.

You may have long suspected that the very fashionable, very *fashion* editors of internationally syndicated glossy women's titles who crossed your path were frauds. And you would be correct. There are still exceptions out there, but so many just have it written all over them: the name-dropping; the decibels-makes-up-for-intellect conversation; the mistaking of conspicuous adornment with big-brand accessories for style; the internationalist pretence when actually she's just Miss Ordinary from Didcot. We've all seen it, so let's condense this amorphous heap of label-clad humanity into an imaginary individual. We'll call her Square Bob Spray Pants.

Whatever your take on the feminist credentials of Gurley Brown or the elitist reserve of Wintour, it is hideously apparent that Square Bob Spray Pants carries no revolutionary agenda or cultural insight with her in her Gucci bag, and she doesn't really know where she might find it. In fact, she doesn't actually know that much at all.

What she knows is what the big advertisers and their PR jackboots are up to, because that's who she spends her time with. And invariably it is only the advertisers who are doing 'divine' and 'stunning stunning stunning' things, as she will have you know on her Instagram feed. She knows what's big this year because the PR folk from Louis Vuitton and Prada and Rolex and BMW and Zegna and Cartier and Hackett and Mercedes-Benz and Tag Heuer and the Sheraton Group and British Airways have told her what's big this year – or else. Which is pretty much all she needs to do her job.

And this is what the reader of the average women's glossy magazine needs to know: that the vast majority of the 'editorial' she's reading, the fashion shoots she admires and the car reviews she studies, the in-depth look at a Swiss watch manufacturer, that cute little feature on sunglasses, on accessories, on fragrances – it's all been bartered for advertising. You get a sense of this if you cast a critical eye over virtually any magazine today, women's glossy or otherwise.

These magazines are ruthless businesses. They're up against the digital revolution and they're using its tactics (rather than finding other ways to progress) in the fight to stay alive – so what they sell is you. They sell you, your demographic and your potential spend, to advertisers. As smart people, you probably know this already, but perhaps you don't now how clinically commercial it is.

Meetings between magazine editors and their 'clients' deliver carefully prepared spreadsheets that give detail on their readers. Household income, age groups, favourite shops, number of overseas holidays a year, disposable income, family status, number of cars, home ownerships status, what kind of phone you have, gym memberships, field of work, where you live. It's all there. How did they get it? Well, from you of course! Every time you enter a competition or accede to their request to 'tell us a bit about yourself' or even just subscribe, you're arming the magazine with more capacity to sell *you* to an advertiser. Why do you think they run competitions?

Many will know this, or at least understand that the readership of a magazine is of enormous commercial value to its proprietors. It is therefore understandable that advertisers might spend vast amounts on celebrity-driven spreads with breathtaking production values for high-end perfumes and designer labels, and that some readers may even enjoy the advertisements themselves – as advertisements. But the unwritten deal we make (or used to make) with the editors of our favourite monthlies is that the editorial is curated by some metric beyond who funds the ads. It's done to a style, or a taste, or a price bracket, or indeed because it is a story of genuine interest on some kind of genuine trend, or just simply because the editor thought her readers might like it. This is the expectation that the likes of Gurley Brown and Wintour built up in the last decades of the 20th century: an expectation built on trust. (By contrast, there are no such delusions on the internet; it takes a gobemouche of the highest order to ever trust anything online. See the following entry…)

But that's not how it goes down now. Now feature articles may be entirely conceptualised according to advertisers' needs, or are appropriated and jimmied to provide 'value-add'. Do this enough and all of a sudden Square Bob Spray Pants finds herself in a Business Class seat to Paris Fashion Week – because in an era where long boozy lunches have gone the way of *Mad Men*, 'gifting' is the thing. (Where do you think she got the Gucci bag?) And once she's received a gift or two, the capture is complete.

So, yes, it's corrupt. Fabulously corrupt, and often incompetent too. But the crimes of Square Bob Spray Pants run deeper than this. Because Square Bob also seeks importance as a commentator and as a 'feminist activist', an important part of her ruse. The fact is many of editors of women's magazines, glossy and otherwise, are the most anti-feminist creatures on God's earth. Just look at the messages they peddle.

You're too fat! Try this diet! OMG have you seen how skinny/fat Britney is looking? Your skin is a disaster! Your clothes are frumpy – look at these insanely expensive clothes and the way they hang so beautifully on this teenaged girl with no arse and tiny prepubescent boobs! Why aren't you getting more done in a day? Why do you have so little sex? Is your man cheating? Look at this sex position that only a 19-year-old gymnast could ever achieve! Why are you so poor? Have you considered these massively condescending ideas to stretch your wallet? Here's something really scary that will almost certainly happen to your kids! Are you a psychopath? We've got the answer!

Now, cue the Photoshopped cover shoot, which is where the Big Fat Evil Lie comes into undeniable focus. Because if they're airbrushing and boob-enhancing and bum-altering the cover models – literally the most perfect physical specimens in the world – then it's apparent that there are no qualms at all. That nothing in the magazine is practical, attainable or real. And that they really are running stories to keep their readers feeling relentlessly crappy about themselves so they keep coming back for their 'solutions', brought to you fresh from a big ad agency in London.

One notorious incarnation of Square Bob Spray Pants wrote as indictable an editor's letter as there could possibly be. Feminist facades need to be burnished from time to time, so Square Bobs do sometimes try to be serious and clever. Being thin on ideas, this particular one had returned to a theme she'd covered several times before, about bumping into refugees from the Syrian Civil War while jogging on a Greek beach, and how these handsome Syrian men wanted selfies with Herself in her short running shorts. Having managed to centre a great tragedy of our times onto herself, this:

> What would you wear if the clothes on your back were the only thing between your devastating reality and an uncertain future? The answer for most people seems to be denim — the great equaliser. Hardy, durable, stylish, can dry on one with pleasing results and instantly recognisable as a contemporary marker of modernity. For refugees from Syria, Iran and Afghanistan it was the garb of choice.

What the f–? you may ask. And indeed, *What the f–?* is the correct response, a widely echoed sentiment at the time of publication. But the thought processes that produced this kind of embarrassment are simply a logical extension of the notion that you can publish worthy feminist polemics and then 'showcase' fashion editorials in which the models are plainly ill or feature black celebrities with their skin artificially lightened.

There's a solution, of course. Women should break the abusive cycle and stop buying magazines that are curated by people who don't like them and

'[T]hese are the things that make women self-conscious, that create the unrealistic ideals of beauty that we have.'

— 19-year-old actress Zendaya, on photographs in Modeliste magazine, in which her hips and torso had been digitally slimmed, November 2015

have no scruples. They'll be happier the moment they do. Fortunately, this has been happening in recent times, with the might and influence of the magazine industry declining in lockstep with the rise of the internet and its free content. As a result, it is the editors who still value personal integrity – their own and their readers' – who appear to be making the last stand of the glossy mags, while natural selection sees the Square Bob Spray Pantses of the world migrating to the weekly gossip rags or, even worse, into the cybersphere, where the perpetuation of human insecurity and abuse of 'journalistic standards' has taken on exponential dimensions... (But that particular morass is over the page.)

In 1994, not long before the world hit what we might term 'peak magazine' – when the models were real and revered, the fashion was absolutely fabulous, the talent was abundant, the message was strong and sincere, and the sales were off the charts – Anna Wintour's *Vogue* presented a mythical vision in a shoot: supermodel Nadja Auermann in steamy embrace with a swan, as shot by Helmut Newton. It was inventive, original, provocative, beautiful, tasteful and clever – elements that are conspicuously absent in the majority of magazines (and almost all mainstream media) today.

The glossy women's magazine editor we speak of here is neither the heiress to Helen Gurley Brown nor the protégée of Anna Wintour, though she wishes she were. Square Bob Spray Pants may conceive of herself as the scion of these iconic women – while belittling them when expedient ('slut' and 'bitch', respectively) – but she is the poorest of imitations. Someone who hasn't just lost track of the line between editorial integrity and turning a profit, but who has ensconced herself in a land of personal plenty in which this trade-off is no longer a consideration. Someone who sees sex as a means to sell magazines to women instead of a means to empower the women she's selling magazines to. Someone who barely knows what classical Greek mythology is, let alone gets a Leda and the Swan reference.

Mark Zuckerberg

b. 14 May 1984

Morally questionable developer of Facebook; daddy of social media; disturbingly influential curator of the way you see the world (assuming you're on Facebook, which you probably are); wannabe president

IN JULY 2017 MARK ZUCKERBERG, the founder and CEO of Facebook, invited Facebook's two billion users to a barbeque at his house via the social network's live-streaming service. It was hopeless, and demonstrated so brilliantly several of the failings of social media.

Over the course of an interminable ninety minutes, Zuckerberg had to restart the broadcast because his phone's connection was interrupted by the Bluetooth connection to the thermometer in the grillers. Then he banged on about how much fun he was having hanging out with his family, when he was actually quite visibly alone in his garden most of the time. He made some comments about artificial intelligence that started a fight with Elon Musk, who jumped on Twitter to say that 'I've talked to Mark about this. His understanding of the subject is limited.' And when his heavily pregnant wife, Priscilla Chan, did make an appearance, she appeared massively unimpressed with the whole situation and told him to sort out the barbeque. 'Okay, I got it, I got it,' Zuckerberg whined as he was dragged off by his wife to fix the family lunch.

So, then, a fairly normal day on social media, where you ruin what should have been fun events, get into fights with people over stuff you didn't even plan to talk about, and irritate your nearest and dearest by being entirely disengaged. It's good to see Facebook is ruining Zuckerberg's life too.

In case you glossed over the stat in the first line above, here it is again: two billion people use Facebook. This is a potentially terrifying concept, the biggest collective in the history of *Homo sapiens*, unless perhaps you want to say male and female – difference being that neither men nor women have a platform to tell each other what they've just eaten for lunch.

Why are we on it? Well, it starts because we can stay in touch with our friends and family. And, you know, it's free! Well, actually, the hell it is. There's a very simple often-repeated rule in publishing: if a service is free to you then it is you, the user/reader/viewer, who is the product. Those publishers and broadcasters are selling *you* to advertisers. This is a concept we've just covered in the previous entry on magazine editors, where the betrayal is in the way the editor pretends to offer a considered and objective filter between the reader and the product. Online there are no such niceties. We are resigned to the abuse.

The scary thing about Facebook is, of course, the detail. Whereas in the old days a publisher might say to advertisers that the readers of *The Telegraph* are usually batty old retired brigadiers who live in Harrogate and wear red trousers, or that the readers of *The Guardian* are generally smug 35-year-old Londoners who think The North starts in Muswell Hill, Facebook actually knows where you live, even when you turn off Location Services and ratchet up your privacy settings. It knows who you're married to or sleeping with. It knows your hobbies and your favourite foods and holiday destinations and quite possibly your preferred brand of jeans. It knows who you work for and how much money you have (or at least how much you have to spend online). It knows your 'ethnic affinity' (its own term), your politics, your sexual orientation, your travel schedule, how many children you have and their ages. Facebook knows all this because you tell Facebook this. Or you tell the internet, which tells Facebook. (NB: when you log into anything using your Facebook details.) You think you're sharing with friends and browsing online, but what you're actually doing is helping Mark Zuckerberg compile the most valuable source of data on human consumption ever created. Can you imagine what that's worth to marketers and anthropologists and product developers?

If you can't, here it is: Facebook's market capitalisation eased past $500 billion in 2017. Which is about the GDP of Sweden.

Nobody knows more about you than Mark Zuckerberg, and if you're still not convinced then don't forget that Facebook is the big daddy of social media and owns four of the top seven social-media platforms in the world: Facebook itself, Messenger, WhatsApp and Instagram. (Zuckerberg's purchases of the latter two were particularly far-sighted.) As of mid-2017 they had more than five billion active monthly users between them, an astounding figure, and a measure of how social media has changed the way human history is unfolding. It is also rather a lot of information to mine.

Zuckerberg says they don't sell the information his company collects to anyone, unless they're app developers and you've said it's fine. But Facebook's vast and endlessly changing privacy policy is as easy to negotiate as Cape Horn in a bathtub, so if you can't be sure whether your information has been passed on to advertisers, perhaps check to see just how targeted the ads you're getting are before you decide.

What is the young Mr Zuckerberg, net worth $70 billion or thereabouts, doing to society in the process? Well, not to put too fine a point on it, but social media is ruining literally everything, starting with Zuckerberg's Sunday barbeque. You can't go to a concert or a children's school play without having to lift your head above a sea of iPhones as they record, Snapchat, Periscope, Instagram Story, live Tweet or, of course, Facebook Live the event to the two viewers not present who wanted to see dear little Molly's starring turn as the back end of the donkey in the Nativity scene.

Then, because it's 'free' and you can, it offers space for everybody to express their views on everything. Now, freedom of speech is absolutely non-negotiable, as anyone not living in North Korea can agree, but your right to say what you like absolutely does not translate into a right to an audience. Except on social media. And because this is social interaction in the form of digital ones and zeros pinging about the cybersphere, without any physical interpersonal engagement, people feel they have the right to behave appallingly – so if you happen to disagree on what is, in the final analysis, some trivial point about university admissions policy or pyramid-scheme marketing, it gets conflated into enormous showdowns that result in unfollowings and the end of that real-world friendship you thought you had with that nice guy Mike in accounts.

And that's on a good day. On a bad day the trolls are out in force, the abusive and anonymous – or sometimes couldn't-even-be-bothered-to-be-anonymous – bullies who say things designed to offend, intimidate and hurt; things they would never say in real life because someone would eventually punch them in the nose if they did.

God, it's boring – and that's if you can handle it. If you can't, all this online meanness can take a real mental toll.

In the face of growing concerns from doctors, mental health professionals, NGOs, politicians and generally sensible people, numerous studies have started reporting that social media increases anxiety, body-image concerns, sleeping problems, loneliness and depression among younger users. One 2017 survey of 14- to 24-year-olds showed that Instagram was the worst of five platforms studied, with Facebook, Snapchat and Twitter a notch or two below. (YouTube was fine, they reckon.) Another study put it more plainly:

'All of us, when we are uploading something, when we are tagging people, when we are commenting, we are basically working for Facebook.'
– *Professor Vladan Joler, head of SHARE lab in Serbia, which uses cyber-forensic analysis to understand how Facebook really works, 2017*[2]

the more time kids spend on social media, the less happy they are. And we're not even getting started on cyber-bullying.

It all elicits the obvious question: do we really need to know all this stuff about each other? All it seems to do is create bubbles of shared politics and grievance fetishism, and throws out the rest of the important stuff in life, such as shared beliefs or shared hobbies or family affiliations. The idea that you used to love going sailing with your brother-in-law Charles but now he's come out as a Brexiteer/Remoaner and you can't be friends is a very silly modern phenomenon, perhaps an indication that we have allowed politics to overwhelm everything else of importance in the online discourse. This may not be social media's fault, but you'd have to be blind not to see how it exacerbates it all.

The problems mentioned to this point are serious ones, enough even to merit Zuckerberg's entry in the book alone as the single individual who most popularised the idea of hanging out with mates online, the figurehead of social media and online 'image crafting'. The guy responsible for the sheer vexation of having to put up with all your friends and family and acquaintances and ex-work colleagues and old schoolmates you haven't seen in two decades in so much detail. For having to consume the particulars of their daily ministrations; the chrome-filtered photos from their 'perfect holiday'; the public exhortations of love between husbands and wives who are no doubt sitting next to each other in bed and can't just say it to each other's faces; the lectures from guilt-peddling virtue-signalling botherers who need desperately to tell you what you're doing wrong in your life and by the way you should eat more kale.

But perhaps this is the price we have to pay for all the fun and friendship that Facebook provides. You get to interact with your friends at will and with people you wouldn't otherwise, especially those in other cities and countries – and this can be a good thing. If you have to show a bit of discipline by occasionally culling friends who aren't actually friends and leaping clear of the InstaTwitFace vortex before it sucks you in late of an evening, then that's a worthy skill to learn. You could even – if you dare countenance the notion – simply delete yourself when it all gets too much.

What harm is Mark Zuckerberg then?

Ah, but here's the thing. The *real* problem with Facebook goes beyond the everyday annoyances that affect you or your wife or your kids or your friends. It goes to how the world – two billion people on Facebook alone, remember – receives and consumes news these days. Because if you're on Facebook/YouTube/Twitter, you very likely get your news through Facebook/YouTube/Twitter. A 2016 Pew Research Center study showed that, while traditional newspaper circulation continues to decline, 44 percent of adult Americans regularly get their news from Facebook, while nearly two-thirds get it from social media in general. These are astounding and ever-increasing figures, revealing that Facebook is now a virtual newspaper. But what news is it delivering?

In short, it's the worst kind of sensationalised 'you'll be shocked to see!' and 'it'll give you goosebumps!' journalism imaginable. These are articles – supposed news – that have more time and money spent on their 'packaging' than on their content because it's all about 'engagement'; that is, getting you to click on stories so the advertisers will pay in spades. And they are fed to you through your News Feed, which has followed your every click, like, share, hovered-over image and watched video since the day you signed up, and is powered by a constantly refined algorithm that has been described, for the reason we're discussing, as 'the most significant and influential pieces of code ever written'.[3] Its influence? It is powerful enough to affect your state of mind: Facebook's own studies have shown that it can make people happy or sad by feeding them more positive or more negative information. Its significance? It changes the way you – and everyone else on Facebook – see the world.

So the News Feed offers you cat videos and your next-door neighbour's view on immigration law, but also unbalanced, error-strewn, scandal-mongering news articles that entrench all your worst fears and biases and keep you in your safe little online echo chamber because that's how best to engage you and send advertisements your way. The actual money-making isn't the problem; it's the death of human-curated balanced news reporting.

So when you see people shouting past each other online, as they inevitably do, remember that Facebook, along with all its related social media platforms, isn't just feeding *off* our enormous capacity for online rage and combativeness; it's actually feeding it in the first place.

What's additionally scary is that Facebook will get better at this. Better at delivering what it thinks you want to read, better at hammering away at your pet peeves and your hobby horses, better at shielding you from difficult and challenging ideas, better at farming data from you – better, ultimately, at dividing us and boxing us, as it sells us to advertisers. Facebook will become so powerful that it will be able to sway elections – if it hasn't already, as has been credibly claimed of Trump's success. In case we're not being clear here: if Facebook gets to decide the outcome of democratic elections then, we're sorry to say, we're all doomed.

Which brings us neatly to Mr Zuckerberg himself.

For a man who controls, to some extent, the news feeds of billions of people, and for all his geek-done-good ordinary guy act, Mark Zuckerberg has made some highly questionable ethical decisions in the past, not least the one in which it is alleged he stole the idea behind Facebook while a student at Harvard. This story was made famous in the movie *The Social Network* which depicted Zuckerberg as 'an insecure jerk who screws over people and becomes a much richer insecure jerk', as one review had it.[4] On the day of the film's launch, Zuckerberg appeared on *Oprah* and announced a $100-million donation to a New Jersey schools project, which was not, we're pretty sure, a coincidence. In the end Facebook had to 'settle' with (read: pay to go away) his former Harvard mates at a cost of $65 million – hardly a financial hardship for the company, and yet the moral judgement is hard to ignore. (For some perspective, this is about 10 percent of what Zuckerberg will be worth once he gives away 99 percent of his wealth, as he has promised to do.)

And now the man who controls so much of what you read and, indeed, who knows more about you than quite possibly your dearest family and friends, wants to be president. Oh look, he says he *doesn't*, but the Zuckerberg journey through real America has been as obvious as it has

'The News Feed Editor has literally changed the way news is written. It has become the number one driver of traffic to news sites globally, and that has shifted the behavior of content creators. To get a story picked up by the News Feed Editor, news producers (and human editors) have changed their strategies to stay relevant and stem losses. To do this, many news organizations have adopted a traffic-at-all-costs mentality, pushing for more engagement at the expense of what we would traditionally call editorial accuracy.'

– *Tobias Rose-Stockwell, effectively explaining the rise of fake news*[5]

been nauseating. The man himself is politically nowhere. He doesn't own any issues and he hasn't done any hard political yards; he's merely thrown money at projects he likes. He appears to be a standard-grade US-style elitist liberal with a load of money and a patrician view, so he's going to need to work on his positioning if he wants to shake this impression. His sudden renouncement of atheism at the end of 2016 was a blunderingly obvious start, but he's hired a senior guy from Obama's campaign team and a former Clinton pollster, so we're guessing it will get slicker with time. This is hardly mould-breaking stuff in American politics, and we've seen super-rich CEOs try their hand and come painfully short before; Ross Perot, for instance.

There's one difference, though. Zuckerberg owns Facebook, probably the single most influential tool in the world. That fact alone is an enormous argument for the joys of news and comment to be edited by a human being of your particular choosing, not an algorithm designed, more than anything else, to keep you within the walls of Castle Facebook and to make money off you in the process.

It's just another reason to delete the app and all your other social media apps – or, at the very least, to use them less. This is hard, because they are literally designed, by very clever people, to make you use them *more*, to become addicted to them. And yet you don't need them. There's so much more to be had from the real world, a world where it's okay to agree to disagree on the occasional thing and to go sailing with Charles and not stream it live because actually things *do* happen even if you don't record them and post them online. A world where incredible satisfaction is to be had from complicated, nuanced and tangible interactions with real people.

As for thinking the world couldn't get worse than Trump in the White House, what about Zuckerberg as president of the United States in, say, 2024? Perhaps as a chilling vision of the dystopian future he has in mind for us, Facebook now offers users six emoji options when responding to News Feed items. Your permitted reactions are LIKE, LOVE, HAHA, WOW, SAD or ANGRY.

One day – way before 2084, at this rate – you may only be able to describe yourself in President Zuckerberg's world as SAD-ANGRY. In the meantime, while we still can, we're going to say we're BLOODY TERRIFIED.

Endnotes

Endnotes are included primarily for those readers interested in sourcing specific contemporary quotes. Where quote references are missing, we consider them historical/factual or quoted widely and easily accessible from various credible sources.

Lance Armstrong

1. Armstrong's 'alcoholic' and 'whore' descriptions quoted in www.telegraph.co.uk, 20 January 2013. Hamilton line quoted in www.theguardian.com, 11 October 2012. 2. Hamilton's 'fraternity' description quoted in www.theguardian.com, 16 April 2015. Greg LeMond description quoted widely, including www.cyclingnews.com, 21 October 2013. Kathy LeMond description from her Twitter account, quoted in www.cnn.com, 24 October 2012.

Justin Bieber

1. Lennon explanation from *All We Are Saying: The last major interview with John Lennon and Yoko Ono* by David Sheff. 2. Bieber quoted widely, including www.bbc.com, 14 April 2013. 3. Jeff Ross quote from 'The Comedy Central Roast of Justin Bieber'.

Osama bin Laden

1. Maureen Santora quote from 'Robert O'Neill: The Navy Seal Who Killed Bin Laden', A Hannity Conversation.

Ritt Bjerregaard

1. Quote from 1995 European Commission Press Release 'Reducing CO_2 emissions from cars: Commission outlines strategy'. 2. Greg Archer, clean vehicles manager at Brussels-based NGO Transport & Environment, quoted in www.ft.com, 22 January 2015.

Tony Blair

1. Jan Moir quotes from her article 'Diamond geezers' in *The Spectator*, 27 August 2016. 2. Ross Clark quote from his article 'Tony's toxic legacy' in *The Spectator*, 24 January 2015. 3. Peter Oborne, Noam Chomsky and Clare Short quotes in this entry all from *The Killing$ of Tony Blair*. 4. Blair speech widely available, including www.cnn.com, 2 May 1997. 5. Blair speech widely available, including www.newstatesman.com, 6 July 2016.

Nick Bollettieri

1. Navratilova quote and sentiment widely available, including www.news.com.au, 29 August 2014. 2. Description from www.thetennisspace.com, 4 January 2012. 3. Bollettieri quoted in www.tennisworldusa.org, 7 January 2016. 4. Navratilova quote from 'Nine-time Wimbledon champion Martina Navratilova on grunting in tennis', from Wimbledon YouTube channel.

George W Bush

1. Bush speech widely available, including www.cnn.com, 2 May 2003. 2. Chomsky description quoted in www.sputniknews.com, 28 October 2015.

Hugo Chávez & Nicolás Maduro

1. See full speech transcript of 'Decline and Fall of History' by Niall Ferguson at www.goacta.org.

Bill & Hillary Clinton

1. Carl Benjamin description from his interview with Dave Rubin, 'Sargon of Akkad LIVE: Internet Trolls and Brexit Polls'. 2. RW Johnson description from his article 'Why Trump won' in www.politicsweb.co.za, 13 November 2016.

Jack Dorsey

1. Dorsey quoted widely, including www.latimesblogs.latimes.com, 18 February 2009. 2. Delingpole quote from his article 'I'm trying to block out the suppurating vileness of Twitter' in *The Spectator*, 29 October 2011.

Mohammed Emwazi

1. Begg quotes in www.middleeasteye.net, 21 July 2015. 2. Begg quote as per www.newstatesman.com, 5 February 2015. 3. Bary quoted widely, including www.thesun.co.uk, 13 August 2015. 4. Spokesman quoted widely, including www.theguardian.com, 18 October 2015. 5. Qureshi quoted widely, including www.bbc.com, 26 February 2015. 5. Colonel Warren and Diane Foley both quoted widely, including www.thesun.co.uk and www.theguardian.com respectively, both 13 November 2015.

Enver & Talat

1. Quote by Daniel Jonah Goldhagen from his book *Worse Than War: Genocide, eliminationism and the ongoing assault on humanity*. 2. Marozzi quote from his article 'Too little, too late' in *The Spectator*, 18 April 2015.

The guy who killed Concorde

1. Marshall and Blanc quotes as per 'Hooked on Supersonics' by David Kemp in *Vanity Fair*. 2. Putman and Pearlson quotes as per 'Supersonic airplanes and the age of irrational technology' by Dara Bramson in *The Atlantic*, 1 July 2015. 3. Bussell quote as per 'Jeremy Clarkson on the death of Concorde' in www.topgear.com, 1 January 2004. 4. Eddington quoted widely, including www.cnn.com, 30 October 2004.

Rolf Harris, Jimmy Savile & friends

1. Description quoted widely, including www.themirror.co.uk, 10 June 2014. 2. See *The report of the investigation into matters relating to Savile at Leeds Teaching Hospitals NHS Trust* by Susan Proctor et al. 3. Hunt quoted widely, including www.telegraph.co.uk, 26 June 2014. 4. Pullman quotes as per www.independent.co.uk, 15 July 2009.

Joseph Hazelwood

1. Amero quoted widely, including www.latimes.com, 19 April 1989. 2. Bookchin quote from his article 'Death of a small planet' in *The Progressive*, August 1989.

Adolf Hitler

1. Hinsley quote as per *The Better Angels Of Our Nature* by Steven Pinker.

J Bruce Ismay

1. Descriptions of Ismay: 'skulking coward' quoted in *Titanic 100th Anniversary Edition* by Stephanie Barczewski; 'J Brute Ismay' quoted widely, including www.titanicberg.com; 'one of those human hogs whose animal desires swallow up all finer feelings … whose heart is atrophied by selfishness' quoted in *The Restless Sea* by Cynthia Harrod-Eagles.

The Israel-Palestine letter writer

1. Godwin's Law, first outlined in 1990 for Usenet groups and now in the Oxford dictionary, can be considered a glib or lightweight dismissal of an argument. We prefer Andrew Sullivan's view on the law as 'a reflection of the collapse of the reasoned deliberation the [US] Founders saw as indispensible to a functioning republic' (from his article 'Democracies end when they are too democratic' in www.nymag.com, 1 May 2016). This interpretation is intrinsic to the point of the Israel-Palestine letter writer entry. See www.knowyourmeme.com for more on Godwin's Law.

Kim Kardashian

1. Rogan quote from his standup routine (Comedy Central, November 2014), accessed at www.youtube.com.

Mao Zedong

1. Wolfe quoted in *From Benito Mussolini To Hugo Chávez* by Paul Hollander.

Diego Maradona

1. Maradona quoted in *Maradona: The Hand of God* by Jimmy Burns. 2. Valdano quoted in www.theguardian.com, 4 October 2004. 3. Alejandro Chacoff description from his article 'The Fall: how diving became football's worst crime' in www.theguardian.com, 6 April 2016. 4. Cantona quoted widely, including www.the42.ie, 12 June 2014.

Charles Saatchi

1. The 'abused and humiliated' description as quoted by a bystander who witnessed the incident in www.mirror.co.uk, 18 June 2013. 2. Beckman quote from his article 'Pretentiousness isn't a crime' in *The Spectator*, 20 February 2016. 3. There are many wonderful Sewel quotes on Emin, Hirst and other modern artists, often collated in obituaries and reminiscences. These examples taken from www.theguardian.com, 19 September 2015; www.standard.co.uk, 21 September 2015; www.spectator.co.uk, 12 December 2015.

Steven Spielberg

1. Full Bray quote – 'But she [critic Molly Haskell] doesn't add that since that criticism can be made of all Spielberg's work – indeed, that he isn't really interested in the relations between men and women, period – he is therefore crippled as an artist, and his movies only ever likely to be of sociological interest' from his article 'How Steven Spielberg ruined the movies' in *The Spectator*, 28 January 2017. Full Kael quote – 'I was very skeptical of [Charlie] Chaplin, because I thought he pushed too hard. In some ways, he did what Spielberg has been doing: he pushes buttons. And because people like that button pushing, they think Spielberg is a great director. But he's become, I think, a very bad director' from 'The Perils of Being Pauline', interview with Francis Davis at www.paulrossen.com,

October 2001. 2. Schatz quote from his essay 'The New Hollywood' in *Movie Blockbusters*. 3. Perryman quote from his book *Adventures With The Wife In Space: Living with Doctor Who*.

Stalin & Lenin

1. Hastings quote from his article 'Red with the people's blood' in *The Spectator*, 10/17/24 December 2016. 2. Peterson quote from his podcast '2014 Personality Lecture 13: Aleksandr Solzhenitsyn (Existentialism)'.

Donald Trump

1. Roth quoted in www.newyorker.com, 30 January 2017. 2. Shapiro quote from his article 'Antifa and the alt-right, growing in opposition to one another' in www.nationalreview.com, 15 August 2017. 3. Andrew Sullivan is credited with the phrase 'extinction-level event', from his article 'Democracies end when they are too democratic' in www.nymag.com, 1 May 2016. 4. Quote from Sullivan, *ibid*.

HF Verwoerd & DF Malan

1. Roper description from his article 'Zombie Verwoerd stalks internet' in www.mg.co.za, 4 January 2011. 2. Lee quoted widely, including www.nymag.com, 25 February 2014.

Mark Zuckerberg

1. Duffin quote from www.chicagotribune.com, 6 January 2017. 2. Joler quote from www.bbc.com, 26 May 2017. 3. Description from Tobias Rose-Stockwell in his article 'This is how your fear and outrage are being sold for profit' in *The Mission*, 14 July 2017. 4. Description from a *MediaMemo* review, quoted in www.nymag.com, 17 September 2010. 5. As above (3.), from *The Mission*, 14 July 2017.

Bibliography

The following (no doubt incomplete) bibliography consists of the most important books, papers, articles, videos and websites we've used in the compilation of the book. We have not included all individual webpages visited which would, we feel, extend this list to unnecessary and impractical lengths, but would like to take this opportunity to thank all those quality websites that make available good and reputable journalism and writing. Apologies to the various authors or sources who deserve a specific reference that we may have left off. All oversights are ours.

BOOKS

23 Things They Don't Tell You About Capitalism by Ha Joon Chang (Penguin, 2011)

50 People Who Stuffed Up South Africa by Alexander Parker (Mercury, 2017)

Adventures With The Wife In Space: Living with Doctor Who by Neil Perryman (Faber and Faber, 2013), accessed at www.books.google.com

Africa: A biography of the continent by John Reader (Penguin, 1998)

All We Are Saying: The last major interview with John Lennon and Yoko Ono by David Sheff (St Martin's Press, 2010), accessed at www.books.google.com

Ambassador Morgenthau's Story by Henry Morgenthau (Blackmask Online, 2001), accessed at www.books.google.com

American Prometheus: The triumph and tragedy of J Robert Oppenheimer by Kai Bird and Martin J Sherwin (Vintage Books, 2005)

Atrocitology: Humanity's 100 deadliest achievements by Matthew White (Canongate Books, 2011)

The Better Angels Of Our Nature by Steven Pinker (Viking Books, 2011)

Bloodlands by Timothy Snyder (Basic Books, 2010)

Development As Freedom by Amartya Sen (Oxford University Press, 1999), accessed at www.books.google.com.

Down With The Old Canoe: A cultural history of the Titanic disaster by Steven Biel (WW Norton & Company, 2012), accessed at www.books.google.com

Film As Social Practice by Graeme Turner (Routledge, 2009)

The Finish: The killing of Osama bin Laden by Mark Bowden (Grove Press UK, 2012)

The First World War by John Keegan (Vintage Books, 2000)

Fools, Frauds And Firebrands by Roger Scruton (Bloomsbury Continuum, 2016)

From Benito Mussolini To Hugo Chávez by Paul Hollander (Cambridge University Press, 2016)

The Great War For Civilisation by Robert Fisk (Harper Perennial, 2006), accessed at www.spokesmanbooks.com

The Gulag Archipelago by Aleksandr Solzhenitsyn (Collins & Harvill Press, 1974)

Heart of Darkness by Joseph Conrad (Penguin, 1995)

Hillbilly Elegy by JD Vance (HarperCollins Publishers, 2017)

History's Worst Decisions by Stephen Weir (Zebra Press, 2011)

The Holocaust: The Jewish tragedy by Martin Gilbert (HarperCollins, 1989)

How Much Is Enough? by Robert and Edward Skidelsky (Penguin, 2012), accessed at www.books.google.com

The Idea of Justice by Amartya Sen (Penguin, 2010)

It's Not About The Bike by Lance Armstrong (Yellow Jersey, 2004)

King Leopold's Ghost: A story of greed, terror and heroism in colonial Africa by Adam Hochschild (Papermac, 1999)

Lenin: A Biography by Robert Service (Pan Macmillan, 2010)

Life's Rich Tapestry by Matthew Holt (Utter Tosh, 2012)

Living History by Hillary Clinton (Headline, 2003)

Long Walk To Freedom by Nelson Mandela (Macdonald Purnell, 1994)

Manhunt by Peter Bergen (Vintage, 2013)

Mao's Last Dancer by Li Cunxin (Penguin, 2009)

Maradona: The Hand of God by Jimmy Burns (A&C Black, 2011), accessed at www.books.google.com

Mein Kampf by Adolf Hitler (Hurst and Blackett, 1939)

My Life by Bill Clinton (Vintage Books, 2005)

No Easy Day by Mark Owen (Michael Joseph, 2012)

North Korea Undercover by John Sweeney (Transworld Publishers, 2014)

Not For Turning: The life of Margaret Thatcher by Robin Harris (Corgi, 2014)

Origins of Political Order by Francis Fukuyama (Profile Books, 2012)

Outliers: The Story Of Success by Malcolm Gladwell (Penguin, 2009)

A People's History of Britain by Rebecca Fraser (Pimlico, 2004)

The Politics Of Climate Change Negotiations: Strategies and variables in prolonged international negotiations by Christian Downie (Edward Elgar Publishing, 2014), accessed at www.book.google.com

The Private Life of Chairman Mao by Li Zhisui (Chatto & Windus, 1994)

The Restless Sea: The Morland Dynasty by Cynthia Harrod-Eagles (Hachette Digital, 2004), accessed at www.books.google.com

Sapiens: A brief history of humankind by Yuval Noah Harari (Vintage Books, 2014)

A Short History of Nearly Everything by Bill Bryson (Black Swan, 2016)

Stalin: The court of the Red Tsar by Simon Sebag Montefiore (Hachette, 2010) accessed at www.books.google.com

Them: Adventures with extremists by Jon Ronson (Simon & Schuster, 2003)

The State of Africa by Martin Meredith (Simon & Schuster, 2013)

Titanic 100th Anniversary Edition: A night remembered by Stephanie Barczewski (Continuum, 2004), accessed at www.books.google.com

Titans of History by Simon Sebag Montefiore (Quercus, 2012)

Word History: 50 key milestones by Ian Crofton (Quercus, 2011)

Worse Than War: Genocide, eliminationism and the ongoing assault on humanity by Daniel Jonah Goldhagen (Hachette Digital, 2009)

PAPERS, ARTICLES, MAGAZINES & OTHER RESOURCES

'Antifa and the alt-right, growing in opposition to one another' by Ben Shapiro, www.nationalreview.com, 15 August 2017

'At last: a calm, definitive account of the Armenian genocide' by Justin Marozzi, *The Spectator*, 18 April 2015

'Blair witch project' by Rod Liddle, *The Spectator*, 10 September 2016

'Death of a small planet' by Murray Bookchin, *The Progressive*, August 1989, accessed at www.scribd.com.

'Decline and fall of history' by Niall Ferguson (Philip Merrill Awards presented by the American Council Of Trustees And Alumni, 2016), accessed at www.goacta.org

'Democracies end when they are too democratic' by Andrew Sullivan, *New York Magazine*,

2 May 2016, accessed at www.nymag.com

'Diamond geezers' by Jan Moir, *The Spectator*, 27 August 2016

'Edelman Trust Barometer 2007' compiled by Edelman, accessed at www.edelman.com

'Environmental policy as social policy? The impact of childhood lead exposure on crime' by Jessica Wolpaw Reyes (NBER Working Paper Series, 2007), accessed at www.nber.org

'The greatest World Cup tragedies: Diego Maradona, USA 1994' by Marcela Mora y Araujo, www.the42.ie, 12 June 2014

'Hooked on supersonics' by David Kemp, *Vanity Fair*, October 2003

'How Steven Spielberg ruined the movies' by Christopher Bray, *The Spectator*, 28 January 2017

'How to deal with North Korea' by Mark Bowden, *The Atlantic*, July/August 2017, accessed at www.theatlantic.com

'IARC: Diesel Engine Exhaust Carcinogenic' press release from International Agency for Research on Cancer, 12 June 2012, accessed at www.iarc.fr

'I'm trying to block out the suppurating vileness of Twitter' by James Delingpole, *The Spectator*, 29 October 2011

'It all began with OJ' by Lili Anolik, *Vanity Fair*, June 2014

'Jeb Bush: Coming to a free world near you' by Chris Ayres, *GQ UK*, December 2014

'Jeremy Clarkson on the death of Concorde' by Jeremy Clarkson, www.topgear.com, 1 January 2004

'Lessons in sex' by Patrick Skene Catling, *The Spectator*, 8 October 2016

'Licence to kill' by Dominic Green, *The Spectator*, 27 June 2015

'New Hollywood: Classical Hollywood in a new light' by Wesley D Buskirk (Cinesthesia, 2016), accessed at scholarworks.gvsu.edu

'The New Hollywood' by Thomas Schatz, from *Movie Blockbusters*, edited by Julian Stringer (Routledge, 2003), accessed at www.books.google.com

'No Hitler, no Holocaust' by Milton Himmelfarb, *Commentary*, 1 March 1984, accessed at www.commentarymagazine.com

'The not-so-beautiful game' by Giles Coren, *GQ UK*, May 2007

'Presidential IQ, openness, intellectual brilliance, and leadership: Estimates and correlations for 42 US Chief Executives' by Dean Keith Simonton (*Political Psychology*, Vol 27, No 4, 2006), accessed at www.acsu.buffalo.edu

'Pretentiousness isn't a crime' by Jonathan Beckman, *The Spectator*, 20 February 2016

'A Reassessment of Mortality in North Korea, 1993-2008' by Daniel Goodkind, Loraine West and Peter Johnson (Population Association of America Annual Meeting Program, 2011), accessed at paa2011.princeton.edu

'Reconstructing Iraq: The last year and the last decade' by Catherin Lutz, from The Cost of War Project (Watson Institute for International Studies, 2013), accessed at watson.brown.edu

'Red with the people's blood' by Max Hastings, *The Spectator*, 10/17/24 December 2016

'Reducing CO2 emissions from cars: Commission outlines strategy' press release from European Commission, 20 December 1995, accessed at European Commission Press Release Database at europa.eu.

'The report of the investigation into matters relating to Savile at Leeds Teaching Hospitals NHS Trust' by Susan Proctor, Ray Galloway, Rebecca Chaloner, Claire Jones and David Thompson (Leeds Teaching Hospitals NHS Trust, 2014), accessed at www.leedsth.nhs.uk

'Share of diesel in new cars in West Europe (1990-2016)' spreadsheet, accessed at the European Automobile Manufacturers Association at www.acea.be

'Supersonic airplanes and the age of irrational technology' by Dara Bramson, *The Atlantic*, 1 July 2015

'Table 1-23: World Motor Vehicle Production, Selected Countries' spreadsheet, accessed at Bureau of Transportation Statistics at www.rita.dot.gov

'This is how your fear and outrage are being sold for profit' by Tobias Rose-Stockwell, *The Mission*, 14 July 2017, accessed at www.medium.com

'Tony's toxic legacy' by Ross Clark, *The Spectator*, 24 January 2015

'The urban rise and fall of air lead (Pb) and the latent surge and retreat of societal violence' by Howard Mielke and Sammy Zahran (*Environmental International*, August 2012), accessed at www.sciencedirect.com

'What are the Tories for?' by Fraser Nelson, *The Spectator*, 24 June 2017

'Why Trump won' by RW Johnson, www.politicsweb.co.za, 13 November 2016

VIDEOS & PODCASTS

Of the various podcasters we follow or have encountered in our research, we are generally indebted to the YouTube channels of Jordan B Peterson and The Rubin Report. The former has been particularly useful in understanding the nature of crimes against humanity, while the latter has been excellent for moderated assessments of the state of US politics and online engagement today.

'2014 Personality Lecture 13: Aleksandr Solzhenitsyn (Existentialism)' by Jordan Peterson, (Jordan B Peterson, 1 March 2014), accessed at www.youtube.com

'The Armenian Genocide Experiment' (davidmtv, April 2016), accessed at www.youtube.com

'Author, Gerald Posner, and Auschwitz Dr Josef Mengele's only son, Rolf, on Phil Donahue' (originally recorded 1986), accessed at www.youtube.com

'The Comedy Central Roast of Justin Bieber' (Comedy Central, 2015), accessed at www.youtube.com

'The Killing$ of Tony Blair', produced by George Galloway (Journeyman Pictures, 2016)

'Louis Theroux: Savile' by Louis Theroux (BBC, 2016), accessed at www.dailymotion.com

'The Most Evil Men of History: Pol Pot' (Discovery Civilization, 2001) accessed at www.youtube.com

'Nine-time Wimbledon champion Martina Navratilova on grunting in tennis' (Wimbledon, 3 July 2009), accessed at www.youtube.com

'The Pervert's Guide To Ideology' by Slavoj Žižek (Zeitgeist Films, 2012), accessed at www.critical-theory.com

'Pol Pot: The journey to the killing fields' (BBC Timewatch, 2005), accessed at www.youtube.com

'Robert O'Neill: The Navy Seal Who Killed Bin Laden', A Hannity Conversation (Fox News, November 2014), accessed at www.youtube.com

'Rolf Mengele on meeting his father, Dr Josef Mengele' (originally recorded 1985), accessed at www.youtube.com

'Sargon of Akkad LIVE: Internet Trolls and Brexit Polls' (The Rubin Report, 20 June 2017), accessed at www.youtube.com

'Top Tennis Grunts' (Tennis Now, June 2013), accessed at www.youtube.com

'Why Is Modern Art So Bad?' by Robert Florczak (Prager University, 2014), accessed at www.prageru.com

WEBSITES

www.abcnews.go.com, www.academics.wellesley.edu, www.advisorperspectives.com, www.adweek.com, www.aljazeera.com, www.allafrica.com, www.allthingsd.com, www.alternet.org, www.armenian-genocide.org, www.auschwitz.dk, www.autonews.com, www.bbc.com, www.bdlive.co.za, www.bibleresearch.org, www.bjreview.com.cn, www.britannica.com, www.businessinsider.com, www.cage.ngo, www.cambodiatribunal.org, www.candlesholocaustmuseum.org, www.cbsnews.com, www.celebritynetworth.com, www.cia.gov, www.cnn.com, www.concordesst.com, www.cosmopolitan.com, www.counterpunch.org, www.cyclingnews.com, www.dailymail.co.uk, www.dailymaverick.co.za, www.dailyrecord.com, www.deep.social, www.democratandchronicle.com, www.economist.com, www.endthekilling.ca, www.etonline. com, www.eur-lex.europa.eu, www.express.co.uk, www.fivethirtyeight.com, www.fool.com, www.footballtoptens.wordpress.com, www.forbes.com, www.fortune.com, www.ft.com, www.gallup.com, www.gauteng.net, www.greenpeace.org.uk, www.haaretz.com, www.harpersbazaar.co.uk, www.herald.com.au, www.heralddlive.co.za, www.hiroshima-spirit.jp, www.history.com, www.history.state.gov, www.historyofrussia.org, www.historyonthenet.com, www.hollywoodreporter.com, www.holocasut.com.au, www.hrlibrary.umn.edu, www.huffingtonpost.com, www.icanw.org, www.independent.co.uk, www.indexmundi.com, www.infowars.com, www.instagram.com, www.internetlivestats.com, www.investor.gov, www.irelandchauffeurtravel.com, www.jewishvirtuallibrary.org, www.journalism.org, www.jta.org, www.knowyourmeme.com, www.kvinfo.dk, www.lamag.com, www.latimes.com, www.latimesblogs.latimes.com, www.lead.org.au, www.madoffvictimfund.com, www.marketrealist.com, www.measuringworth.com, www.medium.com, www.mengele.dk, www.metro.co.uk, www.mg.co.za, www.middleeasteye.net, www.militaryhistorynow.com, www.mirror.co.uk, www.monitor.co.ug, www.monster.co.uk, www.motherjones.com, www.msnbc.com, www.mtstandard.com, www.nasa.gov, www.nbcnews.com, www.newhistorian.com, www.news.bbc.co.uk, www.news.com.au, www.newstatesman.com, www.newsweek.com, www.newyorker.com, www.nymag.com, www.nytimes.com, www.nzherald.co.nz, www.outsideonline.com, www.paulrossen.com, www.people.com, www.physicsoftheuniverse.com, www.politico.com, www.politico.eu, www.politicsweb.co.za, www.recode.net, www.resetdoc.org, www.ritt.dk, www.rollingstone.com, www.saatchigallery. com, www.sahistory.org.za, www.salon.com, www.sciencedaily.com, www.scnc.ukzn.ac.za, www.scribd.com, www.slate.com, www.slatergordon.co.uk, www.smithsonianmag.com, www.spectator.co.uk, www.spirit-concorde-tours.com, www.sputniknews.com, www.static.guim.co.uk, www.statista.com, www.stuff.co.nz, www.sunderlandecho.com, www.techcrunch.com, www.telegraph.co.uk, www.tennisnow.com, www.the42.ie, www.theatlantic.com, www.thebalance.com, www.theguardian.com, www.theonion.com, www.therichest.com, www.thespacereview.com, www.thetennisspace.com, www.thoughtco.com, www.time.com, www.timeslive.co.za, www.timesofisrael.com, www.transcripts.cnn.com, www.twitter.com, www.usnews.com, www.uspolicymetrics.com, www.vanityfair.com, www.vogue.com, www.vox.com, www.vulture.com, www.warefarehistorynetwork.com, www.washingtonpost.com, www.web.archive.org, www.web.facebook.com, www.wholetruth.net, www.wikipedia.org, www.wired.com, www.world.bymap.org, www.wsj.com, www.ww2today.com, www.youtube.com, www.zoomph.com

Acknowledgements

From Alexander:

The cobbling together of this book was the product of about a year's work, if sitting at a computer and hacking out 100,000 words may be considered work. Perhaps obviously, though, there's a bit more to it than that. The entire process, for one, was five years in the making, and it is just as much the product of a partnership now a decade old with my co-author and co-editor, Tim Richman. Working with Tim has always been a happy experience for me; he tolerates the months-long silences and the staccato bursts of frantic activity, and as an editor he improves everything he touches.

Equally, the Zapiro cartoons do so much to lift this book. Jonathan Shapiro's sharply satirical style has been offending the right sort of people for years, and he is surely one of the world's most talented political cartoonists. He misses nothing, and this partnership is such a treat.

It's impossible not to mention here two men I miss greatly and who both contributed in different ways: David Rattray, mentioned in the introduction, and Nico Nortje, a wonderful soul who left us far, far too soon.

For their absolutely critical contributions to the improvement of this book, and to the state of the discourse generally, I'm indebted to Tom Eaton and Dr Karen Graaff.

I am grateful to my colleagues at 24.com for their forbearance, and I am forever in the debt of my parents, Jim and Jeannie, and to Greg, Lucy, Ben and Lily Mullins, who have always supported and encouraged my endeavours. I can't thank enough my various friends and family in Cape Town who have over critical periods variously encouraged, helped, fed, watered and consoled me, especially Nick and Shelley Traverso and the boys, Nick Holleman, Ed, Zara and Rose Roman, Catherine Luckhoff, Gareth Nortje, Jackie Nortje, the Dalling clan, Nolufefe Mahlombe, Stephen Grootes, Nick Clelland and Chris Lazari.

I'm so grateful to my children – Olweyn, Elizabeth and Dair – for tolerating my absences, and to Olweyn for lending me her bedroom as a study. Most of all, though, I'm grateful to my wife Bronwyn Nortje, whose boundless support and intelligence constantly challenges me to be better. I'm a lucky fellow.

From Tim:

To Alex, thank you for the experience. This is our fourth book together, in some or other form, and it is quite easily the most ambitious of the lot – our light and entertaining, sometimes amusing and hopefully enlightening, ever-so-slightly meaningful take on the world... It has been an enriching and truly enjoyable experience, for which I am most grateful.

Jonathan, once again thank you for playing along and offering your cartoons, along with your wisdom. Eleanora, you are a saint, and Alex and I are both indebted for all your assistance.

There is a long list of people to thank, whose contributions, both great and small, have been hugely important, and I apologise to those I've omitted. My gratitude to: Francesca Beighton, Matt Dalby, Guy Dviri, Holger Bernt Hansen, Tom Eaton, Jonathan Phillips, Liz Sarant, Brooks Spector and Eihorere Wesigye. Also to Rob Ambler-Smith, Brett Aubin, Greg Boyes, Jon Burnett, Mike Dixon, Edward Durrant, Ceddie Eachus, Azad Essa, Michael Furter, Oliver Genthe, Steven Loubser, Bronwyn Nortje, Roberto Pharo, James Price, Michael Rosholt, Chris Warncke and Greig Wilson. Often the loudest voices of dissent were the most useful!

To the members of SASASU, your insight is humbling.

At the production grindstone in Cape Town, thank you to Chelsea Petersen, and Deborah Louw, Simon Richardson and Ania Rokita. And in London, to Duncan Proudfoot, and Tom Asker, John Fairweather, Felicity Robinson, Rebecca Sheppard, Charlotte Stroomer and everyone else at Little, Brown.

To my close family, for their support and feedback, thank you, Leigh Herringer, Liz Parker, Simon Richman, Bob Rowand and Tricia Rowand.

To Rupert Butler, I owe you lunch.

The concept of this book was right up my father's street and I know he would have loved to see the finished version, though I'm sure he would have disagreed with the final fifty. To Ritchie, sorry you missed it.

Finally, to my son and wife: Nicholas, thank you for contracting glandular fever four, and not two, weeks before deadline. And, Jules, thank you for dealing with the former – and, of course, for everything else.

www.50peoplewho.com